Romania

TOPOGRAPHICS

Romania
Borderland of Europe

Lucian Boia

Translated by
JAMES CHRISTIAN BROWN

REAKTION BOOKS

Published by Reaktion Books Ltd
33 Great Sutton Street, London EC1V 0DX

www.reaktionbooks.co.uk

First published 2001, transferred to digital printing 2006

Printed and bound in Great Britain by Antony Rowe Ltd

British Library Cataloguing in Publication Data

Boia, Lucian
    Romania: borderland of Europe. – (Topographics)
    1. Romania – History 2. Romania – Civilization
    I. Title
    949.8

ISBN 1 86189 103 2

Contents

Introduction

This book is an attempt to answer the question 'What is Romania?' What I hope to do is to describe and explain a country. But can a country be contained within a book? Yes and no. Reality is multiform and inexhaustible, while any representation of it cannot avoid being limited and simplified – and inevitably subjective. One country, but so many viewpoints! One history, but so many ways of reconstructing and interpreting it! No image can ever be identical with the object it represents. We can only see things from one point of view. And the more complex the reality, and the more numerous the vantage points from which it can be observed, the more our collection of images gains in diversity. To the adaptation (and distortion) of reality through the image, we must also add its adaptation (and distortion) through the word. Without words, we could express nothing, but these very words force reality into certain pre-established mental moulds. Words are too abstract, too poor and too rigid to give a faithful rendering of the endless richness and depth of the universe.

We can, of course, summarize things, and we do so all the time, by means of a few selected images and symbols. A dichotomy of archetypes has operated for as long as human communities have existed: identity versus alterity. We, with all our characteristics, are who we are, and others are different; they have characteristics of their own. In fact, people resemble each other more than they differ, and so do communities. But can we do without distinctions? It would appear not. So we pick out differentiating features, bring them into the open and turn a spotlight on them. Thus we construct ourselves and the 'other'. There is a considerable element of caricature in this process. People and communities end up differing from each other much more in the realm of the imaginary than they do in reality.[1]

Such simplified geographical and anthropological reference points can be found in the minds of all of us. They may not be entirely untrue, but they are not entirely true either. How far do they represent the country or people of which we are speaking, and how far do they represent us, our manner of seeing and understanding things? Nearly 2,500 years ago, Herodotus, the father of history, sketched a complete picture of the known world for the first time. One after the other, he paraded a multitude of lands and peoples before his readers. But is this the real world, we may ask, or is it a Greek adaptation of the real world, an image of 'others' seen from a Greek point of view? To ask such a question is already to answer it. Nowadays, we are certainly much better informed, but I doubt if we are any more objective or detached from our prejudices than Herodotus was. We may be looking at 'something' that is well defined, but we are still looking at it with our own eyes.

A country can be multiplied endlessly. It is made up of a multitude of people and things, each with their own individuality. It is a history – that is, not a static picture, but a film made up of multiple sequences. And it is not only what we see now and what once was but also the consciousness of people about the present and the past, about themselves, indeed about anything. What people think and imagine is as significant as (if not more significant than) what actually happens. Reality and the imaginary are bound together in a host of lives, acts and thoughts. And all of these continue to multiply, in all sorts of variants, distorted to a greater or lesser degree in relation to reality according to the perspective of the observer. How are we to make a synthesis? What is worth retaining and what is not? There are no simple answers to these questions. To imagine that a country is *one* is to ignore the diversity of the elements that make it up and the fact that these can be combined in countless syntheses.

Like any other country, Romania can be simplified and can be multiplied into all sorts of images and symbols. Seen from the West, its location alone is enough to make it seem an almost exotic land: somewhere 'out there', on the margins of Europe. We can recognize here the same logic that we met in Herodotus: the further away 'others' are from us, the more different they are perceived to be. The tale of Dracula fits perfectly into this system of representations. When the famous novel first appeared, Transylvania belonged to Hungary, and Count Dracula himself was a Magyar, not a Romanian, aristocrat. Romania inherited the myth, along with the respective territory, in 1918. Dracula's home could not have been placed in the Alps (too close to the heart of Europe) or in Tibet (too far away). The Carpathians offered just the right setting: on the edge of Europe, where Western civilization gives way to something already different. The Romanian space represents, for the West, the first circle of otherness: sufficiently close for the curious configurations and disturbing forms of behaviour which Westerners find there to be highlighted all the more strongly.

Two Western writers give us striking portrayals of Romania as it was shortly before the Second World War: a country looking back on a century of modernization which had brought it ever closer to the structures and culture of the West. Romania had never been better integrated into Europe. Bucharest had long been spoken of as a 'Little Paris'. Our two authors are very different: Paul Morand, an urbane Frenchman married to a Romanian and with many impressive connections in Romanian society, and Olivia Manning, a young Englishwoman, withdrawn, frustrated and little inclined to look favourably on things. The former published his essay-volume *Bucarest* in 1935, while the latter's *Balkan Trilogy*, the first two volumes of which (*The Great Fortune* and *The Spoilt City*) are set in Romania in the period 1939–40, appeared somewhat later, in the 1960s. The former treats the country sympathetically; the latter cannot conceal her antipathy.

What is remarkable, given the differences between these two writers, is their fundamental agreement regarding the character of Romanian civilization. To both, Romania presented itself as a country only partially integrated into European civilization, a country of the margins, still characterized by a pronounced substrate of primitivism and a strange amalgam of modern urban life and rustic survivals. In Bucharest, Morand noted with amusement, Ford automobiles shared the road with ox-carts. So much for 'Little Paris'! Manning saw the citizens of Bucharest more or less as peasants, some openly so, others as peasants dressed up in city clothes. Her Romania was a fluid, insecure world, where nothing was really taken seriously. For Morand, on the other hand, the un-Western mentality was a positive quality, a lesson Romanians could offer Westerners about adaptability, indulgence, optimism, the ability to pass through history without caring – precisely the things which irritated Manning!

What we are left with is the fact that the Romanians are perceived as a people *apart*, animated by a different spirit to that of Western nations: a certain 'lightness' in living which separates them from the responsible seriousness of the West. While the West defines itself as an ordered and predictable world, Romania occupies a vague and unpredictable space.[2]

Unfortunately for the Romanians, the seductive side of this exoticism has tended to fade, giving way to darker images. In this connection, top marks must go to Dracula, amply assisted by Ceauşescu with his extravagant variety of Communism. And there has been so much in recent years to confuse or repel Western observers: a bloody revolution still cloaked in mystery, the miners' devastating onslaughts on Bucharest, the intolerable situation of children abandoned in the street or infected with AIDS . . . All of these, taken out of context, have become negative symbols of Romania. At the other extreme, we have the enticing bucolic image of the country promoted by the tourist industry: the beauties of nature, picturesque locations, the hospitality of the people, the originality of traditional crafts and folksongs . . . In between these extremes, there are, of course, all sorts of other images. How much is true, and how much is untrue?

What can I do myself but select and interpret in the light of my own opinions? At least I can try not to make excessive simplifications, and to explain as much as possible. Romania is certainly more 'normal' than the more extreme interpretations would make it seem. Of course, it has its specific characteristics. But these should not be thought of as absolutes. I doubt if there is such a thing as a 'typical Romanian'. Romanians differ among themselves, and at the same time they have much in common with people everywhere. The regions of Romania also present a varied picture. When all of these elements are brought together, the resulting synthesis will present certain characteristic traits – perhaps, for a Westerner, even oddities. There is no timeless Romania, however. It is my view that the country's distinctive characteristics are to be explained by history and by the current social situation. Today's Romania does not much resemble yesterday's. Nor will the Romania of tomorrow be much like that of today.

What follows, then, does not pretend to present 'Romania in all its aspects': it is a personal interpretation, *my* Romania.

1 A Look at the Map

The first difficulty with Romania is deciding where it belongs on the map of Europe. In which zone are we to place it: Eastern Europe, the Balkans, Central Europe?

From a strictly geographical point of view, it is not hard to see that the Balkan peninsula does not include Romania. Its northern limit is formed by the Danube, and Romania, with the exception of Dobrogea – the region framed by the Danube to the west and north and the Black Sea to the east – lies north of the Danube. And yet it is not just land, mountains and rivers that define a space of civilization. In fact, as the result of a long history and many human and cultural contacts, Romania is in many ways a Balkan country. The Danube unites more than it separates. In Antiquity, Thracian tribes occupied both the northern half of the Balkan peninsula and the present territory of Romania. Roman expansion and the process of Romanization took place on both sides of the Danube. In the Middle Ages, Byzantium offered the Romanians their principal political, cultural and religious model, largely through the intermediary of the Balkan Slavs. The Turks, too, advanced through the Balkans, and, like other peoples of the region, the Romanians came under their domination for hundreds of years. The Greeks, another Balkan people, had an extremely powerful cultural influence on Romania at the beginning of the modern period. It is clear that Romania cannot be separated from the Balkans, but since it cannot strictly speaking be called a Balkan territory either, Romanian historians and geographers have opted for the formula 'South-eastern Europe', a useful way of referring to the Balkans plus Romania. So we have a solution, at least from the point of view of terminology.

In fact, things are even more complicated than this, since Romania is not, or at least until recently was not, a homogeneous country. Present-day Romania (which first came into being in 1859,

11

and then doubled its territory in 1918) is, broadly speaking, made up of three historical lands: Wallachia (known in Romanian as *Ţara Românească*, the 'Romanian Land') to the south, between the Danube and the southern Carpathians; Moldavia to the east, between the Dniester and the eastern Carpathians; and Transylvania to the west, separated from the other two by the curve of the Carpathians. At the risk of gross simplification, we might say that Wallachia, bound as it is to the Danube, is predominantly Balkan; Moldavia looks not only south but also north, towards Poland, and east, in the direction of the Russian steppes; and Transylvania is part of Central Europe and belongs appreciably to the space of Western civilization. Many waves of population and culture have come from the east, from ancient Scythians to modern Russians, and many others have come from the west, from Celts and Romans to Hungarians (who came originally from the Urals, but settled in the Pannonian plain, to the west of the Romanian space) and Germans.

So Romania is, at one and the same time, Balkan, Eastern European and Central European, without belonging wholly to any of these divisions – which are in any case somewhat artificial.

Important as geographical location may be for the destiny of a country, it does not determine an unwavering process of evolution. Changing historical circumstances also play their part. As a result of Communism, for example, a large part of Europe – extending right into the heart of Germany – came to be perceived as 'Eastern', because of its attachment to the Soviet Union. Having emerged from Communism, these same countries are now regarded as 'Central European'. At times, a decisive choice may intervene. Such a choice was made by the Romanians in the first half of the nineteenth century, when they decided to break away from the East and to reorient themselves towards the West. Within a short period of time, Romanian society adopted broadly Western cultural and political models. Romania became, to a partial extent in reality, and even more in the realm of the imaginary, an extension of Western Europe.

So here we have a country that looks towards all the cardinal points of Europe. Its individuality lies in the fact that it has not yet opted decisively for a single direction.

The Romanian space presents itself as a marginal one. Throughout history, it has always been on the edge of great political units and civilizations. The margin of the Roman Empire was here –

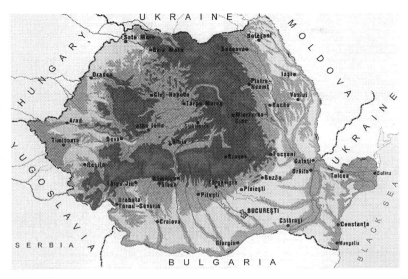

Romania today.

the frontier between the Roman and barbarian worlds divided ancient Dacia, the Romania of modern times, into two parts. Here too were the margins of the Byzantine, and later the Ottoman, empires. Western civilization, too, extended just this far. At the beginning of the modern period, three great empires – Ottoman, Habsburg and Russian – met precisely where Romania now lies. Whether in relation to Russia, Germany and Austria, or Turkey, the Romanians have always been on the margins, and now they stand on the margin of the European Union, as candidates whose chances of being integrated into the European construct remain uncertain.

This permanent 'frontier' situation has had two complementary and contradictory effects. On the one hand, it gave rise to a certain degree of isolation, an attenuated reception of outside models, the perpetuation of traditional structures and a mentality attached to indigenous values. On the other hand, it produced an extraordinary combination of ethnic and cultural infusions from all directions. Romania is a country which has assimilated, in different periods and in different ways from one region to another, elements as diverse as Turkish and French, Hungarian and Russian, Greek and German. It would be hard to find such a varied mixture anywhere in Europe, a synthesis of so many different colours. Situated as it is at a crossing point of roads and civilizations, the Romanian space is an open

13

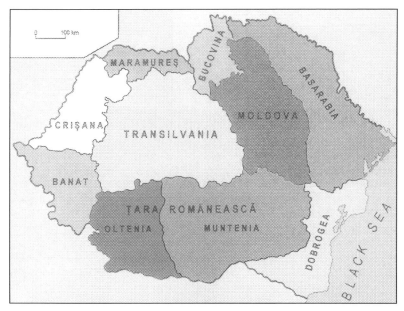

The historic Romanian provinces contained within the borders of Greater Romania in the inter-war period.

space *par excellence*, characterized by a permanent instability and a ceaseless movement of people and values. There is a proper measure in everything, and exceeding that measure may provoke adverse reactions. The Romanians are receptive to foreign models, but they may sometimes feel overwhelmed by them and turn to the preservation of their indigenous identity as a means of self-defence. Some Romanians look towards Europe, while others do not want to look outside at all. This tension between Europeanism and autochthonism illustrates an intellectual polarization that is typical of Romanian society. The confrontation between these opposing tendencies has accompanied the process of modernization over the last two centuries. Of course, the dramatization of relations with the 'other' is a universal feature of the imaginary. However, it may be that Romanians dramatize to an exceptional extent, admiring or rejecting, accepting wholesale or refusing on principle. This is the contradictory outcome of a contradictory history.

To complicate matters still further, it has to be said that the three lands which make up modern Romania can themselves be divided into a number of regions. Wallachia comprises Oltenia, Muntenia and Dobrogea; Moldavia, as well as the core region of Moldavia itself, includes Bessarabia and Bukovina; and 'Transylvania' is used as a generic name for all of the lands west of the Carpathians, including the Banat, Crişana and Maramureş, as well as the historical principality of Transylvania. In the course of their historical evolution, these ten provinces have acquired distinctive characteristics. They differ from each other to a greater or lesser extent: the last half century has reduced the differences, but they are still perceptible. The element which brought them together was the presence almost everywhere of Romanians as a majority of the population. But there are differences among Romanians, and even greater differences in the general ethnic composition of the regions, and in their relations with other European spaces. Some regions have traditionally looked westwards, others towards the Balkans, others to the north or east. There are regions with an almost exclusively Romanian population, while others are home to numerous other peoples (and were even more so in the past). These peoples are themselves very different from each other in language, culture and religion: Turks and Tatars, Hungarians, Germans, Serbs, Russians, Ukrainians, Jews – almost a synthesis of Europe!

In order to understand Romania better, it may be useful to look first at these ten geographical, historical and human units. But from which historical moment should we begin? Physical geography remains relatively unchanged over the centuries, and is easier to place within a synthesis than the historical and cultural constructions established by people. These are everywhere in permanent motion, and even more so in a space like that of Romania, characterized as it is by a high degree of historical instability. My choice for a starting point, especially where social and demographic statistics are concerned, is 1930. This is a less arbitrary choice than it might appear to be at first sight. In 1930, the first (and only) census of Greater Romania was conducted.[1] The records of this census bring together all the Romanian, or formerly Romanian, provinces and make it easy to compare them. Moreover, at that time, Romania was not yet at a very advanced stage of modernization. Traditional structures, the result of centuries of history, were still very much alive, in a way that they were not to remain for much longer. A short time later, the Communist experiment began, with an aggressive policy of social and territorial homogenization. Today, there are still differences between the provinces, but they are considerably reduced.

15

Urbanization and the massive emigration of certain ethnic groups (Germans, Jews and Turks in particular) have radically modified the traditional human landscape. The year 1930 represents the last moment at which modernity had not yet covered over the traces of previous history.

THE SOUTH: WALLACHIA

Wallachia is the historical and geographical unit that forms the south of present-day Romania, and around which modern Romania was created.[2]

Approaching in an easterly direction, we come first to Oltenia, the region framed by the Carpathians, the Danube and its tributary, the Olt. In its south-west corner, the Carpathians meet the Balkan mountains, forcing the Danube to carve its way through the Iron Gates gorge. Oltenia is a region of mountains in the north and plains in the south, with predominant hilly relief in between. It is the most purely Romanian of all the Romanian territories, exceptional in that very few foreigners have settled here over the years. The census of 1930 records that 97.5 per cent of the population were ethnic Romanians. This was also one of the most rural areas of the country, with an urban population of only 13 per cent (compared with a national average of 20 per cent). Consequently, many features characteristic of traditional cultures could be recognized. The level of literacy was lower than in most of the other provinces, and the disproportion between male and female literacy was the highest in the country: 70.4 per cent of men could read, compared with only 31 per cent of women. This weak degree of engagement with modernity had allowed the survival of an extremely lively folklore, and Oltenia offered one of the most dense and original variations on Romanian folk art. It was from the mountains of Oltenia that Constantin Brâncuşi set out into the wider world to revolutionize modern sculpture, simplifying and abstracting forms in a way reminiscent of traditional Romanian motifs.

Continuing eastwards, we cross the Olt into Muntenia, a province twice the size of Oltenia, the nucleus of Wallachia and, later, of Romania. Like Oltenia, Muntenia occupies the space between the Carpathians and the Danube, and its relief is marked by a similar drop in altitude from the mountains of the north through hilly country to the plains of the south. As we move eastwards, however, the plain

The highest place in Romania: the Făgăraş mountains in the southern Carpathians.

becomes more and more extensive, until it covers the greater part of Muntenia. This plain is the granary of Romania. It is also here, where trade routes crossed, that the greatest urban centre of the province developed, the capital first of Wallachia and later of Romania: Bucharest. Bucharest lies in the plain of the Danube, just 60 km from the river that marks the northernmost extremity of the Balkan peninsula. Muntenia, too, had a large Romanian majority in 1930, but the proportion of foreigners was higher than in Oltenia: Romanians accounted for 93.4 per cent overall, but only 82.3 per cent of the urban population. Of the total population, 27.1 per cent lived in towns, a proportion well above the national average. This relatively high level of urbanization was partly due to the presence of the capital. Bucharest, and other towns like Brăila, a bustling port on the Danube, were marked by a pronounced cosmopolitan note (with significant proportions of Jews, Greeks, Hungarians, Germans and Gypsies alongside the Romanian majority).

The Danube forms the border of Muntenia not only to the south but also to the east. The great river changes its course abruptly to flow north and then east again before entering the Black Sea in three branches, which form the largest delta in Europe. The region between the Danube to the west and north and the Black Sea to the

17

Romania's lowest-lying area: a view of the Danube Delta.

east is known as Dobrogea. Conventionally, Dobrogea is considered part of Wallachia, at least as far as the three great divisions of the country are concerned. However, it is really a region in its own right, both geographically and historically, and in an ethnic and cultural sense as well. It is one of the most interesting areas, not just of Romania but of the whole continent. Here, some of the most recently formed land in Europe – the world of the delta, with its amazing wealth of plant and animal life, where earth and water are not yet completely differentiated – lies close to some of the oldest – the time-worn mountains of Dobrogea. The rest of the region consists of plateau and plain. The climate is generally harsh and dry, with the Black Sea's influence felt only near the coast.

Dobrogea only actually belonged to Wallachia for some three decades, during the reign of Mircea the Old (1386–1418). In Antiquity, it was the home of the Getae, a Thracian people akin to the Dacians. The Scythians, a people of Iranian origin from the steppes to the north of the Black Sea, settled among them, while the Greeks founded colonies on the coast. The ruins of one of these, Istros (Histria), are today the site of an important archaeological excavation and a major tourist attraction. Tomis, the largest and busiest city of the region in

Another mountain landscape: the gorge of the Dîmbovicioara, a tributary of the Dîmboviţa.

19

the Hellenistic and Roman periods, lies under the modern city of Constanţa, the principal seaport of Romania. It was to Tomis that the poet Ovid was exiled in the time of Augustus, for reasons which remain obscure, and it is there that he died, still pining for Rome; his statue stands today in the central square.

Dobrogea was Roman, then Byzantine, after which it belonged to the first Bulgarian tsardom, then to the Byzantines again and back to the Bulgarians. In the fourteenth century, it emerged as a small state in its own right, ruled by Dobrotici (from whom it probably received its name). It was then incorporated into Wallachia for a time before being conquered by the Turks, who ruled it for four and a half centuries. Dobrogea was acquired by Romania in 1878, after the Russian-Romanian-Turkish war of 1877–8. By this time, it had a mixed population, in which Muslim Turks and Tatars were more numerous than Romanians. Hitherto, the territory had been merely a neglected borderland of the Ottoman Empire; the Romanians colonized it and made it profitable. Settlers included Romanians from the south of Transylvania, arable and livestock farmers known as *mocani*, and Aromanians from the Balkans. At this time, Constanţa was little more than a village; it was to grow into one of the great ports of Europe. In 1930, the population structure in Dobrogea (including the so-called 'Quadrilateral' – two counties taken from Bulgaria in 1913 and lost again in 1940) was as follows: Romanians: 44.2 per cent (only a relative majority); Bulgarians: 22.8 per cent; Turks: 18.5 per cent; Tatars: 2.7 per cent; Russians: 3.4 per cent; Germans: 1.5 per cent; and Greeks: 1.1 per cent. However, almost all of the nations of Europe and the East were represented here in smaller numbers. Dobrogea was – though sadly it no longer is – an extraordinary ethnic and cultural mosaic. Nowhere else in Europe was it possible within such a restricted space to encounter such an amalgam of languages, religions and lifestyles.

THE EAST: MOLDAVIA

The second great historical-geographical unit in Romania, Moldavia, evolved as a unified territory for centuries. In 1775, the Habsburg Empire annexed the northernmost part of the country, which came to be called Bukovina. A few decades later, in 1812, the Russians took possession of the eastern part, Bessarabia. Moldavia thus entered the modern period divided into three parts, each of which developed distinctive characteristics.

The Moldavia which remained after the loss of Bukovina and Bessarabia represented less than half the previous extent of the principality. It is a land of gentle hills between the parallel north–south lines marked by the eastern Carpathians and the Prut, a tributary of the Danube. In 1930, the proportion of Romanians here, 89.8 per cent, was slightly lower than in Muntenia; it was lower still in the towns: 70.8 per cent. In the course of the nineteenth century, there had been a significant increase in the Jewish population, largely as a result of emigration from Galicia. Jews made up 6.5 per cent of the total population, 23.1 per cent in the towns. In the Moldavian capital, Iaşi, and in some of the other towns, they accounted for a third of the population. (In 1900, the proportion of Jews in Iaşi had been even higher: around half the total population.)

The hills and forests of Bukovina, one of the two northernmost provinces of Romania (along with Maramureş), form a poetic setting for Suceava, the old capital of Moldavia, and a cluster of monasteries of the fifteenth to the seventeenth century, famous for the exterior frescoes of their churches. Alongside their religious function, these are major tourist attractions today. Annexation by Austria complicated the ethnic make-up of this former Moldavian territory. In 1930, Romanians accounted for 44.5 per cent of the population: Bukovina and Dobrogea were thus the only provinces in which they were not an absolute majority. They were followed by Ukrainians: 27.7 per cent; Jews: 10.8 per cent; and Germans: 8.9 per cent. In the towns, only 33 per cent of the population were Romanian; 30 per cent were Jewish and 14.7 per cent German. As in Dobrogea – though the components were very different – there was thus an interesting ethnic and cultural mosaic in Bukovina, which might have produced an original synthesis if history had permitted it. Nowadays, the province is cut in two; the northern part, with its majority Ukrainian population, became part of the Soviet Union as a result of the Second World War, and now belongs to Ukraine.

Bessarabia is bordered to the west by the Prut, to the east by the Dniester, and to the south by the Black Sea. After occupying the territory in 1812, the Russian authorities applied a policy of Russification. Thus in 1930, the ethnic make-up was as follows: Romanians: 56.2 per cent; Russians: 12.3 per cent; Ukrainians: 11 per cent; Jews: 7.2 per cent; Bulgarians: 5.7 per cent; Gagauzians (a Turkish-speaking Christian people): 3.4 per cent; and Germans (the

Voroneț, the most famous of the externally painted churches of Bukovina (15th–16th centuries).

descendants of nineteenth-century colonists): 2.8 per cent. In the southern counties of Ismail and Cetatea Albă, and in the northern county of Hotin, Ukrainians and Russians were in the majority. Bessarabia was annexed again by the Soviet Union in 1940 and divided. The northern and southern extremities were assigned to Ukraine, while the central part of the territory, with the addition of a strip of land on the left bank of the Dniester (Transnistria), where a substantial part of the population was Romanian, made up the Soviet Republic of Moldova. With the break-up of the Soviet empire in 1991, it became an independent state. Consequently, there are two Moldavias today: the Romanian region (*Moldova* in Romanian), and the independent Republic of Moldova, which corresponds substantially, but not completely, to historical Bessarabia.

Even within the old Moldavian principality, Bessarabia was a marginal territory. The centre of gravity in political and cultural terms lay in the area between the Prut and the Carpathians, in the part of Moldavia which has remained within the borders of contemporary Romania. In the Greater Romania of the inter-war period,

Bessarabia was the most economically and culturally backward province. The urban population was proportionately the lowest in the country (12.9 per cent), and only 31 per cent of those living in towns were Romanians. The level of literacy was only 38.1 per cent compared with 57 per cent for the whole country. Such figures set Bessarabia apart. Having previously been oppressed (as they were soon to be again) by the Russians, the Bessarabians had good motives to complain of an attitude of superiority on the part of other Romanians and a lack of interest in their problems. This was indeed a factor that contributed to Bessarabia's failure to become reintegrated into Romania after the break-up of the Soviet Union (others being the presence of a large Russian-Ukrainian minority, who have a higher economic and social standing than the Romanians; the continuing effects of years of Soviet anti-Romanian propaganda; and the reservations or even direct opposition shown by Russia and Ukraine towards the possibility of a union of the Republic of Moldova with Romania). It seems that the current trend of evolution is towards the emergence of a distinct 'Moldovan nation'. What was known in Soviet times as the 'Moldavian language' is simply Romanian with a few regional peculiarities and a sprinkling of Russian neologisms, but it is clear that the cultural difference between Romanians and Moldovans has deepened.

THE WEST: TRANSYLVANIA

Finally, we come to the third great component of Romania, the 'land beyond the mountains' (seen from the perspective of Wallachia and Moldavia). This part of the country is commonly known as Transylvania, although strictly speaking Transylvania is only a part – albeit the central part, and the part with the clearest historical and political individuality – of a complex of territories. These are regions whose past does not belong to the history of the Balkans or of the East, but to that of Central Europe, as a result of their association first with Hungary and later with the Habsburg Empire.

Transylvania proper (the former principality of Transylvania) may be imagined as a mountain stronghold surrounded by the Carpathians. The majestic peaks of the southern Carpathians, sometimes known as the Transylvanian Alps, rise in places to over 2,500 m, and separate Transylvania from Wallachia, while the eastern Carpathians mark its border with Moldavia. The 'Carpathian arc' is completed in the west by the massif of the western Carpathians (or Apuseni Mountains), which formerly separated the principality from the kingdom of Hungary. From an ethnic point of view, Romanians made up 57.6 per cent of the population in 1930, Hungarians 29.1 per cent and Germans 7.9 per cent. In the towns, Romanians were still in the minority (although the balance had shifted in their favour since 1918): they accounted for 35.9 per cent of the urban population, alongside Hungarians (39.8 per cent) and Germans (12.7 per cent). Even today, when the towns of Transylvania have been considerably Romanianized, their architecture gives away their origins. Cluj (Kolozsvár) and Tîrgu Mureş (Marosvásárhely) were purely Hungarian towns, while the Saxon foundations of Sibiu (Hermannstadt), Braşov (Kronstadt) and Sighişoara (Schässburg) retain the appearance of typical German burgs. Religious divisions also contributed to the area's ethnic complexity. In 1700, the majority of Romanians in Translylvania left the Orthodox Church to become Uniates (also known as Greek-Catholics) under the authority of Rome: Blaj, the seat of the Uniate Metropolitan, was nicknamed 'Little Rome'. The Germans (Saxons whose ancestors had migrated mainly from the north-western regions of Germany from around the mid-twelfth century, some of them distantly related to the Saxons who had earlier colonized England), were by then Lutheran. The Hungarians were Reformed (Calvinist), Roman Catholic or Unitarian. The census shows the following religious distribution: Uniate: 31.1 per cent; Orthodox: 27.7 per cent (only here and in historical Maramureş were Orthodox not in the majority); Reformed: 15.5 per cent; Roman Catholic: 12.8 per cent; Lutheran: 7.6 per cent; Unitarian: 2.1 per cent; and Jewish: 2.5 per cent.

In its mountain setting, tripartite ethnic composition and religious diversity, Transylvania somewhat resembles Switzerland. In contrast to the Swiss situation, however, the ethnic zones were not clearly defined: in Transylvania, the groups were much more inter-mixed. Moreover, their social conditions were not equal. The aristocracy was largely Hungarian and the bourgeoisie German, while most of the peasants were Romanian. Switzerland was formed by juxtaposed ethnic communities, producing a combination of solidarity and indifference in inter-ethnic relations, while the unequal mixture of Transylvania gave rise to frustrations (for the Romanians) and tensions. The result could not be a new Switzerland: rather it was the orientation of the Romanian majority towards incorporation into Romania.

Between Transylvania and Hungary, between the mountains and the plain of the Tisza, may be distinguished three more regions, which never reached the degree of geopolitical coherence and historical continuity attained by the principality of Transylvania. All three are nowadays cut across by the borders which separate Romania from Serbia, Hungary and Ukraine.

The Banat, the south-western province of Romania, is delimited by the mountains to the east, the Danube to the south, the Tisza to the west, and the Mureş, a tributary of the Tisza, to the north. Its relative historical autonomy is due to the fact that it was a frontier territory with a clear military role. In the Middle Ages, it belonged to Hungary. In the sixteenth century, it was conquered by the Turks, who lost it again in 1718 to the Habsburgs. The war-ravaged territory was colonized and made viable again by its new masters. From the end of the seventeenth century, Serbs from south of the Danube took refuge here. Large numbers of Germans were also brought especially from the south and west of Germany; they became known as Swabians and were Catholics, in contrast to the Lutheran Saxons of Transylvania. Timişoara, the provincial capital, became a typically Austrian town, as its nickname of 'Little Vienna' suggests. In comparison to Transylvania, with its political and ethnic structures crystallized over centuries, the Banat seemed to be a shifting frontier zone, a substantially new land made fruitful by colonists. This may explain the fact that ethnic tensions on the scale of those in Transylvania have never been seen here. There have been disagreements, of course, not only between Romanians and Hungarians but also between Romanian and Serbs; however, the Banat has also seen the formation of a culture of ethnic diversity. In 1918, the region was divided between Romania and Yugoslavia (the latter taking the part known as Voivodina). In 1930, the Romanian portion had a population that was 54.3 per cent Romanian. The second largest ethnic group was the Germans (23.8 per cent) followed by Hungarians (10.4 per cent, much fewer than in Transylvania), and Serbs and Croats (4.3 per cent). The religious configuration was also different from that of Transylvania. There were few Uniates, Reformed or Lutherans; almost all of the Romanians and Serbs were Orthodox (56.1 per cent of the total population), while the Germans and Hungarians were Roman Catholic (34.2 per cent).

A wooden church from Maramureş, built in 1722 and now in the Village Museum in Bucharest.

To the north of the Banat lies a territory that is more vaguely defined geographically and historically, the area which the Romanians call Crişana, after the three Criş rivers that flow through it before joining as a single tributary of the Tisza. Crişana is bounded to the east by the Apuseni Mountains, to the south by the Mureş, and to the west by the Tisza. The Romanian-Hungarian border cuts it in two. Historically, this area belonged to Hungary, without having any special status like that of Transylvania or the Banat, but, as in these other territories beyond the mountains, the majority of the population (in the portion assigned to Romania in 1918) was Romanian. In 1930, Romanians made up 61.2 per cent of the population, Hungarians 25.1 per cent and Germans 5.8 per cent.

Maramureş, too, the region on the northern edge of Romania, belonged to Hungary for centuries, but preserved its individuality thanks to its relative isolation. It consists of a hilly depression of some 10,000 sq km, surrounded by mountains. Only a third of Maramureş went to Romania in 1918; the rest (with a majority Ukrainian population) was incorporated into Czechoslovakia and now belongs to Ukraine. The Romanian part of Maramureş had a population in 1930 that was 57.5 per cent Romanian. There were relatively small numbers of Hungarians (7 per cent) and Germans (2 per cent). On the other hand, there were a considerable number of Ukrainians (11.9 per cent) and even more Jews, who had settled there relatively recently (20.6 per cent). Another distinctive feature was the small proportion of Orthodox: Uniates (both Romanian and Ukrainian) made up 65 per cent. This was a strongly rural region, with an urban population of only 17 per cent and a low level of literacy (38 per cent). (These figures refer only to the historical land of Maramureş. Nowadays, the name is applied to a larger area, the western part of which extends outside the mountains and has a less traditional and more urban character.) A traditional rural environ-ment and a lifestyle little touched by modernity were preserved in Maramureş better than anywhere else in Romania, and indeed they can still be found there, despite the industrialization and urbaniza-tion of recent years. The specific character of Maramureş comes from many elements: costume, dance, religious and folk art, and espe-cially the craft of woodcarving. There are the famous Maramureş carved gates, and wooden churches with tall, slender spires. Next to the Danube Delta and the monasteries of Bukovina, the landscape of Maramureş is one of the most unique and authentic sights which Romania offers the visitor.

A single country, ten regions: ten regions, a single country. Romania is a synthesis, the product of a vast diversity. To understand it, we need to explore its history, starting with the hazy and much mythologized problem of origins and ending with the Romania of today, a country still in search of the way ahead.

11 An Island of Latinity

The Romanians are much preoccupied with their origins. So much so that the past sometimes seems to be more important to them than the future. When, how and where was the Romanian people formed? What are its component elements? To such questions mythology gives much more certain answers than any prudent and critical historical approach could ever do.[1]

The first difficulty arises from the very concept under discussion. What is a people? What unites individuals into a people? The term is somewhat vague, and highly loaded politically. The anthropological concept of *ethnic group* seems more neutral and appropriate, but ultimately this is just a matter of a semantic shift and casts no fresh light on the problem. The principal bond uniting a people is usually linguistic, the possession of a common language. But even here, there are all sorts of complications and exceptions: a people may extend beyond the limits of a linguistic space, while a single linguistic space may be divided between several ethnic solidarities (with the fragmentation of languages into dialects introducing yet another note of complexity). However, ethnicity is not just a matter of language; there are other social and cultural structures which contribute to the cohesion of a people. Can these be defined with any degree of precision?

We may also add – indeed, it is essential – a repository of symbols. A people, or ethnic group, recognizes itself in certain symbols, in particular historical, cultural and political reference points. First and foremost, it has a name! How can we speak of a people when the population in question has no awareness of belonging to a community, when, indeed, it has no name for itself? For the Romanians to be Romanians, is it sufficient that they speak Romanian? If so, the problem of the formation of the Romanian people can be reduced to the problem of the formation of the Romanian language. It becomes a purely linguistic matter. But if we insist on other common reference points, things become more complicated. When did all the Romanians start to call themselves and each other Romanian, to consider themselves a common body, distinct from other ethnic entities? It is not easy to say. The Scots, for example, speak English, but they are not English. They may be called British, but here we have to introduce the concept of nation, a modern political concept which incorporates and transcends strictly ethnic criteria – the democratic principle of popular sovereignty, the idea of the nation-state, the 'sacralization' of the nation above all other values and structures, and so on. It is easy enough to say when the Romanian nation first emerged (as with most other European nations, it was in the nineteenth century), but it is much harder to define the stages in the formation of the Romanian people, for the simple reason that 'people' is a much vaguer concept than 'nation'. The Moldavians are as much a component part of the Romanian nation as are the Muntenians – the Romanians of Wallachia. But until the nineteenth century, not only did they have their own state and their own distinct history, they did not even call themselves Romanians, but Moldavians. They were nonetheless very close – and conscious that they were – to other Romanians in terms of language, culture and other forms of solidarity. From a present-day perspective, they were undoubtedly Romanian, but what about their own perspective, in their own time?

There is one fixed point in the midst of all of this confusion over Romanian origins: no linguist will contest the fact that the Romanian language is of Latin origin. It is a Romance language, like Italian, French, Spanish and Portuguese, but one that stands somewhat apart in that it evolved not in the west of Europe like the others but in the east, in the zone where Slavic languages predominate. It is all that remains of the eastern realm of Latinity, which in Antiquity also included the northern part of the Balkan peninsula. Furthermore, the Romanians bear a remarkable name. They are the only Romance people, apart from the small Romansch community of Switzerland, which has preserved the name of the one-time conquerors of the world. The original form of the name was *rumân* (hence forms like *Rumanian* and *Roumain* in other languages); it was modified in modern times to *român*, so as to come closer in spelling and pronunciation to *roman*. At first, this name applied to the people of Wallachia (the 'Romanian Land'); later, it became generalized. (It is interesting

The peoples of South-eastern Europe, according to a German map of 1918. The map shows the complex ethnic mix that made it so difficult to trace 'national' borders. It is nonetheless easy to recognize the shape of Greater Romania, which generally corresponds to the area where Romanians ('Rumänen') were in the majority. Hungarians are represented in the area labelled 'Magyaren'; a substantial group lies at the centre of the Romanian space. Note the numerous German 'islands', marked 'Sachs.' and 'D.', which are practically gone today. 'Osmanen' indicates the Turkish population of the Balkan peninsula, including Dobrogea; nowadays, Dobrogea is almost entirely Romanian. Towards the west, the Romanians barely reach the Tisza ('Theiß'), while in the east, there are Romanian 'islands' beyond the Dniester ('Dnjestr'), and even beyond the Bug. Today, the shadings would be rather more uniform everywhere; with a few exceptions (Kosovo), the percentage of minorities has fallen.

that in Wallachia, *rumân* was also the term for a dependent peasant – a curious linguistic conflation of the name of the lowest social class with that of the people and the country.)

Small wonder that at an early stage of historical enquiry, the nature of the Romanian language and the name of the people pointed scholars in search of origins first of all, and even exclusively, towards the Romans. For historians of the Renaissance, the Romanians were direct descendants of the Romans. The Romanians themselves began to show an interest in their Latin origins somewhat later. While the Renaissance was flourishing in Western Europe, they were fully integrated in the Slavonic culture of the East. Their cultural reference points were not Latin but Greek and Slavic, determined by their membership of the Orthodox Church. At the time, Europe was divided into two zones, Catholic and Orthodox, regardless of language and ethnicity. Latin Europe was Catholic Europe (or Catholic and Protestant Europe from the sixteenth century onwards). The Poles were Slavs but belonged through their Catholicism to the Latin cultural space, while the Romance-speaking Romanians belonged through their Orthodoxy to the Slavic space. They even wrote, as they were to do until well into the nineteenth century, in Cyrillic characters, just like the Bulgarians, Serbs and Russians. What counts more: distant origins or the cultural synthesis of a particular period? In a sense, the Poles were more Latin then than the Romanians!

The Romanians discovered their Latinity in the seventeenth century. This was the period when the Slavonic language, which had been omnipresent in the Church, in chancery documents and in the earliest historical writings, began to give way to Romanian. A first, and still limited, opening towards Western culture occurred; a few young boyars went abroad to study and acquired a knowledge of Latin. Moldavia had strong connections with Poland, and it was there that Grigore Ureche and Miron Costin, the greatest Moldavian historians of the seventeenth century, went to study. In the *Chronicle of the Land of Moldavia*, written in the 1640s, Grigore Ureche noted the striking similarity between certain Romanian words and their Latin equivalents, and concluded that all the Romanians (Moldavians, Muntenians and Transylvanians alike) had a common origin in Rome. A few decades later, Miron Costin devoted one of his works to the formation of the Romanian people, thus initiating what was to become a constant, and even obsessive, preoccupation of Romanian

Dacia and the other Danubian provinces of the Roman Empire.
The Roman province of Dacia included only a part of ancient Dacia
or modern Romania (more precisely, Transylvania, Oltenia and the
Banat; Muntenia, Moldavia, Bessarabia, Bukovina, Maramureş
and Crişana remained outside the Empire, while Dobrogea was
included in Moesia). Note Dacia's identity as an 'outpost' in the
'barbarian world'; it was the only Roman province situated north
of the Danube and surrounded by territories not controlled by the
Romans. Hence, it was exposed to attack and could not be
maintained for long.

historiography. Although his title, *On the Moldavian People*, illustrates the distinction between Moldavians and Muntenians, he
attributed the same Roman origin to both. Around 1720, the most
erudite of all of these Moldavian writers, Dimitrie Cantemir
(1673–1723), a former Prince of Moldavia, dealt with the same
problem of origins in a substantial and thoroughly documented
work entitled *Chronicle of the Antiquity of the Romano-Moldo-
Wallachians*, in which the Moldavians and Wallachians were placed
together in a direct line of descent from the Romans.

The historical facts were – or appeared to be – simple enough.
Dacia had been conquered by the Romans in the time of the Emperor
Trajan, in the course of two wars fought in AD 101–2 and 105–6. After

the final decisive defeat, Decebalus, the Dacian King, had committed suicide. Trajan and Decebalus came to constitute a double symbolic image of Romanian origins, in which their roles varied from one interpretation to another. In the first version, only Trajan's triumph was recalled, while Decebalus lost everything. As late as the nineteenth century, Romanian historians, with a few exceptions, would not even hear of a Dacian component to the Romanian people. The sacrifice of Decebalus had been pointless. The Dacians had disappeared without a trace. The Romanians were pure Romans.

We are dealing here, of course, with the particular logic of *foundation myths*. All communities, whether traditional or modern, construct a mythology of their origins. The 'foundation' is for a community what the birth certificate is for an individual. Without it, you do not exist, or you exist in a diminished and marginal manner, not recognized for what you are. This is why communities hold so strongly to their foundation myths, endlessly commemorating and re-actualizing them. Hence the inclination to ideologize and politicize these first moments. Nothing is more present than the beginning! But which beginning? We are faced with a choice, not something objectively given.

There was a time when nobility of origins counted above everything else. An outstanding hero from a far-off land had greater worth than a foundation grounded on native soil. Thus foundations were attributed to external, prestigious acts of creation. At the origin of Rome, we find the Trojan Aeneas. The French and the English of the Middle Ages likewise invoked two Trojans, Francus and Brutus, whom they considered to be the distant ancestors of their respective monarchies. For medieval and modern Europe, the principle mythological reference point was Rome. The imperial and the Christian ideas – the two great components of European civilization – found their starting point here, at the symbolic 'centre of the world'. For the people of the Renaissance and of the eighteenth century, Latin culture lay at the base of any intellectual training, and Roman history constituted an apparently unsurpassable model. The new imperial syntheses set out only to perpetuate (albeit imperfectly!) the Roman model: such was the case with Byzantium, with the Holy Roman Empire and even with Moscow, which began its imperial policy by considering itself the 'third Rome' (in other words, the inheritor of the world empire).

How could the Romanians resist such a temptation? If this sort of mythology has seemed particularly essential to them, it has largely been because of certain complexes and frustrations. The two Romanian lands of the time, Wallachia and Moldavia, were relatively insignificant on the map of Europe, subject territories of the Ottoman Empire whose rights were frequently disregarded by more powerful states. For the Romanians of Transylvania, the situation was even worse: they were peasants dominated by the Hungarian aristocracy. How could they fail to be seduced by the prospect of vengeance through history? This nation, whose present situation seemed so precarious, had once, through its Roman ancestors, been master of the world! And it could be presumed that a new glorious future awaited it.

The Latinist orientation was continued and amplified by the intellectual movement known as the 'Transylvanian School'. This movement appeared in the context of the annexation of Transylvania by the Habsburg Empire, closely followed by the adhesion to Uniate, or 'Greek', Catholicism (Catholicism of the Eastern Rite) of part of the Romanian population. The Greek Catholics enjoyed certain cultural and religious facilities which were denied to the Orthodox. Greek Catholic Romanian schools were established, and a number of young men were able to continue their studies in Vienna or Rome. The result was the emergence of the Transylvania School, which sought to enlighten the Romanians and obtain for them a status similar to that of the Hungarians and Germans. In their arguments, a key position was occupied by history, and especially the history of origins. They insisted on the antiquity of the Romanians (who antedated the other ethnic groups in Transylvania) and on their Latin, indeed purely Latin, origins. What better response could there be to the contempt with which the Magyar aristocracy regarded their Romanian subjects? In Hungary more than in other European countries, Latin continued to be an official language (used in administration and education) until well into the nineteenth century. What respect for Roman tradition! But in fact, the Romanians were the real Romans!

The three great historians of the Transylvanian School – Samuil Micu (1745–1806), Gheorghe Şincai (1754–1816) and Petru Maior (1761–1821) – did everything in their power to annihilate the Dacians and highlight the Latin purity of the Romanians. The reality was not quite so simple, of course. The Dacians had not all perished, nor was there any way in which the Romanians could be pure

Romans (where could anyone have got hold of so many pure Romans in the cosmopolitan Roman world of the second and third centuries?). In order to get rid of the Dacians, the historians either simply annihilated them (arguing that the Dacian wars had been conflicts of unimaginable brutality, veritable wars of extermination) or considered that they had fled or been banished from Dacia. In his *History for the Beginning of the Romanians in Dacia* (1812), Petru Maior proposed a demonstration – by *reductio ad absurdum* – which is not without a certain charm for today's readers.[2] The question of whether some Romans might not have married Dacian women was answered negatively by Maior, because, in his view, there were no Dacians left at all. But even if a few women had survived, the Romans would not have looked at them; in general, they did not marry women of other races, least of all the 'savage' women of Dacia. The Romanians, Maior continued, had inherited this form of exclusivity and did not marry foreign women either. Thus he was able to demonstrate in an impeccable way that the blood of the Romanians was Roman in its totality. The Hungarians, in contrast, presented a quite different aspect. First of all, their origins were far from noble. Then, having come to the Pannonian plain, they mixed with other peoples, as they had no women of their own race. They were a 'mongrel' people. The antithesis was perfect!

The approach of the Transylvanian School survived well into the nineteenth century, not only in Transylvania but throughout the Romanian space, in the hands of the Latinists, who were dominant until after 1870. The most influential of these, the historian and linguist August Treboniu Laurian (1810–1881) – note the Latin fore-names: the Transylvanians liked to give such names to their children – began his *History of the Romanians* (1853) with the foundation of Rome in 753 BC, adopting a dating system to match. The history of the Romanians was presented as a continuation of Roman history. The Romanians were Romans – no more and no less.

This Latinism was also fed by the affirmation of national ideology in the nineteenth century. Until the 'age of nations', the Romanians felt no need to delimit themselves clearly from the Slavs surrounding them. They too were Orthodox, and religion, with its reflections in culture, counted more than ethnic origin. Once they had entered the national phase, however, separation from the Slavic world and closer links with 'Latin sisters' in the West entered the agenda. Rome became a more powerful symbol than Byzantium, not only for the Transylvanian Greek Catholics, but for all Romanians. The Romanians discovered that they were 'a Latin island in a Slavic sea', isolated in the east of Europe and eager to break loose and navigate towards the West. The invocation of Rome indicated a strong insistence on Romanian identity, but it also showed a desire for Westernization.

ROMANS, DACO-ROMANS OR DACIANS?

And yet, towards the middle of the nineteenth century, Latin 'purism' began to be questioned. This was a sign of political and intellectual maturity. With the foundation of Romania (1859), and the proclamation of independence (1877) and of the Kingdom (1881), the Romanians saw that they could manage on their own, that they represented something in their own right, without the support of the Romans. At the same time, historiography and linguistics began to move beyond the national-romantic phase and become increasingly professionalized. By the end of the century, Maior's tale of Dacian women ignored by Romans could hardly be upheld by responsible historians. In the first place, the Roman colonization began to be seen in all its complexity. With some regret, but rather more realism, it was accepted that all too few pure Romans would have settled in Dacia at that time. The colonists were a mixed population, brought, according to the fourth-century historian Eutropius, 'ex toto orbe romano' (from the whole Roman world). The common factor among them was, of course, the use of Latin.

There could be no more talk of the 'disappearance' of the Dacians either. In 1860, the linguist and historian Bogdan Petriceicu Hasdeu (1838–1907) published an article with the provocative title 'Did the Dacians Perish?' His answer was simple and logical: there was no way the Dacians could have disappeared. Archaeological discoveries subsequently provided material evidence pointing in the same direction. Latinism was abandoned, at least in its extreme forms, and a consensus was reached on the Daco-Roman, rather than pure Roman, origin of the Romanian people. The Romanians began to feel less ashamed of the Dacians, discovering all sorts of qualities in them: nobility, courage, a spirit of sacrifice and so on. Herodotus in particular was cited, with his eulogistic appreciation of the Getae as 'the noblest as well as the most just of all the Thracian tribes'. (The phrase was taken out of context, however: Herodotus was in fact underlining the otherness of the Getae in relation to the Greeks, attributing to them a certain primitivism and pointing out their more passionate than rational character.) The spirituality of the Dacians and especially their religion, the cult of Zalmoxis, could likewise be developed into arguments in their favour.

Zalmoxis, certainly an interesting case, also came on the scene in the *Histories* of Herodotus.[3] The father of history reported, without particularly believing it, that this divinity of the Getae was said to have been a slave of the philosopher Pythagoras who, having been freed, returned to his own people and spread among the Getae the idea of immortality (which he had acquired, of course, from his master). Already in Antiquity, a legend began to take shape around this passage. Since all of the relevant texts are Greek (or, later, Roman), it is impossible to say what the real beliefs of the Getae and Dacians actually were. No representation of Zalmoxis of any kind is known in Dacia, either from pre-Roman or Roman times, even though the latter period was otherwise so rich in all sorts of divinities. A whole library has been written, and a complex ancient and modern mythology has grown up, on the basis of almost nothing. This is a good illustration of the way in which 'mythological logic' functions.

In modern Romanian culture, Zalmoxis provided support at one time for the theory that Dacian religion was monotheistic. From this point of view, at least, the Dacians were thus more advanced than the Greeks and Romans, and closer to Christianity. One single god to set against the host of divinities in Greco-Roman mythology! Belief in the immortality of the soul! Some more excitable enthusiasts went so far as to see in Zalmoxis a precursor of Jesus Christ. Even the young Mircea Eliade (1907–1986) dared to claim that 'When the first Christian missionaries arrived to bring the new faith to the Daco-Romans, the latter embraced Christianity at once and before others did so: Zalmoxis had paved the way for the new faith for centuries.'[4] There is no evidence to support such a statement. In the end, the notion of Dacian 'monotheism' gave way to the conclusion that the Dacians were polytheists like the majority of ancient peoples. Indeed, it is possible that what is attributed to Zalmoxis is no more than a projection into the Getic space of Greek Pythagorean conceptions. (In any case, nothing is more naïve than to accept ancient accounts about the composition of the world *ad litteram*; they are not realities but 'images', often highly distorted and even invented. It is difficult, and sometimes impossible, to extract the 'truth' from them.)

The revival of interest in the Dacians fits the general typology of modern foundation myths. In contrast with the traditional approach, preoccupied with nobility of origins and dependent on providential intervention from outside, the modern interpretation inclines towards indigenous continuity (going further and further into the past, even into prehistory). This is an evolution stimulated by the great ideologies of recent centuries – democracy and nationalism – in the sense that indigenous masses now count for more than conquering élites, while present-day national territory is projected back into a distant past. This new approach has also been supported by the development of archaeology. Classical archaeology was interested in works of art and the monuments of the great civilizations. In these terms, Dacia could not compare with Greece or Rome. Modern archaeologists, however, are interested in any trace of life, however modest. For them, there is no longer a distinction between 'interesting' and 'uninteresting' cultures.

And so the Dacians entered Romanian history. The Latinists had begun the national history with the Daco-Roman wars and the Roman conquest of Dacia, or even with the foundation of Rome. By the end of the nineteenth century, however, the first chapter belonged to the Dacians. The most important work of synthesis published in this period, *The History of the Romanians in Dacia Traiana* (1888–93) by Alexandru D. Xenopol (1847–1920), took as its starting point the year 513 BC — the first mention of the Getae in the *Histories* of Herodotus. Until then, the Romanians had benefited from the great virtues of the Romans. Now, they benefited from the combined virtues of the Dacians and the Romans (and from the additional historical right provided by the former as the earliest masters of the land).

It was not easy to reconcile the Romans and the Dacians, however. Which of them, after all, was to have priority? Once this game had been embarked upon, five answers were possible: 1) the Romanians were Roman (this previously dominant response no longer convinced anybody); 2) the Romanians were Daco-Romans, but more Roman than Dacian; 3) the Romanians were equally Dacian and Roman; 4) the Romanians were Daco-Romans, but more Dacian than Roman; 5) the Romanians were Dacian! Each solution had its adepts (and the discussion is not yet closed – how could it be?). The issue has provided an interesting ideological indicator. Romanians inclined towards the West prefer the Romans, while nationalists are more attracted to the Dacians.

Around 1900, and even later, the dominant discourse continued to give a privileged place to the Romans. For the Romanian nation and state, at the height of the process of modernization and Westernization, Rome offered a symbol that could not be neglected, and the Roman connection had to be preserved. This was far from simple, once it was acknowledged that the Dacians had not just disappeared. Despite the fact that the natives of a place are normally more numerous than its colonists, Xenopol argued that the importance of the Romans had been greater than that of the Dacians, and that 'the finest examples of the Romanian race of today do not derive from the Dacian so much as from the Roman character'.[5] Nicolae Iorga (1871–1940), considered to be the greatest Romanian historian, had a theory of his own on this matter. Long before the conquest of Dacia, he claimed, there had been a significant demographic flow from Italy towards the Balkans and the Danube. To begin with, Italian peasants had Romanized the Thracians and Illyrians; then together they had extended Romanizing influences north of the Danube, where, in Roman Dacia, they had become superior in numbers to the relatively small Dacian population.

In this connection, we might consider the great fresco of the Romanian Athenaeum in Bucharest, one of the city's emblematic monuments. This mural, by Costin Petrescu, inaugurated in 1937, presents a pictorial history of the Romanians. The Daco-Roman fusion is symbolized by the idyll of a Dacian woman and a Roman legionary. The Emperor Trajan is presented as a conqueror. But Decebalus is missing! On the other hand, Apollodorus of Damascus, the architect who built the Danube bridge over which the Roman legions passed, is represented. Although the Dacians have not been excluded entirely, Roman symbols are clearly dominant.

The point of perfect equilibrium may be found in the writings of Vasile Pârvan (1882–1927), the founder of the modern Romanian school of archaeology. Both in his great work *Getica* (1926) and in *Dacia: An Outline of the Early Civilizations of the Carpatho-Danubian Countries* (1928), the shorter book in English which resulted from a series of lectures delivered at Cambridge, Pârvan presented Dacia as a great kingdom with a homogeneous ethnic base, an advanced civilization and a well-defined political and national identity. The Dacians were valorized to the full. But so were the Romans! Pârvan argued that a long process of Westernization had occurred prior to the Roman conquest, which prepared and eased the way to effective

39

The birth of the Romanian people: a sketch for the great historical fresco in the Romanian Athenaeum in Bucharest, painted by Costin Petrescu between 1933 and 1937. In this symbolic composition, the Romans advance triumphantly while the Dacians are crushed to the ground. In the background can be seen the monument erected by Trajan at Adamclisi (known in Antiquity as *Tropaeum Traiani*) in Dobrogea in memory of his victory over the Dacians. In the foreground, a Roman soldier and a young Dacian woman (bending over the tomb of her loved ones who perished in the war) appear as the Adam and Eve of the Romanian nation.

Romanization. In Roman Dacia, in the midst of a reduced indigenous population and in conditions of massive colonization, the Roman element was dominant. However, Romanization also spread by means of a multiplicity of connections through the remainder of Dacia, the part not annexed by the Romans and whose population remained Dacian. The Romanians were thus, according to Pârvan, both Dacians and Romans to the highest degree, and modern Romania found its counterpart in ancient Dacia both before the Romans arrived and during the Roman period.

Belief in the primacy of the Dacians continued to advance, however. Mircea Eliade's generation – the young intellectuals of the 1930s – felt closer to the Dacians than to the Romans. Constantin C. Giurescu (1901–1977), representative of this generation, shifted the balance in favour of the Dacians in his *History of the Romanians* (1935). Even in the Roman province, he considered, in spite of wartime losses, Dacians remained in the majority. Their 'biological' weighting among Romanians was thus greater than that of the Roman colonists.

40

This theory marked a significant evolution. The Romanians had started by considering themselves Romans, then passed through a Daco-Roman phase, and now they ended up as Romanized Dacians. This last expression seems to correspond best to present-day historical consciousness. Stimulated by archaeological discoveries, but also by an inclination towards autochthonist nationalism, the Dacians have distanced themselves from the Romans. The Romanian language may be Romance, but Romanian blood is Dacian – the common perception of Romanian origins could be summed up in this way. Decebalus has thus had his revenge on Trajan.

Some have gone even further, to the extent of completely eliminating the Romans. This is a solution symmetrical to that attempted by the Latinists, who sought to remove the Dacians from history. But at least the Latinists had the argument of language on their side. In order to be convincing, the 'Dacianists' have had to demonstrate that Romanian does not derive from Latin but from Dacian, a hypothesis that could only provoke indignation and hilarity among linguists. However, mythology knows no impediments. Some Romanians consider themselves to be pure Dacians (and seem very content with their choice!). The tone was set by Nicolae Densuşianu (1841–1911), an erudite fantast and the author of a massive volume entitled *Prehistoric Dacia* (published posthumously in 1913). The thesis he supported, by drawing on a bizarre amalgam of information and deduction, was that around 6000 BC Dacia had been the centre of a world empire incorporating Europe, the Mediterranean, Egypt, North Africa and a good part of Asia. It was from here, between the Danube and the Carpathians, that civilization flowed out over the whole world. It was from here too that the Romans' ancestors set out for Italy. Dacian and Latin were merely dialects of the same language; it was not the Dacians who had ended up speaking Latin, but the Latins who spoke Dacian! In fact, all the Romance languages had their origin in Dacia. Among the evidence Densuşianu cited was Trajan's Column, the monument constructed by the Emperor in Rome after the Dacians' defeat, decorated with bas-reliefs illustrating the two wars (somewhat in the manner of strip cartoons). Here, Densuşianu noted, the Dacians and the Romans engaged in dialogue without interpreters, thus proving that they could make themselves understood perfectly while speaking their respective languages! Much can be said about the Dacian language for the simple reason that nobody knows it; the few surviving words are sufficient, however, to show that it was not at all similar to Latin!

From Latinists to 'Dacianists', the actors had changed, but the strategy remained the same. Through mythological identification with the Romans, first of all, and then through an even more mythological amplification of Dacian civilization, the Romanians were compensating, in their imaginations, for the marginality of their history; they were shifting themselves from the periphery to the centre. The imaginary past offered what the real present could not offer.

On the ideological level, the Daco-Roman synthesis meant the creation of an equilibrium between nationalism and Europeanism. The rejection of the Romans and the claim to an exclusively Dacian inheritance meant a distancing from the West and an immersion in autochthonism. It was just such a historical interpretation that the extreme Right promoted in the inter-war period. Paradoxically but understandably, these theories were revived some decades later, in the 1970s and '80s, by nationalist Communism. In both variants, the Dacians were on the side of a Romania closed in on itself, with its own values. The Latin island isolated from its non-Latin neighbours became a Dacian island isolated from the whole world.

The Dacians were put to work by Communist ideology in its intensification of nationalism, around 1980, the year in which the 2,050th anniversary of the foundation of the first Dacian state ruled by Burebista was celebrated with great pomp. (Chronology was 'arranged' in order to permit this commemoration, as it was impossible to say exactly when the Dacian King had actually begun his reign.) The Institute of History of the Communist Party, which had hitherto specialized in researching revolutionary workers' movements, underwent a radical shift of profile and started (with a degree of competence that may be imagined!) to deal with the problem of origins. The line the Institute adopted was decidedly pro-Dacian. Densuşianu's theses were brought back to life, including the famous argument based on the absence of translators on Trajan's Column. Thus Romanization was done away with, while the value of Dacian civilization was amplified beyond measure, not in the religious sense of the Zalmoxis cult, as the Communists were atheists, but through the highlighting of the Dacians' scientific knowledge and even their philosophical interpretations. (The ideal source for such an understanding is the sixth-century historian Jordanes, the author of a history of the Goths. Seeking to place the latter in a favourable light, he assimilated them to the Getae, to whom he attributed a brilliant civilization. Quite against their will, the Dacians were of service both to the Goths and to the Romanian Communists!)

No authentic specialist upheld the thesis of pure Dacianism; it was propounded by false researchers – Communist Party activists and various nationalist intellectuals lacking in historical training. Some Romanians succumbed nonetheless, and thus a current of opinion developed which can still be encountered today in all sorts of pseudo-historical interpretations. There is a sort of nationalist religion for which Dacia represents the centre of the world. Novels are written on this theme, and of course we still hear the ritual invocation of Zalmoxis, slave of Pythagoras, god of the Getae and protector of the Romanian people.

A COMPLICATED SYNTHESIS

So the battle of origins has been fought out. The mythological approach tends towards simplification and promotes racial purism: the Romanians cannot be other than Romans, Dacians or Daco-Romans. The idea of a more complex ethnic and cultural mixture, indeed one which has varied from one period to another, rarely enters the discussion. And yet what is striking about Romania is precisely the multitude and variety of the elements which have gone to make it up.

First of all, even the apparently simple components, the Dacians and the Romans, conceal a great diversity. The ancient writers distinguished between Dacians and Getae, both of whom were branches of the Thracian people. The Getae lived beside the Danube, especially to the south of the river, in the northern part of today's Bulgaria, but also in the Muntenian plain and in Dobrogea. The nucleus of the Dacians was in Transylvania. At a certain point, the phrase 'Geto-Dacians' was coined in Romanian historiography to suggest a unity of Getae and Dacians, the existence of a single people. Among the authorities invoked was the first-century-BC geographer Strabo, who had written that the Getae and Dacians spoke the same language. But it would be naïve to imagine that Strabo (or Poseidonius, from whom his information probably derived) knew Thracian dialects as well as all that. Once again, it was a case of the uncritical use of ancient sources. A Geto-Dacian people may exist from the modern, national point of view, but it certainly did not exist in Antiquity. The individuals concerned did not call themselves 'Geto-Dacians', and a people without a name is hard to imagine. In fact, the Dacian space was fragmented, even if the tribes spoke similar languages (or dialects of the same language). Moreover, the Dacians were not alone. The Scythians, a people of Iranian origin who came from north of the Black Sea (in present-day Ukraine), settled in the eastern part of their territory, and especially in Dobrogea, known in Antiquity as Scythia Minor. From the west came the Celts, some of whom remained in Dacia. Somewhat later, Bastarnians and Sarmatians (peoples of Iranian origin, like the Scythians) also settled in Dacian territory. Not to mention the Roman colonists, who themselves had a wide variety of origins.

In the thousand years that followed the Roman withdrawal, an impressive series of migrations affected the present-day territory of Romania. Many of the 'migratory peoples' in question did not simply pass through but settled, cohabiting, and finally mixing with, the native population. Indeed, sources of the time speak only of them, ignoring the Daco-Romans. The list is long, featuring Goths and Gepids (Germans), Huns and Avars (from Central Asia), Slavs, Magyars, Pechenegs and Cumans (of Turkish origin) and, finally, Tatars, the great invasion of 1241 being the last migratory wave before the foundation of the Romanian states. However, even after this millennium of migrations, the Romanians were not left alone; their space continued to attract foreigners from all directions, whether as guests or as conquerors. Although, as I have already shown, this ethnic, cultural and religious mosaic was still apparent around 1930, the tendency in Romanian historiography has been to regard all of these elements as superficial and transitory with the possible exception of the Slavs.

The file on the Slavs is, indeed, significant. While they settled in the present territory of Romania in the sixth and seventh centuries, they crossed in larger numbers to the south of the Danube (especially after 602, when the Byzantine defences on the river collapsed), Slavicizing the northern half of the Balkan peninsula. Thus were born the Bulgarians, the Serbs and the other Slavic Balkan peoples. Had it not been for the Slavs, Romanity might well have survived both north and south of the Danube, and today there might have been a vast Romania incorporating its own present territories plus

Bulgaria and former Yugoslavia! On the other hand, the opposite process might have been brought to completion: total Slavicization, north as well as south of the Danube, resulting in a purely Slavic land. What is certain is that the assimilation of the Slavs did not mean their disappearance without trace, but rather the enriching of the Romanian synthesis. While this may seem a natural conclusion, it was hard for modern Romanian historiography to accept it in a period when the Romanians had decided to finish with the Slavic world and to look exclusively westwards.

It goes without saying that the Latinist School, having eliminated the Dacians, did not wish to hear about the Slavs. When, in a subsequent phase, the Dacians were rehabilitated, the Slavs were not. Hasdeu, the tireless upholder of the Dacians, showed no inclination to treat them with the same good will – an apparently curious choice for the first Romanian Slavicist! Hasdeu, however, was a native of Bessarabia, then under Russian rule; he did not like the Russians at all and saw Pan-Slavism as a threat (in response to which he urged the Romanians to adopt a 'pan-Latin' policy). In his view, Slavic influence had come relatively late and was the result not of ethnic mixing but of borrowing in the political and religious spheres. In other words, the Slavs had not affected the essence of the Romanian people and culture.

A few decades later, when the critical spirit had progressed and the problem of origins had been de-dramatized to some extent, Ioan Bogdan (1864–1919), the first truly professional Romanian Slavicist, presented things in a quite different light. For him, the Slavs were a constitutive element of the Romanian synthesis. 'The influence of the Slav element in the formation of the Romanian nation', he wrote in 1905, 'is so evident that we may say, without exaggeration, that it is not even possible to speak of a Romanian people prior to the absorption of Slav elements by the native Roman population in the sixth to tenth centuries.' Bogdan's arguments included the 'enormous number of Slav elements' that had entered the Romanian language, both directly, through cohabitation, and by way of political and literary channels; the use of Slavonic (the old Slav language) in both church and state contexts, and even in 'the everyday affairs of the Romanians', as late as the sixteenth and seventeenth centuries; and the Slavic origin of the majority of medieval Romanian institutions. The strongest influence was that of the southern Slavs, more precisely of the Bulgarian state (the Slavic language used in the

45

Romanian lands being essentially 'middle-Bulgarian').[6]

These considerations were never taken to their logical conclusion: the placing of the Slavs alongside the Dacians and Romans. Even if they were granted a certain role, the Slavs remained in a secondary position: an addition, perhaps an important one, but no more than an addition, to a synthesis that had already taken shape. The exception was the first period of Romanian Communism (the 1950s), when the Slavs were put in the spotlight, given the relationship of subordination to the Soviet Union and the promotion of 'brotherhood' among Communist countries (which were mostly Slavic). However, with the affirmation of a nationalist brand of Communism under Ceauşescu, things went to the other extreme. If even the Romans were no longer favoured, how much less the Slavs! The conclusion was advanced that the Romanian people and language had already been formed, at least in broad terms (as 'proto-Romanian'), by the sixth century. This meant that subsequent influences, including that of the Slavs, could not have affected the basic Romanian stock in any profound way.

It is not at all easy in Romania to evoke the role of the Slavs in the past with scholarly detachment, as they are all too present around Romania today. The Romanians' identity in the modern period has been affirmed precisely by distancing them from the Slavic world. The fact that Communism, in its anti-national phase, also made use of the Slavs in its attempt to destroy Romanian national feeling does not make things any simpler. However, I believe that Ioan Bogdan was right. Where the Romanian language is concerned, the Slavs' contribution was clearly more important than that of the Dacians; moreover, it is far from certain that the Slavs were any less numerous than the Roman colonists. However, it is important to remember that a people cannot be reduced to biological data ('blood'), or even to linguistic data. The racial-linguistic approach of the Romantic period now seems completely out of date. In speaking about the Slavs, we cannot ignore the profound cultural impact of the Slavonic model in the Romanian Middle Ages. With the exception of language (and even here we must note a significant Slavic infusion and the use of Slavonic as a language of culture), the Romanian lands in the Middle Ages come across as similar to the Slavic countries of the region. It is not France and Italy that Wallachia and Moldavia resemble so much as Bulgaria and Serbia.

A people does not remain fixed over time. It is a fluid synthesis and in any case a cultural, not a biological, one. Ancestral inheritance is continually diluted, and contemporary connections are more important than origins. Ancestors end up counting less for themselves and more for the ways in which we use them to mark our identity. It is certain that the Romanians of today resemble the British (different as they are) more than they do the Dacians and the Romans. In fact, they do not resemble the latter at all: they lived 2,000 years ago, and had a quite different mentality and way of life than we do. Marc Bloch's remark, quoting an Arab proverb, is very apt: 'People resemble their times more than they resemble their fathers.'[7]

THE DISPUTE OVER CONTINUITY

However complicated the origins of the Romanians might be, they seem simple in comparison with the famous and endlessly controversial problem of continuity. At a certain point, the idea took shape that the Romanians came from south of the Danube, from an area hard to pinpoint exactly but probably in the north-west of the Balkan peninsula. This migration, it was argued, happened either quite late, around the thirteenth century, or somewhat earlier, beginning in the ninth century. The 'immigrationist' theory was first proposed towards the end of the eighteenth century by the Austrian historians Franz Joseph Sulzer and Johann Christian Engel and, again, with a more modern historical and philological apparatus, by the Austrian Robert Roesler in his book *Romänische Studien* (1871). It has become a veritable dogma in Hungarian historiography and a permanent bone of contention between Hungarian and Romanian historians.

Why did this situation arise? For a wide variety of reasons, both historical and political.[8] From the very beginning, there appears to have been a discrepancy between the effective process of Roman expansion and Romanization and the present ethnic configuration of south-eastern Europe. The northern half of the Balkan peninsula was part of the Roman Empire for some eight centuries, long enough to permit the consolidation of a thriving Roman lifestyle. To the north of the Danube, on the other hand, in the present-day territory of Romania, the Romans ruled only half of Dacia; moreover, the extent of Romanization in this province is open to question, as it belonged to the Empire for only 165 years (from AD 106 to 271, when it was abandoned as the Romans withdrew to the Danube).

Meanwhile, the un-annexed half of Dacia had no way of being Romanized (even if some historians claim the contrary). Yet the result turned out to be the opposite of the starting point: Romania, the 'successor of Rome' in this part of Europe, lies to the north of the Danube, not to the south.

Then there is the problem of the so-called 'dark millennium' between the withdrawal of Roman rule in 271 and the foundation of the Romanian states in the fourteenth century. Here, the most diverse hypotheses have free rein, given the paucity of sources referring to the area north of the Danube during this period. Internal written sources are particularly lacking. But even external ones tell us very little, or at least very little that is reliable, about the Romanians. (It is true that the *Gesta Hungarorum*, the chronicle written in the later twelfth century by an anonymous notary of King Bela III of Hungary, the so-called 'Anonymus', mentions the presence in Transylvania of Romanians, and of small Romanian states, at the time of the Hungarians' arrival around 900; however, as the text was written long after the events it describes, the adversaries of Romanian continuity accord it no credit in this respect, while Romanian historians, of course, consider it a precious and trustworthy source.) For some aspects of the period, archaeology has been able to make up for the lack of written sources. We now know that the territory of Dacia continued to be densely populated, and we can reconstruct the inhabitants' way of life. Unfortunately, archaeological material cannot tell us what language they spoke.

Finally, but no less significantly, ideological and political factors have come into play. It is obvious that the denial of Romanian continuity corresponded to Austro-Hungarian objectives in the eighteenth and nineteenth centuries. And it continues to be the sole interpretation espoused by contemporary Hungarian historians, for whom it serves to ensure chronological priority for the Magyars in Transylvania. Of course, the affirmation of Romanian continuity is no less politicized an option, though this time, one that favours the Romanians, Romanian national ideology and the Romanian nation-state (in other words, the identification of ancient Dacia with Greater Romania). It is interesting that some arguments are common to both immigrationists and Romanian nationalists. The notion that the Dacians were exterminated, invoked by the Latinists in their obsession with the purity of Romanian blood, has served the purposes of the immigrationist thesis equally well: what better argument could there be for immigration than the emptying of Dacia of its indigenous inhabitants? Conversely, the non-Romanization of the Dacians, upheld by the nationalist extreme of pure Dacianism, has provided a further argument in support of the hypothesis that the Romanians and their language expanded from outside the present space of Romania, given that all serious linguists consider Romanian to be a Romance language.

On what do the immigrationists base their thesis? The 'silence of the sources' may not be a sufficient argument in itself, but it certainly gives cause for thought. And what about the similarities between Romanian and Albanian (in particular a series of words common to both)? These tend to suggest that the two peoples were neighbours in an initial phase. The Slavic element in the Romanian language (and in Romanian culture and society) is likewise Balkan in nature. The Macedo-Romanian or Aromanian dialect (spoken in Greece, Albania and Macedonia) is sufficiently close to Romanian to 'draw' the Romanians back towards the Balkans.

The Romanian upholders of continuity have ready replies to all of these arguments. They explain the similarities to Albanian in terms of a common Thracian, or Dacian, substrate. The words in question are thus precisely the Dacian element in the Romanian language. This is unfortunately an unverifiable hypothesis, as the Dacian language (and indeed the language of the Thracians in general) is unknown. The only certainty remains the similarity to Albanian (which moreover includes a number of words of Latin origin, some of them almost identical in the two languages). The Slavic elements in Romanian, and the Slavic influence on the Romanians in general, can, on the other hand, be explained by the assimilation of the Slavs north of the Danube, a process completed and amplified by the later influence of the Slavonic political and cultural model. Thus the silence of the sources cannot be considered an argument against continuity. Medieval documents generally refer to the dominant elements in military and political terms. In any case, the Balkan Vlachs also appear late in the sources. A migration on such a large scale hardly seems credible. And if the sources do not mention the presence of Romanians north of the Danube, they also do not mention any migration of Romanians from the south. In other words, they say nothing about the formation of the Romanian people north of the Danube, but they also say nothing about its formation in the Balkans. And yet the Romanians exist!

It is difficult for immigrationists to identify the place from which the Romanians set out and when they did so. Romanian historians, the upholders of continuity, have likewise elaborated very different scenarios. On top of this, historians and linguists have not been in perfect agreement on the matter. A number of Romanian linguists – including some of the most famous – have even embraced the immigrationist theory (in general, linguists cannot ignore the Balkan character of the Romanian language). The fact is that, broadly speaking, Roman Dacia comprised Oltenia, Transylvania and the Banat. This is where Roman colonization and Romanization, the necessary premises for the formation of the Romanian language and people, took place. The greater part of Muntenia, Moldavia and Maramureş remained under the control of the free Dacians. The map of Romanization does not, therefore, correspond to the map of today's Romania. It includes half of Romania and, on the other side of the Danube, half of the Balkan peninsula. It was within these limits that the solution had to be sought.[9]

Hasdeu had a special preference for Oltenia: the region's pure Romanian character impressed him. This, he decided, was the region where the Romanian people had been formed, and from where it had gradually spread between the fourth and fourteenth centuries. Xenopol gave the privileged role to Transylvania. During the thousand years of migrations, he believed, the Romanians had taken shelter in that 'mountain fortress'; from the thirteenth century on, they had come down to the hill country and plains, where they had founded the two states of Wallachia and Moldavia. In 1885, Dimitrie Onciul (1856–1923), the founder of the new critical current in Romanian historiography, published an important study on the 'Roesler theory'. Both Roesler's and Xenopol's interpretations seemed unsatisfactory to him. Why, he asked, must it be a case of *either* south *or* north of the Danube, and not one of *both* south *and* north? The Danube was not a frontier: the Romans ruled, and the Latin language was spoken, on both banks of the river. The cradle of the Romanian people was thus, according to Onciul, Roman Dacia together with Moesia (the northern part of the Balkan peninsula, part of the present-day territory of Bulgaria and Serbia). His was therefore a compromise or synthesizing solution between continuity and immigrationism. The debatable points in the theory of continuity were dealt with (those curious similarities to Albanian, for example) without sacrificing what was essential: the persistence of the

Romanian element in the territory of Romania, or at any rate in part of it (certainly in Transylvania, the principal bone of contention).

Thus the Romanians became heirs to the whole of eastern Romanity (a conception strongly supported by Nicolae Iorga). Alongside its role in historical argumentation, this 'Balkan inheritance' also served to justify Romanian policy in the region: at the beginning of the twentieth century, Romania appointed itself arbiter of the Balkans, and in any case protector of the Romanian element there (the Aromanians). The main emphasis continued to be placed on the territory north of the Danube, however, as historians were preoccupied, naturally enough, with marking out the country's contemporary borders. The area south of the river remained a 'reservoir' of secondary importance. At the same time, there was a tendency to blur the border between Roman Dacia and that part of the territory which had remained Dacian (a border that cut across modern Romania). Pârvan considered that, in one way or another, Roman life had also penetrated the Dacian villages of Muntenia and Moldavia. Iorga, too, identified an early (but hypothetical) Romanian Land, which embraced all of the Romanian territories. Gheorghe Brătianu (1898–1953), on the other hand, in a book often cited on the issue of continuity, *Une Enigme et un miracle historique: Le Peuple roumain* (1937), accepted that Moldavia and Bessarabia had represented a later phase of Romanian expansion in the Middle Ages. Whatever some historians say, it is still difficult to understand how regions that were not colonized by the Romans could have become Romanized. Commercial contact alone, however close it may be, is not sufficient to make people give up their language and adopt another. There must have been a Romanian expansion in the Middle Ages, if not from south of the Danube, then at least from the south-west of Romania (corresponding to Roman Dacia) towards the north and east.

Communism did not trouble itself with such subtleties; instead, it took radical steps, as was its wont. On the one hand, it gave up the trans-Danubian connection (partly to avoid feeding the immigrationist theory but also on the principle of not intervening in others' affairs, so that they would not intervene in return). On the other hand, it decided that the Romanian people had been formed precisely in the entire territory of present-day Romania. Especially under nationalist Communism, the dispute with Hungarian historiography caused a pronounced emphasis to be placed on continuity.

The archaeologists were put to work in order to prove absolute continuity, in every corner of Romania, and this they did, or at least so they claimed. In fact, they confused material traces and ethnic characteristics (including language), and the results they obtained were equivocal and two-edged. Following a first phase of Daco-Roman continuity, there is a complete change in the archaeological record around the year 600, with the arrival of the Slavs. Everything is different: the character of dwellings, their contents, even funerary customs. Curiously enough, the archaeologists of the Communist period concluded from this that there had been uninterrupted Romanian ethnic continuity! In strictly archaeological terms, in fact, there was discontinuity.

Much ink has been spilled over the Dridu culture (named after a village in the Danube plain), which can be identified from the eighth century in both Romania and Bulgaria. Romanian researchers consider it to have been Romanian; the Bulgarians, on the other hand, along with other non-Romanian specialists, regard it as a Slavic cultural synthesis. Some see the Romanians present everywhere, while for others they have disappeared! According to the second variant, they were simply swallowed up by the Slavs, much as happened in other places where the Roman imprint was wiped out as a result of invasions (Britannia, Pannonia, the north of the Balkan peninsula, North Africa etc.). Ultimately, the archaeological discoveries lend support to both theories: continuity and immigrationism. The result of the match is a nil-nil draw. Two perfectly opposed scenarios, constructed out of the same material, stand face to face. This, too, is an original aspect of Romanian history, a special case in European historiography. According to the multitude of divergent interpretations, Romanian and foreign, old and new, the Romanians were either formed all over the territory corresponding to modern Romania, or only in part of this territory, or over a territory considerably larger than that of today's Romania, or completely outside the country's present borders! The Romanians remain, in the words of the French historian Ferdinand Lot (borrowed by Brătianu in the title of the book referred to above), 'an enigma and a historical miracle'. Will the enigma ever be resolved? We have to accept the fact that history does not provide answers to all our questions, and, even worse, it sometimes confuses us with contradictory answers.

But what would happen if it were proved that the Romanians really did arrive from somewhere in the Balkans? Nothing would happen! I do not believe that anyone would think of returning them to the other side of the Danube, evacuating the Serbs and Bulgarians in the process! This would be a stupid game. But it could also become a bloody one. In Kosovo, too, there was the pretext of a dispute over continuity, with the Serbs claiming that the territory was the 'cradle' of their nation and state, while the Albanians considered themselves to be a much older presence in the area, the descendants of the Thraco-Illyrians. History is used as an alibi everywhere; the real problems are those of the present, not the past. Romania is what it is not because Dacians and Romans lived there two thousand years ago, but because Romanians are nowadays in the majority in all of its provinces, including Transylvania, and because they wanted, and still want, to live in a Romanian state. If they were to become a minority in Transylvania, like the Serbs in Kosovo, what use would historical continuity be to them? Although they are less numerous than the Romanians, the Hungarians are also at home in Transylvania, regardless of when they arrived there. The peoples of Central and South-eastern Europe have to learn to leave the majority-minority dichotomy behind and look towards the future rather than back to the past.

A LANGUAGE DIFFERENT FROM OTHERS

While it is far from certain how Romanian blood breaks down into proportions of Dacian, Roman, Slavic or other origin, and it is not easy to say how the Romanian language and people crystallized, one thing remains clear: Romanian is a Romance language. The extravagant theory that it is actually Dacian does not even merit serious discussion. For Romance scholars, it is a fascinating language which has evolved far from the other members of its family, and independent of them. It has assimilated specific elements (Slavic, Turkish, Greek and Hungarian) which differentiate it even more from the western Romance languages (while largely lacking the Germanic borrowings which predominate in these). Certainly, it is the most original of the Romance languages.[10]

The structures of Romanian (its morphology and syntax) are Latin to an overwhelming degree. Where vocabulary is concerned, however, things are rather more complicated, and there has been no shortage of polemics around the subject. Between 1870 and 1879, the linguist Alexandru Cihac published a Romanian etymological dictionary, *Dictionnaire d'étymologie daco-romane*, in Frankfurt. The results of his study were surprising – the more so as the Romanians had hitherto been educated in a spirit of respect for their Latin inheritance. Cihac's conclusion was that out of a total of 5,765 words studied, 2,361 were Slav, 965 Turkish, 635 borrowed from modern Greek, 589 Hungarian, 50 Albanian – and only 1,165 were Latin. In other words, Romanian vocabulary was two-fifths Slavic and only one-fifth Latin. Latin words were hardly more numerous than those of Turkish origin. It can be imagined what emotions were aroused by this calculation in Romania. Either Cihac was mistaken, or the Romanians were no longer Roman, even in linguistic terms! It was noticed later that many words were missing from Cihac's dictionary, and that not all of the etymologies were correct. It is an illusion to imagine that statistics is an objective and exact science. Accuracy depends upon *what* is counted and *how*! A study dated 1942 and based on a much larger number of words (over 40,000) reduced the proportion of Slavic words to 16 per cent (compared with almost 41 per cent according to Cihac); in fact, their 'statistical' trend is one of continual decline.

But the real problem does not reside here, as B. P. Hasdeu showed in a fundamental study.[11] In English, for example, there are more Romance words (from French or Latin) than Germanic, but this does not prevent English from belonging to the Germanic family. It is the same with Romanian: what matters, Hasdeu argued, is not so much the number of Latin words (which varies in any case from one 'head count' to the next) as their circulation value. In his theory of the 'circulation of words' (their 'frequency', we would now say), Hasdeu made an important contribution to general linguistics. (It is not surprising that it should have been a Romanian who came up with this idea; at the time, a fierce battle was raging in Romania around the question of origins.) Who uses all the words of a language? Most of them we do not even know; others occur only occasionally in normal speech. There are, however, words we use again and again. In Romanian, it is possible to formulate whole sentences using only words of Latin origin, but it is impossible to put together a sentence using exclusively Slavic, Turkish, Greek or Hungarian elements.

The essential Romanian vocabulary is thus to a large degree Latin – though this claim should not be exaggerated. *Om* ('man', 'person'), *bărbat* ('man'), *femeie* ('woman') and so on are Latin words. Some other Latin words have taken on quite different meanings in Romanian compared with the western Romance languages. *Pămînt*, for example (meaning 'earth', in the sense both of soil and of the terrestrial globe), comes from the Latin *pavimentum* ('floor'). On the other hand, *terra*, which means 'earth' in Latin (whence the Italian *terra* and French *terre*), gave the Romanian *ţară* ('country'). *Bătrîn* ('elderly') comes from *veteranus*, the word for an old soldier. *Sat* ('village') is from *fossatum* ('ditch' in Latin), conjuring up an image of settlements protected by defensive ditches.

Slavic words incontestably form the second constitutive element of the Romanian language (despite the marginalizing of some of them, or their doubling, and even replacement, with neologisms, usually of French origin). Grammatical structures and phonetics have also been touched by Slavic influence. While *om*, *bărbat* and *femeie* are Latin, *nevastă* ('wife') is a Slavic word. Also Slavic are *dragoste* and *iubire* (both meaning 'love'). A large number of words concerned with the human body, elements of nature, the peasant household, agriculture and cattle rearing, and social and military organization are Slavic in origin. *Boier* ('boyar'), the term defining the Romanian nobleman, is a Slavic word, likewise *voievod* ('voivode', 'prince'), the title of the medieval Romanian rulers. There are also a number of Slavic prefixes and suffixes which are used to form families of words and which give a more general Slavic colouring to the Romanian language. Often a root is Latin but the added particles are Slavic: thus *ţăran* ('peasant') comes from *ţară*, a word of Latin origin, to which is added the Slavic suffix *-an*; the feminine form *ţărancă* ('peasant woman') involves the addition of a further suffix, *-că*, likewise of Slavic origin. The Slavs also passed many personal names, and an impressive number of place names, to the Romanians. A considerable number of geographical features – rivers, hills, mountains and human settlements – bear Slavic names; these include Moldova (Moldavia), so called after the river of the same name, and Dîmboviţa, the river that flows through Bucharest.

The Turkish stock of words is the third in importance (if we consider only 'traditional' Romanian, without the neologisms adopted in the last two centuries). It is possible, in fact, to speak of a broader oriental influence, as some Turkish words may have been borrowed by the Romanians before the Ottoman period (from the Pechenegs, Cumans and Tatars), while Turkish was the intermediary through which a series of words from Arabic and Persian entered the language.[12] In contrast to the Slavic element, Turkish did not affect the structures of Romanian. The Turkish adoptions consist mostly of nouns with a concrete meaning, denoting material things or elements of civilization. Many entered popular speech as the result of prolonged Romanian-Ottoman contact and the adoption of Turkish products, techniques, customs and fashions from the fifteenth to the beginning of the nineteenth century. *Cioban* ('shepherd'), *musafir* ('guest'), *duşman* ('enemy'), *odaie* ('chamber'), *duşumea* ('wooden floor'), *tavan* ('ceiling'), *dulap* ('cupboard') and *chibrit* ('matchstick') are words of Turkish origin. Romanian gastronomy also takes much of its vocabulary from Turkish, including what are nowadays considered typically Romanian dishes: *ciorbă* (sour soup) and *sarmale* (meat and rice rolled in cabbage). The pre-modern terminology of architecture and urbanism likewise shows a profound Turkish influence, although some of these words have suffered a depreciation as the oriental model has been left behind. Such is the case with *mahala*, for example, which formerly meant 'district'; nowadays, the Romanians use the French neologism *cartier* for 'district', and *mahala* has taken on a pejorative sense, referring to the poor areas on the periphery of a city. Similarly, *maidan* once meant an open space or marketplace; now it means a neglected piece of waste ground.

A considerable number of medieval and modern Greek words have also entered Romanian. In the Middle Ages, the Greeks offered the Romanians an important political, religious and cultural model. Moreover, many Greeks settled in the Romanian lands, a process which culminated in the eighteenth century in the so-called 'Phanariot' period (named after the princes appointed by the Ottoman Sublime Porte, who were mostly Greeks from the Phanar district of Constantinople). This period saw a veritable invasion of Greek words. The majority of them did not resist the modernizing process of the nineteenth century; however, there are still a number of essential words of Greek origin in Romanian: *ieftin* ('cheap'), *folos* ('use'), *frică* ('fear'), *a lipsi* ('to lack'), *a plictisi* ('to bore') and so on.

There is also a body of words of Hungarian origin. Not many are in everyday use, but a few are important. One of these is *oraş* ('town'), from the Hungarian *város* – but note that *cetate* ('citadel') is of Latin origin and *tîrg* ('market', 'small town') is Slavic: yet another illustration of the Romanian lexical mosaic. Others include *hotar* ('boundary'), *neam* ('people', 'nation') and even *gînd* ('thought') – a word full of subtleties of meaning in Romanian.

But where are the Dacians? Did they leave no linguistic inheritance? Hasdeu, who rescued them from the fury of the Latinists, was also the first to try to delimit the Dacian element in Romanian, identifying more than 80 possible candidates. But most of the etymologies he proposed have not stood the test of time. Other researchers have picked up the torch, however. The recent specialist in the problem, I. I. Russu, came to the conclusion that some 160 words belong to the Dacian substrate. Together with their derivatives, they would account for around 10 per cent of the basic word stock of Romanian.[13] Statistics again! Such enthusiasm seems a little excessive, and the ideological dimension of the project is evident. Current exploration is centred on the parallels between Romanian and Albanian, whose shared words (with the exception, of course, of those of Latin origin) are taken to be, in the case of Romanian, Dacian. These include *mal* ('river bank'), *brad* ('fir tree') and *a se bucura* ('to rejoice') – along with the noun *bucurie* ('joy') and the personal name *Bucur*, whence the name of the capital of Romania, *Bucureşti* ('Bucharest'). Ultimately, any word for which no other origin (Latin, Slav etc.) can be established could be Dacian! On the other hand it is clear that the Dacians, and the Thracians in general, adopted Latin after their own fashion. Everywhere the 'substrate' had its part to play in the 'corruption' of the Latin language, pointing it towards the respective modern languages. This is probably the explanation for certain peculiarities shared by Romanian, Bulgarian and Albanian (three languages which otherwise belong to completely different families). To give an example from phonetics, there is the closing of *a* into *ă*, a vowel sound characteristic of all three.

Later on in this book, I will deal with the process of Westernization unleashed in the nineteenth century and the significant effects this had on the language. What remains, apart from the dominant mark of Latinity, is the remarkable and picturesque mixture that is the Romanian synthesis: the reflection of a troubled history, subject to varied influences and interferences. Like Romania itself, the Romanian language is unmistakable, with its predominantly Latin note but also its appreciable Slavic colouring, its oriental words that burst out from time to time, and its specific sounds (*ă*, *î*, *ş* and *ţ*) which are so hard for foreigners to pronounce. Of all other languages, the closest to Romanian is Italian. I would say that, paradoxically, Romanian resembles Italian more than

Italian does Romanian! A Romanian who hears Italian spoken can understand quite a lot (those Roman ancestors count for something, after all!); an Italian will understand much less Romanian, confused by the Slavic and oriental words and by the pronunciation. In any case, an Italian will never speak Romanian perfectly. On the other hand, many Bulgarians learn Romanian very well and speak it without an accent (precisely because the 'tone' of the two languages is similar). Are the Romanians closer to the Italians or to the Bulgarians? Who can say? They are brought close to the Italians, of course, by their Latin roots and by the desire of an élite in the modern period to look towards the West. But the Thracian substrate, the Slavic component, the Orthodox faith, oriental influence and a long common history mean that they are close to the Bulgarians and other Balkan peoples too. In the end, Romania is simply Romania – not an easy country to classify!

iii How Romania was Created

The phrase 'De la Nistru pîn' la Tisa' ('From the Dniester to the Tisza') is well known to Romanians. It defines the limits of an ideal Romania (though we should note that the Romanian population extends in the east beyond the Dniester, while both banks of the Tisza are completely Hungarian for most of the river's length). To the south, the Danube completes this symbolic geography of Romania: an enclosed space between three rivers, with an area of some 300,000 sq km, comparable with that of Italy or the British Isles. Rivers, then, are perceived as natural borders, separating Romanians from Others. But what about mountains? The Carpathians divide Romanian territory in two. Their 'responsibility' has been seen in different ways by historians. Xenopol saw the mountain barrier as the main explanation for the Romanians' division into different states: the Carpathians separated Transylvania from the other two provinces, and moreover obliged Moldavia to look eastwards and Wallachia towards the south. Other historians have attributed a unifying function to the Carpathians, considering them to be the 'spinal column' that structures and supports the Romanian organism. It is possible to claim almost anything about the role of geographical factors in history, as indeed about the causes of historical evolutions in general. It is not easy to say what Romania would have been like without the Carpathians – or the British Isles if they had not been isles! What is certain is that the Danube and the Carpathians are the lines of resistance of the Romanian space. Since Romania as such has not always existed, its present territory can be suggested by the expression 'Carpathian-Danubian space' or, more recently, 'Carpathian-Danubian-Pontic space', to include Dobrogea and the Black Sea coast. (However, the Romanians have not looked towards the sea very much, as it never had anything like the significance which the mountains and Danube have had for them. They are not a 'maritime' people, and the sea only really entered their history with the acquisition of the mouth of the Danube and Dobrogea in 1878.)

Regardless of reasons, there is no doubt that until the modern period the 'Carpathian-Danubian-Pontic space' was not unitary in its evolution but, on the contrary, fragmentary and subject to diverse, even divergent, foreign influences.[1] The Getae and Dacians were only incorporated into a single political unit in the time of Burebista (mid-first century BC), a contemporary of Julius Caesar. And we may be sure that even this 'empire', which extended considerably beyond the borders of present-day Romania, did not have the degree of cohesion imagined by some recent historians, and especially by the historical-political propaganda of the Ceauşescu period (when Burebista's 'centralized and unitary' Dacian state was spoken of in terms suggesting its equivalence with Ceauşescu's Romania). In any case, Burebista's state ended with him and was divided into a number of political entities. It was only towards the end of the first century AD that Decebalus reunited the greater part of Dacia under his rule. But this second attempt to create a Dacian kingdom also came to nothing. As a result of their two wars against the Dacians, the Romans extended their dominion over the Danube and the Carpathians. Three distinct zones now took shape within the present-day territory of Romania. For the next 165 years, the western regions made up Roman Dacia. The east and the north remained in the possession of the free Dacians. Dobrogea, on the other hand, which had been included in the Empire as early as 28 BC, initially formed part of the province of Moesia before becoming a province in its own right, under the name of Scythia Minor; it was to remain under Roman, later Byzantine, rule until the seventh century.

After the Romans abandoned Dacia, the region remained open to invasion, and its fragmented and only vaguely politically structured territory came under the control of a succession of different masters. Almost everything about this millennium remains a matter of hypothesis, beginning, as we have seen, with the presence of Romanians north of the Danube. If we accept the thesis of continuity, there remains the question of what sort of political formations the Romanians lived in, and what their relations were with the dominant peoples and states in this part of Europe. One's initial impression is of an almost 'vegetal' life, a merging with the mountains and forests. (Xenopol argued for a 'withdrawal to the mountains', while C. C. Giurescu, somewhat later, saw the forests as the Romanians' principal refuge in the period of migrations.) These romantic images certainly do not completely correspond to reality, but they have nonetheless fed an entire mythology describing the difference between Romanians and 'Others', the distinct character of the Romanians' civilization, their relation to nature ('the forest, brother to the Romanian') and so on. What is certain is that for centuries, this zone lay on the edge of Europe and knew a 'diminished' historical life.

An interesting hypothesis concerns the socio-political role of the Slavs. According to this thesis, Slav conquerors made up the ruling class. The term *boier* ('boyar', 'noble') is indeed of Slavic origin (having previously been borrowed from the Turkic Bulgars). This would also explain the double sense of the word *rumân*: 'Romanian' but also 'dependent peasant'. The condition of the Romanians would indeed have been that of peasants subject to a Slav aristocracy (which was, of course, assimilated in the course of time, and which later constituted the Romanian boyar class). The hypothesis of the ethnic origin of social categories (supported in the Romanian case by historians such as Petre P. Panaitescu[2] and C. C. Giurescu) was evidently inspired by similar situations in, and interpretations of, the histories of France and England, the French aristocracy having been formed by Frankish conquest, and that of England by Norman conquest from France (such interpretations enjoyed a considerable vogue in the nineteenth century, particularly due to the work of the French historian Augustin Thierry).

The expansion of the Hungarians towards Transylvania began with their settlement in the Pannonian plain in AD 896. The twelfth-century chronicle of Anonymus mentioned in Chapter II refers to three small Romanian or Slav-Romanian principalities which submitted to the Hungarians (though the point is disputed by Hungarian historians). By around 1100, Transylvania had already been organized as a principality (known by the Slavic – or Romanian-of-Slavic-origin – term *voivodate*) within the Hungarian kingdom. The first Bulgarian tsardom held dominion on the other side of the mountains (though it is hard to say in what form and to what extent). This had been founded after the invasion of the Bulgars, a people of Turkic origin, in AD 679, followed by their settlement in the northern part of the Balkan peninsula (where they were Slavicized, leaving only their name to the Bulgarians of

61

today). In the early eleventh century, the Byzantines destroyed this first Bulgarian state and returned to the Danube. In 1185, a rebellion led by the brothers Peter and Asen ended with the expulsion of the Byzantines and the formation of the second Bulgarian tsardom, known in Romanian historiography as the 'Romanian-Bulgarian empire'. Here too there is an interesting historical dispute. Was 'Romania' once ruled by Bulgarians? Or, on the contrary, was Bulgaria itself created by Romanians? In the Middle Ages, the Balkan Vlachs (the descendants of Romanized Thracians – 'brothers' to the Romanians north of the Danube) were still numerous; in time, they would disappear into the Slavic mass. From the point of view of Romanian historians, the fact that the very founders of the new state were Vlachs seemed to justify the label 'Romanian-Bulgarian'. In fact, participation in 'great history' south of the Danube compensated in the Romanian historical imaginary for the lack of such history north of the river.

The Romanian space began to take on a more stable form in the course of the thirteenth century. Around the middle of the century, there is mention of a number of statelets south of the Carpathians, dependent on the Hungarian crown. Their unification, in the first decade of the fourteenth century, resulted in the creation of Wallachia. Just in time, it might be said, as the Hungarians, who already had control of Transylvania, were getting ready to extend their domination beyond the Carpathians too. In 1330, at the battle of Posada, the *voivode* of Wallachia, Basarab, won a resounding victory in the mountains over King Charles Robert of Hungary. This is one of the key dates of Romanian history: the moment when Wallachia was truly born. Around the middle of the same century, Moldavia also came into being, likewise as a result of a process of 'separation' from Hungary.

HISTORICAL LATECOMERS

What is striking is the relatively late formation of the Romanian states. The Romanians were latecomers to history. It was not that they had not been around previously, but it was only now that their presence in Europe became 'visible' and their distinct voice began to be heard. The medieval period effectively began in the Romanian lands in the fourteenth century, at a time when it was coming to an end in the West and the Renaissance was approaching. The historical discrepancy is considerable; the Romanians' problem was (and still is) how gradually to reduce their handicap. On top of this, they were small states which could hardly be compared with Hungary and Poland, the 'great powers' of Central Europe, or even with the kingdoms of Bulgaria and Serbia, south of the Danube, which had known their moment of expansion and glory long before the foundation of the Romanian lands. The latter had, in Western terminology, the status of 'principalities' (with the 'prince' bearing the double title of *voivode* and *domn* – from the Latin *dominus*). They could not – according to the feudal hierarchy of the Middle Ages – be placed on a level of equality with the neighbouring kingdoms. The King of Hungary claimed from the beginning to be the suzerain of the two lands. In order to counter these Hungarian pretensions, the princes of Moldavia, who were initially vassals of Hungary, took an oath of vassalage to the kings of Poland. Wallachia remained closer to Hungary; there, manifestations of independence alternated with periods in which the relation of vassalage was recognized.[3]

This rather modest condition, in relation not only to the West but also to their neighbours, gave rise to an inferiority complex in the Romanians' modern consciousness and, logically enough, to various compensatory tactics. Thus emphasis was placed on the distinctive character of Romanian civilization (not inferior to others but different from them), on the victories won against more powerful opponents, and on the Romanians' role in the defence of European Christendom. One fact that was highlighted was the remarkable vitality of the Romanian lands, which succeeded in maintaining their existence – by war and by diplomacy – in adverse conditions, while formerly powerful countries like Hungary and Poland (not to mention the Balkan states) fell, were swallowed up by even greater powers and disappeared for a time from the stage of history. It is indeed a consolation, but one that cannot completely cancel out the frustrating memory of having played a secondary role for too long.

The unfortunate system of succession to the throne (or rather the lack of any real system) came as a supplementary handicap. The succession was neither hereditary nor simply elective but a mixture of the two: hereditary in principle, with two dynasties (Basarab in Wallachia and Mușatin in Moldavia), but without the Western criterion of transmission of the throne in the direct line. Not only sons but also brothers or more distant relatives could aspire to princedom (women were excluded from the start). The only condition was to be 'princely bone', to belong to the family. At first, selection worked within reasonable limits. In time, however, the pretenders multiplied. Even illegitimate sons succeeded to the throne, and, in these conditions, there were of course men who only pretended to be sons of a prince. (Such was the case with Michael the Brave, the most renowned of all of the Romanian *voivode*s, who declared himself to be the posthumous son of the *voivode* Petraşcu the Good; modern historians seem less than convinced of this relationship, which would in any case be impossible to prove.) In time, very distant relatives appeared who were not really relatives at all; some adopted the name Basarab in order to be more convincing. In a final phase, not even this formality mattered anymore; the rulers were now appointed by the Turks anyway.

How were rulers chosen, whether from within the dynasty or from outside it? In principle, they were picked by an assembly of boyars, sometimes by a larger assembly of the country. However, in the absence of a strict procedure (unless a prince had made his son an associate on the throne, thus theoretically ensuring his succession), conflicts were numerous. In addition, help was sometimes sought from outside, providing an excuse for the Hungarians or Turks to intervene. In these circumstances, not all reigns reached their natural term; some rulers were deposed or killed. There were, however, a few long reigns, and it is to them that the most lasting political and cultural achievements belong. Thus we have Mircea the Old (1386–1418) in Wallachia, and his contemporary Alexander the Good (1400–1432) in Moldavia; then Stephen the Great (1457–1504), whose reign – the longest of all – is considered the most glorious period in Moldavia's history; the parallel reigns of Matei Basarab (1633–54) in Wallachia and Vasile Lupu (or Basil the Wolf, 1634–53) in Moldavia; and finally, in Wallachia, Constantin Brîncoveanu (1688–1714). But these are the exceptions. The norm was frequent changes of rule, short reigns of a few years at the most and an instability which increased with each century that passed.

The general instability of this part of Europe was aggravated by internal instability – too much instability! In fact, there is a marked note of anarchy about the history of the Romanians. How could anything durable be built out of it? We can see here the origins of a distrust of history, a lack of confidence in any long-term project. A dose of fatalism was working its way into Romanian culture, a state of mind expressed memorably by Miron Costin: 'The times are not steered by man; rather poor man is under the rule of the times.'

Relations with the Turks constitute an important chapter in the history of the Romanians, but also in their mythology. The mythological image is of an uninterrupted struggle in which the little Romanian lands won many glorious victories against a vast empire. The Romanians thus preserved their national existence while at the same time defending Christian Europe. The historical reality was, as usual, more complex and substantially different.

The Turks began their expansion into the Balkans around the middle of the fourteenth century. Towards the end of the century, the two tsardoms into which Bulgaria was divided were conquered, and the Ottoman Empire reached the Danube, the border of Wallachia. The fall of Constantinople (1453) sealed the fate of the Balkan Christians. Western attempts at an anti-Ottoman crusade (Nicopolis, 1396; Varna, 1444) had ended in disaster. The Turks were finally stopped at Belgrade, where they were defeated in 1456. However, three-quarters of a century later, they renewed their expansion. The Hungarian army was destroyed at Mohács in 1526, and in 1541 the greater part of Hungary became a Turkish province. The Turks twice laid siege to Vienna, in 1529 and 1683, on both occasions without success; this was the extreme point of their advance towards the West.

The Romanian lands lay in the front line. The wars with the Turks have remained imprinted on the national consciousness more than any other historical theme. The Romanians' vocation in the Middle Ages (and their great contribution to European history) would appear to have been to fight the Turks, in a prolonged struggle from which they emerged victorious most of the time. In reality, the years of conflict add up to only a few decades out of half a millennium of Romanian-Ottoman relations. The Romanians won some battles, the Turks won others. However, winning a battle does not mean winning the war. It was the Turks who won the wars in the end! And their result is indisputable: for a long period, the Romanian lands came within the Ottoman orbit.

Three battles are celebrated above all the others as great Romanian victories: Rovine (1394), Vaslui (1475) and Călugăreni (1595). Our knowledge about Rovine is fragmentary. It may in fact

65

have been inconclusive. What is certain is that in its aftermath Mircea the Old, the Prince of Wallachia, was forced to take refuge in the mountains, and that he only regained his throne with the support of the King of Hungary, Sigismund of Luxemburg. Later, Mircea became involved in politics on a grand scale, intervening in the conflict between claimants to the throne of the Ottoman Empire. However, the Turks had the last word. Towards the end of Mircea's reign, a territorially diminished Wallachia had to accept Ottoman suzerainty and to pay tribute to the Turks.

In the case of Vaslui, there is no possible doubt: it was a clear victory for Stephen the Great. But it was followed the next year by a Turkish victory and the devastation of Moldavia. A decade later, Stephen, too, had to submit and pay tribute, after losing southern Bessarabia into the bargain.

At Călugăreni (between Bucharest and the Danube), the result of the battle was equivocal – for the Romanians, it is a great victory, but the Turks consider it a victory as well. After the battle, Michael the Brave withdrew to the mountains, abandoning Bucharest. He returned with the support of a Transylvanian army, and the two principalities' united forces managed to drive the Turks back across the Danube. However, a few years later the whole edifice was to crumble, leaving Wallachia a dependency of the Sublime Porte.

The Romanian lands repeatedly joined the anti-Ottoman coalitions of the Christian states. Hungary was a key part of this system. The victor over the Turks at Belgrade in 1456 was a *voivode* of Transylvania and regent of Hungary whose origins were Romanian. The Hungarians call him Hunyadi János and the Romanians Ioan (or Iancu) of Hunedoara. Regardless of his origins, he was Catholic and a Hungarian noble; his son Matthias Corvinus became King of Hungary. Ioan's impressive castle can by admired at Hunedoara in southern Transylvania, as can his tomb in the Catholic cathedral of Alba Iulia (Transylvania's medieval capital).

Why did the Turks not conquer the Romanian lands? Romanian historians have continually confronted this question. Why did these areas not suffer the same fate as Hungary, a country so much larger and apparently more powerful? The patriotic answer is easy to guess: the Turks did not conquer the Romanian lands because resistance was such that they were not able to. In this interpretation, the Romanians' history becomes transfigured as heroic epic, a sort of replay of the struggle of David and Goliath. But what if the

Romanian armies were not actually so small? The thesis of a specifically Romanian form of military organization was promoted particularly in the Communist period (and was closely linked to the military doctrine of Ceauşescu: the mobilization of the entire people). It was argued that – in contrast with the Western feudal model – among the Romanians it was the 'great host' that took the field, made up principally of free peasants. By means of this quasi-general mobilization, Wallachia and Moldavia could call up armed forces more numerous than those of the great European powers! The military disproportion between the Romanians and the Turks was thus not as great as had initially been thought.

Some historians tried, all the same, to reach a more realistic judgement. P. P. Panaitescu introduced two arguments into the discussion. The first, which is easy to grasp by simply looking at the map, was that the Turks' route towards the heart of Europe did not go through the Romanian lands; the Romanian theatre was thus rather peripheral for them. The Turkish advance was along the line Belgrade–Buda–Vienna, so Hungary fell rather than the Romanian lands! The second argument concerned the economic exploitation of the Romanian lands; indirectly, through the commercial monopoly which they exercised and through the collection of tribute, the Turks gained more than they could have obtained by direct administration.[4] A recent study has demolished the whole scaffolding of traditional Romanian interpretations: there is no point in trying to answer the question 'Why did the Turks not conquer the Romanian lands?' for the simple reason that in fact they did conquer them![5]

Sporadic Romanian victories did not prevent the gradual passing of the Romanian lands under Ottoman control: first Wallachia, which was the most exposed, and then Moldavia, followed (in a situation of somewhat greater autonomy) by Transylvania, which remained a principality in its own right after the fall of Hungary. At first, it was only a matter of paying tribute. In time, however, the Romanian lands entered the Ottoman political, military and economic system. The Turks interfered more and more frequently in the appointment and deposition of princes, until a point was reached when both the indigenous boyars and the Turks felt equally entitled to choose a prince. Then things became simpler. In the eighteenth century, princes were simply appointed and revoked by the Sublime Porte as mere Ottoman functionaries. The rank of prince was equivalent to that of pasha (and not even pasha of the first category, but of the second!). However, it is no less true that the Romanian lands preserved a certain autonomy, diminished as time passed but never done away with altogether. They had their own institutions and were governed according to their own laws and customs. They kept their own ruling class – their indigenous aristocracy – in contrast to their Slav neighbours to the south. The Turks did not settle on Romanian territory; there was no Ottoman colonization or attempt at Islamization. As a result, modern Romania, unlike the Balkan states, did not inherit Turkish or Muslim minorities (except in Dobrogea, which was effectively absorbed into the Ottoman Empire for half a millennium).

The battles with the Turks – however brightly they may shine in the Romanians' historical memory – were less significant in their consequences than the incorporation of the Romanian lands, for centuries, into the Ottoman system. What took place was not so much a prolonged conflict as an interference of civilizations. It is in this way – and certainly not on the battlefield! – that the many words of Turkish origin entered the Romanian language. And the Romanians' role in defending Europe needs to be seen in its true proportions, especially as the road to Central Europe did not pass through the Romanian lands. By around 1500, the West had become sufficiently powerful to be in no danger of falling into Ottoman hands. The fact that the Turks twice arrived before Vienna and were twice beaten has little to do with the history of the Romanians. What is important is that the latter managed to preserve their existence in historical conditions that were far from favourable to them.

The eighteenth century marked the apogee of Romanian integration into the Balkan and Oriental world. The princes, sometimes Romanians but in most cases Greeks, were now mere administrators on behalf of the Sublime Porte. Along with these 'Phanariot' rulers, many Greeks settled in the Romanian lands. Aristocratic families intermarried. Greek became the language of high culture, just as Slavonic had some centuries earlier. The boyars dressed in oriental style. Their children studied at school in Greek. The urban landscape took on Turkish characteristics. The Romanians seemed firmly anchored in the Orient ... Who could have predicted that from one generation to the next everything would change?

According to the immigrationist theory, the Romanians spread in the Middle Ages over a territory that had not initially belonged to them. Romanian historians consider, in contrast, that the original Romanian territory was even larger than the Romania of today. The fourteenth century was a good one for the Romanians, marked by the foundation and territorial expansion of the two lands. But one loss succeeded another during the centuries that followed. Towards the end of the reign of Mircea the Old (around 1418), the Turks annexed Dobrogea, thus depriving Wallachia of access to the sea. In the same period, they established two bridgeheads north of the Danube, occupying the towns of Giurgiu and Turnu. Around the middle of the sixteenth century, a third Danube port, Brăila, fell into Turkish hands. Now Wallachia no longer controlled even the left bank of the Danube. In 1484, Moldavia lost the towns of Chilia (where the northern branch of the Danube enters the sea, today Kiliya in Ukraine) and Cetatea Albă (at the mouth of the Dniester, today Belgorod-Dnestrovskiy in Ukraine). And in 1538, the entire southern part of Bessarabia was occupied by the Turks, leaving the Romanians with no access to the Black Sea.

In 1541, the Turks occupied the central part of Hungary, and in 1552 the Banat. Transylvania remained a principality dependent on the Ottoman Empire, like Wallachia and Moldavia, but in a slightly more favourable position (with less tribute to pay, fewer Turkish interventions and more freedom of movement). As a result of the war that began with the siege of Vienna in 1683 and ended with the Peace of Karlowitz in 1699, the Habsburgs conquered both Hungary and Transylvania (which now had the status of a principality and, later, a grand principality within the Austrian Empire). A new war with the Turks brought the Banat, Serbia and Oltenia (the western part of Wallachia) under Habsburg rule in 1718. The Austrian occupation of Oltenia lasted only two decades; by the Peace of Belgrade in 1739, the Habsburg Empire gave up Serbia and restored Oltenia to Wallachia; however, it was to keep the Banat, as well as Transylvania, until 1918.

In the time of Peter the Great (1683–1725), Russia too began its expansion towards South-eastern Europe. After the fall of Byzantium, Moscow saw itself as the continuer of the imperial idea, the 'third Rome', and took upon itself the mission of reaching

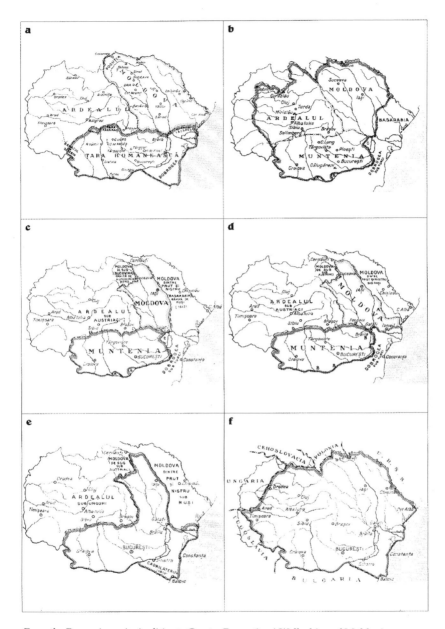

From the Romanian principalities to Greater Romania: a) Wallachia and Moldavia *c.* 1400;
b) Wallachia, Moldavia and Transylvania (Ardeal) in 1600, in the time of Michael the Brave;
c) Wallachia and Moldavia in 1812 (showing Moldavia much diminished following the loss
of Bukovina and Bessarabia); d) Wallachia and Moldavia at the time of the Union of 1859;
e) Little Romania before the First World War; f) Greater Romania in the inter-war period.

Constantinople and crushing the Ottoman Empire. Its route passed through the Romanian lands! Though the Habsburgs did not have such high ambitions, they were also interested in the Balkans. The result was a long series of wars between the Austrians, the Russians and the Turks, which punctuated the eighteenth century and continued – at least between the Russians and the Turks – into the nineteenth. The Romanian lands became a theatre of war. The armies of the belligerents crossed them at will, and one foreign occupation followed another. There was only one good thing in all this: as the competition was three-sided, the opposing forces neutralized each other up to a point, and so the principalities were able to survive. The Ottoman Empire did not collapse all at once. It gave way step by step, resisting much more efficiently than had been anticipated. Having failed to crush the Turks, and with the Austrians watching their every move, the Russians were unable to reach Constantinople. (If the Ottoman Empire had disappeared, perhaps Constantinople would today be a Russian city and South-eastern Europe part of Russia!) So the Romanian lands survived, but with new losses of territory. The Austrians annexed the northern part of Moldavia (Bukovina) in 1775 – by simply making a request to the Turks! – and the Russians took Bessarabia in 1812 (both the southern part, which had long been under Turkish occupation, and the remainder, which had hitherto been part of Moldavia).

The Romanians entered the nineteenth century in a deplorable situation. Half of them were under the rule of various foreign powers, while the two principalities were politically and territorially diminished. Would anyone around 1800 have placed bets on the future of Romania? Even the very word *Romania* did not exist yet!

DIVISION OR UNITY?

How, then, did Romania come into existence? With this question, we touch on a delicate subject. Although the unification of the Romanian territories in the modern period gave rise to a tendency to treat previous history in a 'unified' manner, historians up to the Communist period were not afraid to mention the conflicts between Wallachia and Moldavia, or to acknowledge the particular character of Transylvania in relation to the other two. Under Ceauşescu, however, the absolute unity of Romanian history became the order of the day. The Romanians of the Middle Ages, like their Dacian ancestors, had to be just as united as Ceauşescu's subjects were (or were supposed to be). This sort of highly actualized historical discourse imprinted itself on the minds of several generations. And for many Romanians today, this, and nothing else, is their *real history* – in spite of new interpretations which question the myth of permanent unity.

It is clear that Wallachia and Moldavia were different countries, and that, although largely populated by Romanians, Transylvania as a state (considered in terms of its ruling élite and institutions) was not Romanian but Hungarian. After Hungary's fall, the princes of Transylvania, far from becoming 'Romanianized', set themselves up as the continuers of the conquered kingdom. But why were Wallachia and Moldavia separate countries? The simplest answer to this question, which some Romanian historians have asked themselves, is another question: 'Why should they not have been?' Medieval states were not constructed on the basis of linguistic or national principles. In the Middle Ages, Wallachia was Wallachia and Moldavia was Moldavia, and that was it: the expression 'Romanian lands', which I use here for convenience, is a modern way of designating them. Sometimes, the two lands went the same way, sometimes in opposite directions; they not only fought the Hungarians, the Poles and the Turks but also each other. In the first two centuries of its existence, Moldavia was more closely linked to Poland and Wallachia to Hungary, and as a result their external orientations were quite different – hardly justifying their enrolment in a 'common anti-Ottoman front', to use the expression current in Communist-period historiography.[6] The Turks forced submission on Wallachia first, as it was closer to them. While Stephen the Great's Moldavia continued its resistance, Wallachia, willingly or not, was on the Turkish side. The final armed conflicts between the two lands took place in the middle of the seventeenth century, in the time of Matei Basarab and Vasile Lupu.

The year 1600 is the glittering moment of Romanian history. In 1599, Michael the Brave (1593–1601), the Prince of Wallachia, conquered Translylvania, and a year later Moldavia. For a short time, he ruled all three. But his triumph was followed closely by disaster. The Transylvanian nobility rebelled, the Poles invaded Moldavia and Wallachia, and the Turks crossed the Danube. Forced into exile, Michael went to Prague, to the court of Emperor Rudolf, whose lieutenant in Transylvania he considered himself to be. He

Michael the Brave: one of the Romanians' great symbolic portraits. An engraving made in Prague by Aegidius Sadeler, 1601.

returned with Habsburg assistance and defeated the army of the Transylvanian nobles, only to fall victim a few days later to a plot engineered by the imperial general Basta. The bone of contention was Transylvania, which was desired equally by Michael, the Habsburgs and, of course, the Hungarian nobles.

These are the grand and tragic events which make Michael the most outstanding personality of Romanian history. But what is their significance? What drove him on: thirst for power, a spirit of adven-

73

ture, the desire to create a powerful anti-Ottoman block – or could it have been the idea of Romanian unity? Was he a *condottiere* or a precursor of Greater Romania? Romanian historians of the generation that made Romania in 1859 highlighted what they believed to be Michael's national project. This interpretation was abandoned by the critical historiography of the years around 1900, only to be taken up again and amplified half a century later by national-Communist ideology. The waters are so stirred up that even today it is hard to speak dispassionately about the 'union of 1600'.

In fact, this was not a fusion but a personal unification in which the countries kept their individuality. Again, to speak of 'Romanian lands' at this point is too much. The ruling element in Transylvania was not Romanian, and even the Moldavians were not all that enthusiastic; for them, Michael was not a liberator (from whom?) but a conqueror. Only later was he accredited with a nineteenth-century national project, one that could not have been in his mind in 1600. There may well have been a certain solidarity between the three lands, as a result of their belonging to a common space. Princes of Transylvania, both before and after Michael, tried in their own ways to achieve political 'unity'. They considered themselves, like the kings of Hungary before them, entitled to suzerainty over Wallachia and Moldavia. (In 1595, only a few years before Michael's 'union', the Prince of Transylvania, Sigismund Báthory, obtained the formal submission of Wallachia and Moldavia; Gabriel Bethlen, prince from 1613 to 1629, expressed his intention of rebuilding the kingdom of Dacia, under his own sceptre, of course.) It should not be necessary to point out that the formulas of 'unity' promoted by the Transylvanian princes had nothing Romanian about them. They were reminiscences of Greater Hungary, certainly not first drafts for Greater Romania! Michael the Brave did not unite the Romanians in 1600; what he did was to bring together the three lands in a short-lived political construction, lands which were in similar situations and among which relations had become very close anyway. However, he did unite the Romanians later, long after his death, when he became the great symbol of Romanian aspirations towards unity. It was under the sign of Michael the Brave that Romania was made in 1859 and 1918.

If the invocation of a Romanian project in 1600 proves anachronistic, it is no less true that Wallachia and Moldavia resembled one another in many respects, and as the centuries passed they became even more similar. Their institutions were almost the same. They were in similar relations of dependency to the Sublime Porte. They were very close in language, speaking almost identical varieties of Romanian (the modern literary language developed from the dialect of northern Muntenia). Cultural contacts intensified from the seventeenth century onwards, and the idea of common origins became current in historical writings. In the eighteenth century – the age of the Phanariots (see Chapter 11) – the two countries were under exactly the same regime, with the Turks shifting rulers from one land to the other. (The record is held by Nicolae Mavrocordat, who reigned, intermittently between 1730 and 1769, six times in Wallachia and four in Moldavia!) By then, the Romanian lands had become so close that the next step could only be unification. It is paradoxical that the intensification of this process, which was to lead to the creation of the Romanian nation, took place in a time when the two lands seemed to have blended into the Oriental and Greek world of the Balkans.[7]

THE DECISIVE YEARS: 1821–66

It was in 1821 that the pace of events really began to accelerate. The Romanian lands were the theatre of a twofold revolution. The Greeks, who were by now quite at home there, set in motion a movement for liberation from the Turks, led by Alexander Ipsilanti, the son of a former Phanariot ruler. At the same time, an army of discontents – with a vaguely formulated programme of social demands – set out from Oltenia under the leadership of Tudor Vladimirescu. It is hard to say what exactly this half-peasant/half-boyar figure was seeking – hence the diversity of interpretations. In any event, he reached Bucharest and for a short time was Wallachia's *de facto* ruler. His rapid success is indicative of a generalized social dissatisfaction, from peasants burdened with excessive duties to boyars irritated by competition from the Greeks and the demands of the Sublime Porte. While the Greek rebels, confident of Russian support, were determined to fight the Turks and inflame Greece, Tudor Vladimirescu adopted a more prudent course. Considered a traitor by the Greeks, he was killed on the orders of Ipsilanti, thus putting an end to the revolutionary movement, which lacked coherence without him. The Greeks were defeated in turn by the Turks, who crossed the Danube into Wallachia. Everything seemed to be over; in fact, things had only just begun. The Balkans went into a state of effervescence from which they have yet to emerge! The Greek revolution erupted again in Greece itself, which won autonomy in 1829 and full independence in 1830. The first noticeable change in the Romanian lands was the end of the Phanariot rulers (the Turks no longer trusted Greeks) and the return, in 1822, of 'native' princes.

War between the Russians and the Turks broke out again in 1828–9, and the Romanian lands came under Russian occupation until 1834. This time, their governor was a remarkable man, General Pavel Kiselyov (Kisseleff), the only Russian who retains a positive image in the collective Romanian memory even today: the most elegant boulevard in Bucharest bears his name. Under his supervision, the boyars formulated the first Romanian constitution, known as the 'Réglement Organique', which was almost identical in Wallachia and Moldavia – another step towards unification. Kiselyov took an interest in everything, from the condition of the peasants to the appearance and hygiene of the towns; it was to him that Romanian society owed the first great attempt at its systematic modernization.

Defeated by the Russians, the Turks restored the Danube ports (Turnu, Giurgiu and Brăila) to Wallachia, gave up their commercial monopoly with regard to the principalities, and recognized freedom of navigation on the Danube, all by the Treaty of Adrianople (Edirne) of 1829. All of this served to stimulate the growth of agricultural production for export. The two Romanian lands (and, later, Romania) came to constitute one of the granaries of Europe. The principalities remained vassals of the Sublime Porte, but with an increased degree of autonomy. Their rulers were elected for life by a 'Community Assembly' made up of boyars – a provision intended to put an end to political instability and Ottoman interventions, though in fact no ruler in the period up to 1866 actually remained in power until his death! Turkish suzerainty was complemented by Russian 'protection'. Kiselyov's behaviour had been excellent, but it was hard to say how this 'protection' would manifest itself in the end. Might it not be a first step towards the establishment of full Russian domination? This was the moment when Romanian-Russian relations began to swing in the opposite direction: the Romanians began to fear the Russians.

In 1848, in a Europe caught up in revolution, the Romanians had a revolution of their own. In the Moldavian capital, Iași, only the beginnings were sketched out, but in Bucharest the reigning Prince

Gheorghe Bibescu was deposed, and a provisional government was formed. The Romanians had many problems to resolve, but two objectives took priority, one social, the other national. Society was markedly polarized between land-owning boyars and a landless peasantry burdened by feudal obligations (the rapid growth of agricultural production, stimulated by export, had only served to intensify the exploitation of the peasants). The middle class was very small, which explains the fact that reforming ideas were promoted by liberal boyars and intellectuals (many of whom were also of boyar origin), not by an almost non-existent bourgeoisie. The reformers saw the granting of land to the peasants and their emancipation from feudal burdens as indispensable conditions for modernization and true national cohesion. The other great objective was the principalities' unification, even if the Romanians did not dare to speak of this except in a whisper, fearing the Turks, and even more the Russians. Their fears proved well founded. The Tsar's armies entered Moldavia, and later Wallachia, and the Turks occupied Bucharest. It was the end of the revolution, but not of the ideas which had inspired it.

In Transylvania, the situation was quite different. The principality belonged to Austria. The Hungarian revolutionaries, seeking to remake Hungary within its medieval borders, decided to reunite all of the territories that had formerly been Hungarian, including Transylvania. Thus they came into conflict not only with the Habsburgs but also with the Romanians and the Slavic peoples (Croats, Serbs and Slovaks). There was heavy fighting between Romanians and Hungarians, especially in the Apuseni Mountains, where the Romanian peasants were led by a figure who was to enter into legend: Avram Iancu, 'king of the mountains'. Finally, Russia, taking its role as 'policeman of Europe' very seriously, sprang to the Habsburgs' aid, and the Hungarians were defeated. However, it would later become clear that this was only a temporary setback; in the end, it was with the Hungarians, not with the Romanians or the Slavs, that Vienna came to a settlement. (A powerful aristocracy and the survival of the idea of a Hungarian state were two of their assets.) The Romanians of Transylvania were not yet thinking of a break with Austria; it was still difficult to imagine their land as part of a Romanian national state. What the Romanians wanted was an autonomous Transylvania, perhaps as part of a federalized Austria, and to be treated on a level of equality with the other nationalities.

Romania, initially, was to be made by Wallachia and Moldavia. In the years that followed the crushing of the revolution, Romanian leaders exiled in the West – especially in Paris and London – launched a consistent and efficient stream of propaganda in favour of the principalities' unification. It was ultimately in the European interest that the Romanian space, an unstable zone *par excellence*, should acquire a coherent organization. It was also in the spirit of the 'century of nationalities'. The Romanian patriots found an outstanding ally in Napoleon III, Emperor of France, who dreamed of a Europe of national states with France as their arbitrator.

In the eastern part of Europe, wars between the Russians and the Turks had become a veritable ritual. Approximately every two decades, the Russians would occupy the Romanian lands and try to force their way to Constantinople. This happened again in 1853. Only this time, France and Britain saw fit to intervene. The Ottoman Empire – by this time the 'sick man of Europe' – did not enjoy a great deal of respect. However, its precarious survival seemed preferable to an expansion of Russia into the whole of South-eastern Europe and the eastern Mediterranean. Franco-British forces attacked the Russians on their home ground, landing in the Crimea in 1854. The Russians were forced to withdraw from the principalities. In their place came the Austrians (from 1854 to 1857). All of the surrounding powers wanted control of the little Romanian lands – one more argument in favour of a political solution that would produce greater stability.

Russia's defeat in the Crimean War was followed by the Peace Congress of Paris in 1856, central to which was the problem of the principalities' status.[8] They now passed under the guarantee of the great European powers, with Russia losing its status of protector. The southern part of Bessarabia was returned to Moldavia, not out of any desire to restore Moldavian territory, but in order to keep the Russians away from the mouth of the Danube. The Danube itself came under the control of a European Commission. A degree of order was thus introduced to the region. However, the problem remained of what was to happen to the principalities. France favoured the unification solution, by means of which a buffer state would be created between Russia and Turkey, and, no less importantly, an outpost of French influence in the East. Britain, on the other hand, preferred to rely on the integrity of the Ottoman Empire; a Romanian state might mean the beginning of the end for it (by offering a model to the Balkan peoples) and so ruin the balance of power in Eastern Europe, to the advantage of Russia. It was decided that the Romanians should also be listened to. 'Ad-hoc assemblies' were elected in both principalities in 1857, representing all social levels, including the peasantry. Almost unanimously, they produced an unequivocal response: the Romanians wanted unification in a single state under the name of 'Romania', and a foreign Prince from one of the European ruling families. A foreign Prince would put an end to internal rivalry for the throne and enhance the country's prestige.

Everything depended, however, on the decision of the great powers and, in the first instance, of France and Britain, which were not in agreement on the matter. A meeting was therefore held, at Osborne, between Queen Victoria, accompanied by her Prime Minister, Lord Palmerston, and Napoleon III. The result was a compromise which was not particularly calculated to satisfy the Romanians. The two lands were to be united in a vague manner under the name not of 'Romania' but of the 'United Principalities', each retaining its own ruler (who was to be native, not foreign!), government, parliament and army. Certain common institutions – with a limited role – were to be established in the small town of Focşani, at the border between Wallachia and Moldavia.

The great powers' decisions were not negotiable. Having submitted, the Romanians proceeded to find a brilliantly simple solution to the problem. On 5 January 1859, the electoral assembly in Iaşi chose Colonel Alexandru Ioan Cuza to be ruler of Moldavia. On 24 January, Wallachia, too, elected its ruler, in the person of the same Alexandru Ioan Cuza! The Paris Convention of 1858, by which the European powers had established the political framework of the principalities, had provided for the election of a ruler in Iaşi and one in Bucharest, but nowhere was it stipulated that these could not be one and the same person. After a few months of tension, the *fait accompli* was accepted. In the years that followed, Cuza managed to argue convincingly that it was impossible for him to govern simultaneously from two capitals a considerable distance apart (there were no railways, and the condition of the roads was appalling). On 24 January 1862, exactly three years after the twofold election, a single assembly met, and a single government was appointed, in Bucharest. (Wallachia had come to be appreciably more populous than Moldavia, with 2.5 million against 1.5 million inhabitants, and Bucharest, with a population of 120,000,

A detail from Petrescu's sketch for the Athenaeum fresco of 1933–7. On the right is Alexandru Ioan Cuza, Prince of the Union of 1859 and of the peasants. Beside him is his principal collaborator, Mihail Kogălniceanu. Above is an image of the Metropolitan Cathedral of Bucharest. The Metropolitan hill was the city's symbolic centre, as well as the place where the Union of 1859 was proclaimed. Below, two young women are shown in folk costume, symbolizing Wallachia and Moldavia. Cuza is handing a peasant the title deeds to his land.

was three times larger than Iaşi.) It was at this point that Romania came into existence in reality, with Bucharest as its capital.

Cuza had been a compromise candidate. Not the best known of Romanian politicians, he was regarded as a moderate, and herein lay his good fortune. There is no doubt that he had his weaknesses, however. Among these, he displayed a somewhat excessive partiality for women; although married to Lady Elena, he had a semi-official liaison, which attracted adverse comment, with Maria Obrenović (a member of the Catargiu family of Romanian boyars and the mother of Milan Obrenović, King of Serbia – she also bore Cuza two sons, whom he acknowledged). He imitated Napoleon III in many respects and even resembled him in appearance, thanks to his beard. Like the French Emperor, he showed authoritarian inclinations, and the 'small *coup d'état*' of 2 May 1864, by which he increased his own power considerably at the expense of the 'legislative bodies', could be compared with the *coup d'état* of Louis Napoleon (the future Napoleon III) on 2 December 1851. Perhaps a strong-arm policy was indeed required to put his programme of reform into action. Unfortunately, after the outstanding government led from 1863 to 1865 by Mihail Kogălniceanu, to whom the essence of the reforms was due, Cuza surrounded himself with lesser and corrupt individuals. He managed to unite conservatives and liberals, who otherwise had few points of agreement, in a coalition against him. With the army's support, the political leaders carried out a *coup d'état* on 11 February 1866; Cuza was dethroned and forced to leave the country.

And yet it seems that the Romanians had made the best possible choice in 1859. For all his deficiencies, Cuza has gone down in history as a great statesman. Seen from a distance, his defects fade into insignificance beside his achievements. And it would be hard to find their equal in the entire history of the Romanians. Romania was not made by Cuza single-handed, but it was made under his leadership. He moved skilfully among the European powers, combining persuasion with the politics of the *fait accompli*. He presided over, and where necessary was able to impose, major reforms. The administration, the judicial system, education and the armed forces were all established on new, European lines. The agrarian reform of 1864 finally gave land to the peasants, attempting a compromise between the preservation of the great boyar domains and the consolidation of small peasant holdings. Cuza's seven years were the densest that Romania has ever known. He died in exile, in Heidelberg, in 1873.

FROM THE BALKANS TO THE WEST

I have sketched out, in very broad lines, the crucial events of half a century, from 1821 to 1866. During this period, however, there was also a deeper process going on, which was changing not only the political foundations of the Romanians but also the foundations of Romanian civilization. The Romanian élite opted, in a shift as unexpected as it was radical and rapid, for the values of Western civilization. From the Balkans, Romania suddenly oriented itself towards the Western world. It would be simplifying things too much to say that there were no premonitory signs. Relations with the West were, of course, much older; there had never been an insurmountable wall between East and West. Already in the Middle Ages, relations with Hungary and Poland had opened a window on the Catholic and Latin world. The Latin language was not unknown to seventeenth-century Romanian scholars, one of whom, the politician and historian Constantin Cantacuzino, studied in Italy, at Padua. But let us not confuse contacts and influences with structures. An Orthodox framework of life and traditional atmosphere, still medieval in character, contrasted with the transforming dynamism of the West. In the eighteenth century, however, the first major breach occurred. The passage to Catholicism – of the Greek Catholic variety – of part of the Transylvanian Romanian population led to a rediscovery of Latinity and the affirmation of symbolic links with Rome. But this was more an argument in support of certain national demands than an all-embracing project of modernization. In the principalities, the Phanariots, who were generally cultivated men, carried out some reforms in the European spirit of the time, but these were inevitably adapted to social and mental structures very remote from those of the West. It was through Greek translations that Enlightenment ideas began to penetrate. Around 1800, a number of boyars' sons began to learn French. But Romanian society remained settled in its traditional mould. The eighteenth century even saw an accentuation of Orientalism in the principalities. The Romanians (or at least their élite) dressed in Turkish style, spoke Greek and wrote in Slavonic characters. A few decades later, they would be writing with Roman characters, wearing European clothes and speaking French!

Such a 'transfiguration' calls for an explanation. Two factors played an essential role: modernization and national ideology. The only model of modernity was that of the West. It had already been applied by Russia, and would later be applied by Turkey and even far-off Japan. The nation, too, was a Western creation. The idea of a Romanian nation and of a Romanian national state meant the separation of the Romanians from the Orthodox and Slavic mass in

82

which they had previously been incorporated. Nation now came before religion, becoming – everywhere – a religion itself. This explains why the Orthodox Russians, hitherto seen as liberators, began to be viewed with suspicion, even hostility, as a potential threat to the Romanian nation. The Greeks and Greek culture seemed to represent another danger, threatening the Romanian language and national culture by their massive presence and influence. The far-off West, on the other hand, of which the Romanians had known almost nothing until a short time before, became their ally – with a special inclination towards the Latin countries, particularly the 'great Latin sister', France. The relationship with France, a case of 'love at first sight', became an obsession, holding the Romanians in its thrall for more than a century.

The crucial moment was reached in 1830; from that point on, the process began to accelerate. Forms were, of course, easier to change than content. But even forms have their uses; far from being mere ornaments, they define values and symbols, and profoundly mark people's lives. Styles of clothing, for example, are not just frivolities. 'European' costume was the advance guard of the Western model in Romanian society. Engravings from around 1840 show motley salons, in which, at least in terms of dress, two worlds were meeting. As a rule, the women – who were the most receptive to these changes – and young men appear in 'European' clothes, while the

An engraving showing a soirée at the princely palace in Bucharest in 1843. The ladies and young men are dressed according to Western fashion, while a few older men remain faithful to the oriental style of dress.

older boyars have not yet given up their oriental dress. The transition in clothing was paralleled by a transition in writing. From around 1820, Cyrillic (Slavonic) writing began to be sprinkled with Roman letters. This curious mixture persisted until 1860, when the Roman alphabet was introduced officially. Thus the last relic of centuries of Slavonic cultural influence disappeared.

The Romanians became familiar with the French language during the Russian occupation of 1828–9. It was the preferred language of the Russian officers, aristocrats imbued with Western culture. They had no way of knowing that French would turn the Romanians against them. Young 'Moldo-Wallachians' now began going to study in France in ever-increasing numbers. For the Romanians, French quickly became more than a language of communication or of culture; through it many of them acquired a new soul.[9]

The Romanian language itself came under French influence. Romanian today is no longer quite the same as the Romanian of the eighteenth century, since it has undergone a process of 're-Latinization' in the meantime. Thus in language, too, we find the same desire to break away from Slavic and Oriental influence. The process began with the Transylvanian School (continued by the Latinist trend of the nineteenth century), which appealed to Latin as a source of words to complete the vocabulary of Romanian or to replace words with other origins. In the 1800s, French became the principal language of reference, overtaking Latin by a long way. The need for neologisms was evident: the modernization of society made it a necessity. However, words were introduced not only for new notions but also as replacements or doubles for old Romanian words (especially those of Slavic or oriental origin). Today, the French element in Romanian is immense; it is reckoned at about 40 per cent of vocabulary with a frequency of 20 per cent![10] This means that in everyday Romanian, one word in five is of French origin. (The French element is less noticeable in casual conversation but massive in 'intellectual' expression, as anyone who opens a Romanian newspaper or schoolbook will immediately realize.)

How far could this renewal of the language, almost a reinvention, be taken? The Latinists were ready to go very far, to the extent of completely excluding anything that was not Latin (or, for newer words, French). The *Dictionary of the Romanian Language* published between 1871 and 1876 by August Treboniu Laurian in collaboration with Ioan Massim (under the aegis of the Academic Society) represented an attempt to go the whole way. The dictionary itself included only the Latin element; all other words were gathered in a 'glossary', with a view to marginalizing and ultimately eliminating them. Moreover, Laurian adopted etymological spelling, so as to force words to resemble their original Latin forms as closely as possible.

Spelling had become another headache for the Romanians. As long as they had written in Cyrillic, things had remained simple. For every sound there had been a corresponding sign, as in the writing of Russian today: it was a fully phonetic spelling system. With the adoption of the Roman alphabet, variants began to multiply as writers swung between the rival attractions of etymological and phonetic writing (with some exceptions in the latter case, as the Roman letters covered the range of sounds in the Romanian language less faithfully than the Cyrillic ones). In the end, it was the phonetic approach that carried the day. What was the point of writing etymologically when there was no such tradition (as there is in English or French): the tradition would have had to be invented! In principle, Romanian is written 'as it sounds', but this has not saved the Romanians from at least one spelling reform in each generation. Instability of writing has matched the general instability of Romanian society.

Pure Latinism lost the battle (but not before making a lasting mark on the Romanian language). Laurian's *Dictionary* was rapidly contested and even ridiculed. Some Slavic and oriental words have dropped out of use, but most of the essential ones have been retained. Is there, for example, any other way to talk of 'love' in Romanian? Both *dragoste* and *iubire* are Slavic words; the Latinate *amor* failed to catch on, except to convey a touch of irony. Even today, the Romanians still love in Slavonic. Ultimately, the modernization of the language was a success. Extreme solutions were avoided. Radical steps were taken, but within certain limits. If the process had gone any farther, there would have been a risk of breaking the language in two: one for the common people and another for the élite (as happened in Greece). Romanian underwent a spectacular renewal, but not at the cost of its unity and coherence.

It was also from the West, and especially from the French, that the Romanians adopted new literary and artistic genres. Until 1800, Romanian literature was limited to religious texts, chronicles and 'popular romances' of a medieval-Byzantine character. The story of modern literature began in the nineteenth century, with the writing of romantic elegies, short stories, historical dramas and so on along the lines of French models. Similarly, religious painting in the Byzantine tradition (the only kind of painting practised prior to this time) discreetly gave way to European artistic forms, and Romanian artists began to paint portraits and landscapes suffused with the atmosphere of Paris and Barbizon.

The towns, too, began to modernize (starting around the time of Kiselyov's governership – that Russian general set many things in motion in the Romanian lands!). Their oriental aspect faded gradually, to be replaced by French-inspired architecture and (more important than the architecture itself, which could not transform the urban land-scape overnight) a lifestyle – at the level of the élites – based on that of the West. Bucharest became 'Little Paris', a title of which, justly or not, it was to boast right up to the installation of Communism.

At the same time, a whole range of Western structures were adopted. Political institutions, laws, administration, the judicial system, education, the armed forces ... all came from the West. Romania was leaving its own past behind. It glorified its history, in the romantic spirit of the time, while at the same time breaking away from it. Universities were founded: Iaşi in 1860 and Bucharest in 1864. The year 1867 saw the creation of the Academic Society, which became the Romanian Academy in 1879. The Romanian constitution of 1866 was simply an imitation of the Belgian one of 1833. This was a remarkable performance: Romania was an agrarian country of rural-patriarchal type, while Belgium was one of the most industri-alized and bourgeois countries on the continent. Given all the constitutions available to choose from, the Romanians opted for the most advanced and liberal of them all!

But might this not be too much? Was everything not being done too quickly and superficially? Was a contradiction not emerging between the real country (the majority of whose people were poor and illiterate peasants) and an 'ideal country' imagined by a small élite? A relevant critique emerged from the cultural society Junimea ('Youth'), founded in Iaşi in 1863. Its leader, the literary critic and politician Titu Maiorescu (1840–1917), published his tirade in 1868 under the title 'Against Today's Direction in Romanian Culture'. In it, he launched the theory of *forms without substance*, which was to remain central to political-cultural disputes for a long time. 'In appearance,' he wrote, according to the statistics of external forms the Romanians today possess almost all of Western civilization. We have politics and science, we have journals and academies, we have schools and literature, we have museums, conservatoires, theatre, even a constitution. But in reality all these are dead productions, pretences without foundation, ghosts without bodies, illusions without truth, and thus the culture of the higher classes of the Romanians is null and without value, while the abyss which separates us from the common people become deeper every day. The only real class in this country is the Romanian peasantry, and its reality is the burden of suffering under which it sighs at the phantasmagoria of the higher classes. For it is the peasants' daily sweat that provides the material resources to sustain the fictive edifice which we call Romanian culture ... [11]

As with any polemical text, there is a measure of exaggeration in Maiorescu's article. It might be replied, with some justice, that modern forms still had to be introduced, even if at first their content left much to be desired. However, Maiorescu was right when he denounced mimicry and superficiality. The Romanians' break from one system of civilization and shift into another generated a heightened tendency towards formalism; many Romanians, including political and cultural leaders, considered (and still consider today) that formal adaptation could take the place of committed action. Maiorescu's warning retains much of its validity today; indeed, it is especially relevant as the Romanians return to the Western model – having been removed from the European circuit by Communism – and struggle with the attractions of merely formal adaptation.

THE REIGN OF CAROL I: 48 YEARS OF STABILITY

When they expelled Cuza, the Romanian politicians were determined to put into practice the solution of a 'foreign Prince' which they had unsuccessfully begged Europe to allow them in 1857. They wanted a true dynasty such as they had never really had. The instability of reigns, the lack of clear rules of succession, and the power-struggles between boyars had all contributed to the decline of the Roman lands. The Romanians had hardly ever known anything except instability. It was time to opt for stability.

They began searching Europe for a suitable Prince, preferably a Latin one. Perhaps Amedeo of Savoy, the second son of the King of Italy, Victor Emmanuel?[12] Or Philip of Flanders, the brother of the

Belgian King, Leopold II? For one reason or another, these proposals failed. The solution emerged in the person of Prince Karl of Hohenzollern-Sigmaringen, a member of the southern, Catholic branch of the Hohenzollern family, and so a distant relation of the kings of Prussia. The leading voice in favour of this German option was not that of Bismarck, as might have been expected, but that of Napoleon III, to whom Karl was related in the female line.[13] Indeed, France was the only power prepared to support the Romanians in their desire to have a foreign sovereign. Karl (known in Romania as Carol) arrived in Bucharest on 10 May 1866 and was proclaimed Prince of Romania; once again, Europe woke up to a *fait accompli*. With unexpected efficiency, the Romanians had scored again in the European ball-game.

The most successful aspect of the whole process was the actual choice made. Although he was recommended by France and was half-French by 'blood', Carol proved to be a perfect German, corre-

A late photograph of King Carol I.

Peleş Castle, built by Carol I in the foothills of the Bucegi mountains: the symbol of monarchy in Romania.

sponding exactly to the 'ideal type' of his nation. He was disciplined, methodical and persevering; he had a sense of duty in the highest degree. The Romanians – except perhaps the Transylvanians – had never known anyone like him. In his personal qualities, and in his rigidity, Carol I resembled the Austrian (later Austro-Hungarian) Emperor Franz-Josef. It is no wonder that his wife, Elizabeth (also known by her pen-name of Carmen Sylva), tried – like the Empress Elizabeth, the famous Sissi – to escape, in her case finding refuge in literature and music. Perhaps in different times, someone more open and imaginative than Carol I would have suited the Romanians better. But what they needed above all was not imagination so much as organization and consistency. In the conditions of the time, Carol was the ideal monarch. He was punctual to an exasperating degree for Romanian politicians, who finally learned from him what punctuality meant. He was also extremely distant; he rarely offered his subjects his whole hand, but only one or two fingers, according to the importance he assigned to the person in question! He knew how to place himself high above everyone else. He was, in fact, just what the Romanians had wanted: a true Prince, of a different stuff from the boyars who had succeeded each other on the throne for centuries.

Carol reigned from 1866 to 1914, first as Prince, then – from 1881 – as King.[14] The Romanians thus enjoyed 48 years of stability. This might be said to have been the only long period of true continuity that they had known since the 47-year reign of Stephen the Great, which had, in any case, been limited to Moldavia, and had long become the stuff of legend. Of course, not everything was due to Carol. He was a constitutional monarch, even if his personal authority went beyond the spirit of the constitution. The substantial business of government, especially in internal affairs, was the work of the political class. After Carol, the first name which comes to mind is that of Ion C. Brătianu, the Liberal leader who headed the longest-lasting government in Romanian history (1876–88). The Brătianu government was responsible for important legislative reforms (including the revision of the constitution in 1884, after the proclamation of the Kingdom in 1881) and economic measures (especially concerning the encouragement of industry, which was still in an incipient state). If there was anything that both the King and the politicians could be reproached for, it was their élitist vision of progress and their lack of sensitivity to social issues in a country in which class differences remained very pronounced.[15]

Romania's stability can, of course, be explained by the relative stability of Europe in general in this period. However, it is sufficient to make a comparison with the Balkans – the 'powder keg of Europe', shaken by all sorts of crises – to see the virtues of the Romanian model. (In Serbia, for example, the rivalry between two native dynasties, Karadjordjević and Obrenović, produced a succession of *coups d'état*, and in 1903 King Alexander Obrenović and his entire family were massacred. Such a thing could not have happened in Romania.) Carol was determined to keep strict control of the country's political machinery. Two parties, Liberal and Conservative, alternated in government. This system resembled that of Britain, with the difference that governments were not changed by the decision of voters but by the King's arbitration. When he observed that a government was getting rusty, the King summoned the opposition to power; once installed, the new government would organize elections, which it invariably won! This is yet another illustration of 'forms without substance': the forms were British, the substance Romanian, and the conductor's baton was in the hand of a German, as skilful as he was rigorous!

Carol, Brătianu and Mihail Kogălniceanu (formerly Prime Minister under Cuza, and now Foreign Minister in the Brătianu cabinet) were the principal protagonists at the moment of independence. In fact, Romania had been gaining more and more freedom of movement in the time of Cuza and even more after 1866. It was bound to the Ottoman Empire only by the payment of tribute (which had dropped to 1 per cent of the country's budget) and by a number of largely formal prerogatives in matters of foreign policy. However, two decades had passed since the Crimean War, and it was time for a new war between the Russians and the Turks (the more so as Russia wanted to clear itself of the humiliation of defeat and to undo the consequences of the Treaty of Paris of 1856). This time, it was no longer possible for the Russians to pass over Romanian territory as they had done before. A convention was negotiated with the government by which the transit of the Russian army was permitted, in return for recognition of Romania's sovereignty and integrity. In these conditions, the Russian forces passed through and crossed to the south side of the Danube. Being now in a state of war with the Ottoman Empire, Romania proclaimed its independence on 10 May 1877 (a date chosen to coincide with the start of Carol's reign in 1866). Before long, the Russian advance was halted outside the town of Pleven in northern Bulgaria. Although the Russians had initially refused even to consider Romanian participation, they now requested the Romanian army's urgent intervention. Carol obtained the command of the united Russian and Romanian forces surrounding Pleven. After heavy fighting and a prolonged siege, the town surrendered on 28 November 1877. For the Romanians, it was a symbolic victory: after centuries of subjection, the glorious days of Stephen the Great and Michael the Brave had returned!

The Turks lost the war and were forced to accept a peace settlement the initial terms of which were extremely favourable to Russia, including the creation of a 'Greater Bulgaria' as an outpost of tsarist policy in the Balkans. Concerned at this, the European powers demanded that a congress should be held in Berlin to renegotiate the terms of the peace in such a way that the balance of power in the Balkans would not be upset in favour of Russia. Bulgaria became an autonomous state, but within significantly smaller borders than had originally been proposed. Austria-Hungary took over the administration of Bosnia and Herzegovina, and Britain that of Cyprus. Romania's independence was recognized conditionally (subject to its accepting the right to citizenship of non-Christians, in particular Jews). In addition, Romania acquired Dobrogea – an important territorial gain, as possession of the mouth of the Danube and access to the sea would considerably consolidate its geo-strategic and economic position in the region. However, the Russians, in defiance of their undertaking to respect their ally's territorial integrity, re-annexed the southern part of Bessarabia, which they had been forced to cede to Moldavia in 1856. Indeed, the Russian armies seemed to feel quite at home in Romania, delaying their withdrawal as long as possible. This was enough to reawaken the Romanians' fears. In 1883, Romania adhered to the Triple Alliance, made up of Germany, Austria-Hungary and Italy. Carol I's German origin may well have played a part in this decision. However, the principal reason was the need for protection: with the achievement of independence, the collective guarantee of the great powers, which had largely been a formality in any case, no longer applied. The choice was simple – Russia or Germany – and what Romanian would have opted for Russia? (France, the Romanians' great love, was far away, and more-over it had been defeated by Prussia in 1871 and no longer carried the same weight in Europe as it had done under Napoleon III.)

Excellent relations were possible with Germany. However, with Austria-Hungary the situation was somewhat different. The Austrians had finally given in to the Hungarians in 1867, and Austria had become Austria-Hungary, a state made up of two distinct states. In the Austrian part, even if the German element enjoyed higher status, the autonomy of the various 'lands', among them Bukovina, was preserved. In 1907, universal suffrage was introduced, with the result that the Germans lost their majority in the imperial parliament. Things seemed to be moving in the direction of federalization or of a multi-ethnic state in which discrimination would be a thing of the past. Hungary, however, was constituted on a different basis, proclaiming itself to be a unitary national state. The other nationalities – Romanians and Slavs – were considered to belong to the Hungarian nation. Transylvania lost its autonomy and was simply integrated into Hungary. Universal suffrage was never applied, because it would have put the Hungarians in the minority. A programme of Magyarization was also launched, through administration, the judicial system and education. Although its success was limited, it certainly had the effect of irritating non-Hungarians and provoked continuous protests.[16] The Romanians called for a return to Transylvanian autonomy. (After 1905, they dropped this demand – which in any case would have affected only the former principality, and not the

The two Romanias, I: a village *c.* 1900.

Banat, Crişana and Maramureş – and insisted instead on full political equality.) The culmination of their campaign was the 'Memorandist' movement of 1892, when a large delegation went to Vienna to present the Romanians' complaints to the Emperor. The Hungarians took offence: the Romanians should have gone to Budapest, not Vienna (even though the Emperor of Austria and the King of Hungary were one and the same person). The trial of the Memorandists, which took place in Cluj in 1894, ended with numerous prison sentences. In these circumstances, it is easy to understand that relations between Romania and Austria-Hungary could not be idyllic, and moreover public opinion in the Kingdom of Romania was openly on the side of the brother-Romanians in Transylvania. This situation weighed heavily when Romania had to take sides in 1914.

Carol I's Romania aspired to play the role of arbitrator in the Balkans. It was indeed the largest in area and population, and the most stable, of the small states that had appeared in the wake of the break-up of the Ottoman Empire. In 1912, the Balkan countries (without Romania) went to war with Turkey and emerged victorious; this was the 'First Balkan War'. However, the victors were unable to agree on how to share out their gains; the focus of disagreement was Macedonia, where the population was very mixed. Bulgaria ended up in conflict with all the others, and the

93

The two Romanias, II: the centre of Bucharest (Calea Victoriei in the inter-war period).

'Second Balkan War' broke out. This time, Romania intervened, against Bulgaria. The result was a perfect Romanian victory; its entry into the war led to Bulgaria's surrender and the opening of peace negotiations, which took place in Bucharest and were chaired by the Romanian Prime Minister Titu Maiorescu. By the Peace of Bucharest of August 1913, Bulgaria ceded to Romania the

'Quadrilateral' (two counties in the southern part of Dobrogea). In a broader sense, the Peace meant the recognition of a privileged position for Romania in the Balkans. But would Romania be content with this status as a Balkan power? A century earlier, in 1812, another peace treaty had been signed in Bucharest, between the Russians and the Turks (the treaty by which Moldavia had lost Bessarabia). On that occasion, no-one had paid any attention to the Romanian lands. Much had changed, and to the Romanians' advantage. Romania could now boast that it had managed to become a country which had to be taken into consideration by others.

In August 1914, the First World War broke out. For Carol, the choice was clear. Romania had to take its place alongside Germany and Austria-Hungary, the countries with which it had a treaty of alliance. It was a matter of honour, but also of interest. Germany was sure to win the war. In any case, it was the natural ally of Romania in the face of Russia. While this was a logical attitude in itself, it was not to be confirmed by history. Moreover, it ignored the sensitive issue of Transylvania. When the Crown Council was summoned to make a decision, Carol was surprised to find that the majority of those present opposed him – something to which he was not accustomed! The provisional solution adopted was neutrality. This was a heavy blow for the ageing King. His day had passed; Romania was moving into the troubled waters of a new age.

It was a sad end to his reign. In fact, a shadow had fallen over the picture a few years earlier, in 1907, when Romania had experienced the largest peasant rebellion in twentieth-century European history.[17] This rebellion was provoked by the shortage of land, in spite of the reform of 1864 and subsequent grants of property, and by the precarious conditions of peasant life. The explosion of hatred on both sides was terrible. The peasants killed savagely and were killed savagely. This tragedy, which shook public opinion and the political class, lay at the origin of the major agrarian reform introduced after the war. But above all, it highlighted the polarization of Romanian society and the lack of communication between the 'two Romanias'. This social fissure explains many things, including the later violence of Romanian Communism.

All in all, though, they had been 48 good years, as good as they could have been in the circumstances. Romania's prosperity was largely based on cereals and oil. It was the second-largest cereal exporter in Europe, after Russia. And in the production of oil, which

Oil-wells and a geyser of oil in the Ploieşti area, shortly after 1900. Romania was then one of the world's great oil-producing countries.

had been extracted as early as 1857 around the town of Ploieşti (about 60 km north of Bucharest), it came third in the world around 1900, after the United States and Russia. Its currency was strong and stable; the Romanian *leu* was equivalent to the French *franc* (which was likewise stronger than it is today!). It must be acknowledged, however, that this prosperity was built on the shoulders of the peasants.

Nothing can be judged without comparison. If we compare the 48 years of Carol I with the 48 years before and those after him, we see that between 1818 and 1866 there was a succession of revolutions, wars, foreign occupations, modifications of political status and *coups d'état*. Between 1914 and 1962, there were two world wars, political instability, authoritarian regimes, more foreign occupations and, finally, the darkest years of Communism. Perhaps Romania will find a lasting balance in the future. So far, the only truly balanced period in its history, whatever its failings, remains the 48-year reign of Carol I.

As is so often the case with historical events, the participation of Romania in the First World War has taken on a much simpler shape in the Romanians' memory than it had in reality. It is imagined that there was a quasi-unanimous preference for the consummation of national unity by the liberation of Transylvania. In fact, things were rather more complicated. Until 1914, the union of Transylvania with Romania could not be included in the category of realistic projects. The Romanians there were demanding equal rights with the Hungarians (indeed, negotiations on this issue, between the Romanian National Party of Transylvania and the Hungarian authorities, took place a short time before the outbreak of war). The prospect of federalization was also being considered. Aurel C. Popovici aroused a degree of interest when he proposed the restructuring of the monarchy as a federation of fifteen states in his book *Die Vereinigten Staaten von Gross-Österreich* (1906). Franz Ferdinand, the heir to the throne (whose assassination in Sarajevo led to the outbreak of war), was said to have federalist intentions. Romania itself might even have joined such a hypothetical confederation (a manner *sui generis* of achieving the unity of the Romanians; in the resulting state, they would have been about as numerous as the Germans or the Hungarians!). Of course, this did not mean that there was no dream – however vague and 'atemporal' – of a greater Romania, extending 'from the Dniester to the Tisza'.

The outbreak of war in 1914 changed the terms of the problem. The acquisition of Transylvania now became an achievable objective. The condition was that Romania should go over to the 'right' side, and that that side should win the war. Those inclined to this way of thinking were certainly in the majority, and they won the debate in the end. However, the alternative option was favoured by a far from negligible group of politicians and leaders of opinion. Would Romania align itself with France, Britain, Russia and Italy, or with Germany and Austria-Hungary (and their allies Bulgaria and Turkey)? The partisans of the former option were obviously thinking of Transylvania; in addition, they were sentimentally drawn

97

towards France, the land to which the Romanians felt themselves bound. (There were even voices calling for immediate entry into the war, not for Transylvania but for France!) On the other side were those pejoratively termed 'Germanophiles' (though they were not necessarily any more Germanophile than their opponents were Francophile). They based their reasoning on the fact that Romania did not lie between Germany and France, but between Germany and Russia. Better to be defeated with Germany than to be victorious with Russia! A victorious Russia could only be harmful to Romania (as indeed happened later, after the Second, not the First, World War). However, Germany's prospects seemed safe enough: it was the most powerful country in Europe. In the case of victory along-side Germany, the Romanians would get back Bessarabia (and perhaps also Bukovina, which the Austrians were hinting they would cede if Romania entered the war on their side). Bessarabia or Transylvania? Bessarabia was smaller and poorer, and there were fewer Romanians there than in the lands beyond the mountains. But the Romanians there were in a much worse situation than those in Transylvania. Russification was progressing faster than Magyarization; for all the abuses committed by its government where the issue of nationality was concerned, Hungary was still a liberal state, quite different from autocratic Russia. Moreover, the Romanians had an incontestable historical right to Bessarabia, which had been seized from Moldavia in 1812, whereas Transylvania had belonged to Hungary since its foundation. On the other hand, Transylvania had a different kind of allure. A beautiful and rich country, it had given the Romanians a pleiad of scholars, and it was there that the Romanian national movement had begun. The soul of the Romanians was with Transylvania.

The death of Carol I in October 1914 removed one obstacle. Having no children, he was succeeded by his brother's son, Ferdinand, another German Prince, but one who did not hesitate to embrace the opinion of the majority in his country of adoption. Moreover, his wife, Queen Marie, was British, a granddaughter of Queen Victoria, and her role in the court's new orientation was significant. The process was managed by the Liberal Prime Minister, Ionel Brătianu (son of Ion C. Brătianu), who shifted grad-ually and skilfully from neutrality to commitment on the side of the Entente. Romania's demands were accepted and included in the convention signed with the Allies in August 1916; prominent among them was an expanse of territory extending well beyond the country's present-day western border as far as the Tisza, both in the north of Hungary and in the Banat. A new Crown Council took the final decision, opposed only by the former Conservative Prime Minister Petre P. Carp. 'Sire,' he said to Ferdinand, 'I will send my sons to the front, but I will pray to God that the Romanian army is defeated!'

On 27 August 1916, the Romanian army crossed the mountains into Transylvania and advanced rapidly, occupying about a third of the province within a few weeks.[18] However, the Austro-Hungarians received German reinforcements, and the Romanians were not able to withstand the counter-offensive. The more so as in the south, on the Danube and in Dobrogea, they were attacked by German, Bulgarian and Turkish forces. Romania was surrounded. Allied support was practically non-existent: the Russians remained at the ready, while the British and French forces that landed at Salonika did not launch the promised offensive (which would have put Bulgaria in difficulty). There was heavy fighting in the Carpathian passes; then the forces of Germany and its allies poured into the south of Romania. Bucharest was occupied at the beginning of December 1916, and a short time later a new front line was established in the south of Moldavia. The King and government took refuge in Iaşi. In exceptionally difficult conditions, resistance was organized in Moldavia with the support of a French military mission led by General Berthelot, this time with the participation of the Russian army. Field Marshal Mackensen's attempt to break through the Romanian front line failed. Two important Romanian victories were won in July–August 1917, at Mărăşti (under General Alexandru Averescu) and Mărăşeşti (under General Eremia Grigorescu). Moldavia was saved.

However, Romania was still cut in two. In Bucharest, a German administration was in operation, with the support of 'Germanophile' Romanians, who seemed to have been proved right by events. (This was 'collaboration' *avant la lettre*, prefiguring a phenomenon more characteristic of the Second World War.) In spite of the heroic resistance in Moldavia, the war continued to develop in favour of the Central Powers and against Romania. In Russia, revolution broke out in February and then November 1917, and defeatism and disorder took hold of the army. With Russia out of the reckoning, the Romanians could no longer defend themselves alone on a tiny patch of land like Moldavia. They made a separate peace with the Germans and their allies, which was signed in Bucharest in May 1918. The terms were particularly severe: Romania lost Dobrogea and the Carpathian ridges (as the Austro-Hungarian border was pushed forward). But history was now out of control, and it offered unexpected solutions. The revolution provoked the partial disintegration of the Russian Empire. Bessarabia was liberated and reunited with Romania in April 1918. The Germans now looked set to win the war. For three years, they had managed to wage it on two fronts; now they were victorious in the east and could throw all their forces onto the western front. As everyone knows, they lost nonetheless. On 11 November, they signed an armistice, which amounted to a capitulation.

Austria-Hungary crumbled in defeat, and new political entities emerged from its ruins. Bukovina united with Romania in November 1918, and Transylvania on 1 December, by the vote of a great Romanian assembly held at Alba Iulia. The refusal of Hungary, where a Communist government had been installed under Béla Kun, to recognize its loss of territory led the Romanians to continue military operations. At the beginning of August 1919, the Romanian army entered Budapest. This was the only occupation of an 'enemy' capital by any of the allies, and an extraordinary historical revenge for the Romanians, who had hitherto always been in a position of inferiority in relation to Hungary and the Hungarians!

The peace treaties (particularly the Treaty of Trianon, signed with Hungary in 1920) confirmed these territorial modifications, though not without difficulty as far as the drawing of Romania's western border was concerned. The Romanians did not, as they had requested, obtain territory extending as far as the Tisza. The western part of Crişana remained in Hungary, and the western Banat, where there were more Serbs than Romanians, went to Serbia (Yugoslavia). Even so, Romania's success was extraordinary. Having suffered apparent defeat in the war, it ended up gaining Transylvania and Bukovina, as well as Bessarabia. This was more than the greatest optimists could have imagined in 1914. Accused of having advocated a mistaken course of action, P. P. Carp gave a prompt and memorable reply in his acid style: 'Romania has so much good fortune that it no longer needs politicians!' The good fortune had come, it is true, after centuries in which Romania had been less than fortunate. Though the newly drawn borders could be contested in matters of detail, it is clear that the

King Ferdinand and Queen Marie at their coronation in Alba Iulia in October 1922: a detail from Costin Petrescu's sketch for the Athenaeum fresco of 1933–7. The scene symbolizes the creation of Greater Romania.

provinces now united all had a majority Romanian population. In a Europe of national states, this was the natural configuration of a Romanian national state. It was certainly more coherent, and has proved more viable, than Yugoslavia, Czechoslovakia and Poland, which resulted from the same process of imperial dismemberment. They were multinational states, not so very different in their ethnic structure from the defunct monarchy. (Czechoslovakia, for example, incorporated distinct zones inhabited by Czechs, Germans, Slovaks, Hungarians and Ukrainians.) Romania was on the borderline between being a national and a multinational state. Non-Romanians were numerous, but they were a minority in all of the provinces, although they formed a local majority in several counties of Bessarabia, Bukovina, Transylvania and Dobrogea. Czechoslovakia and Yugoslavia have now broken up, and Poland was shifted on the map at the end of the Second World War, but, apart from some cessions of territory, Romania's borders have remained substantially as they were established in 1918.

The question which must be asked is how useful – in a more general sense – the fragmentation of Central Europe actually was. Austria-Hungary had been an ethnic-cultural mosaic, but so were its successor states (with the partial exception of Romania). Throughout this part of Europe, there were no clear dividing lines. Thus the borders drawn by some have been endlessly disputed by others, and the problem of minorities has become an almost insoluble problem. No less serious was the power vacuum created in the heart of Europe. The First World War completely did away with the old politics of European balance in which a few great powers of approximately equal strength had kept continuous watch on each others' movements. The small countries in the centre of the continent now found themselves caught between Germany and Russia: it was this situation which gave rise to the Second World War. If Austria-Hungary had been replaced by a large confederation, a better balance might have been preserved, and at the same time such a confederation might have been in a position to attenuate national contradictions. For Romania, the conclusion of the war was a triumph, but it was a triumph that concealed many dangers. Little Romania, protected by the game of European balance, was safer than Greater Romania, thrown into the whirlpool of a history that no longer knew any rules.

THE INTER-WAR PERIOD: BETWEEN DEMOCRACY AND TOTALITARIANISM

Compared with Romania before the First World War, Greater Romania was another country. It had more than twice the area: 295,000 sq km compared with 137,000 in 1914. In 1912, its population had been scarcely more than 7 million; in 1930, it was 18 million. Its minorities had multiplied, both in numbers and in diversity, and now represented slightly over a quarter of the total number of inhabitants. (Romanians accounted for 71.9 per cent of the population, according to the census of 1930.) Apart from their number, their insufficient integration was also a problem. Frustration and distrust were manifested on both sides. The Hungarians, previously masters of Transylvania, and the Romanians, their former subjects, had now reversed roles. Time and goodwill would be necessary for relations to settle into a pattern of normality. Relations between Romanians and Russians or Ukrainians, or between Romanians and Jews, were also very delicate. All were Romanian citizens, but in peoples' minds the distinction between Romanians and 'others' remained strong.

Like pre-war Romania, Greater Romania was constructed on the principle of a unitary and centralized state after the French model. The card of federalism or regional autonomy was never played, out of fear that a looser relationship between the various parts of Romania (which started out with considerable differences between them) might lead to the dismemberment of the country. (The same fear is still manifested even today!)

Immediately after the war, two essential political and social changes were implemented. Universal male suffrage was introduced, and a radical agrarian reform was passed in 1921, by which the greater part of the land was transferred to the peasants; the *latifundias* disappeared. The Romania of 1914 had belonged to a restricted élite; with a little cynicism one might say that that was why things had gone so well! Now, everything was more complicated. The era of mass politics had begun, even if the masses served more as objects of manipulation. The two-party system, which had functioned perfectly thanks to Carol I, now fell apart. Parties fragmented and multiplied. The Liberals remained dominant for a time, before having to face the competition of the National Peasant Party (which was partly the continuation of the older Romanian National Party of Transylvania). The constitution of 1923 was an updating of that of 1866: it was liberal, even democratic. However, Maiorescu's famous distinction between form and substance still applied. Instead of elections bringing a government to power, governments which had already been installed, by way of all sorts of combinations, resorted to elections which, as before, they regularly won. The same party which obtained almost all of the seats in one electoral consultation might remain with only a handful at the next! This situation was created both by pressure from above and by the inadequacy of civic consciousness, itself a consequence of the low level of education of the majority of the population. It was, basically, a fluid mixture of authoritarianism and democracy.

The Crown, too, contributed to the accentuation of instability. Gone were the days of Carol I – Maiorescu had expressed the fear that a German Prince might end up becoming too Romanian! When Ferdinand died in 1927, he was not followed on the throne by his son, Prince Carol, who had given up his right to the succession, partly of his own free will – choosing to lead a freer life alongside his mistress Elena Lupescu – and partly under duress – his behaviour had aroused the anxiety of the political class. Instead, the new King was Carol's young son Michael, in whose name a regency was established from 1927 to 1930. In 1930, however, Carol returned and proclaimed himself King. A strong-willed and authoritarian figure, he saw the ruling of the country as his personal prerogative, and eroded the power of the political parties as much as he could. In the elections of 1937, the Liberal government lost (the first time a Romanian government had been voted out of office!), while the Legionary movement – or Iron Guard, a nationalist party of Orthodoxist and anti-Semitic character – won a disturbing 15 per cent of the vote. This was the beginning of a drift towards totalitarianism – far from a Romanian speciality in the period: from Communism to Fascism or Nazism, almost all of Europe passed, at some time or another, through the totalitarian fever provoked by disgust with democracy and by the mythology of a 'new world' and a 'new man'. In February 1938, Carol II established his own dictatorship. A new constitution abandoned the liberal foundations on which modern Romania had been constructed. Political parties were abolished and the separation of powers was practically done away with in favour of the King. Now, the Romanians had their first encounter with a 'single party', in the form of the Front for National Rebirth. The King promised them a new Romania, prosperous and free of social dissension. There were certainly a few good years of economic dynamism and flourishing culture.

On 1 September 1939, however, the Second World War broke out. Since the First World War, Romania had remained allied to France and Britain; the 'Little Entente', made up of Czechoslovakia, Romania and Yugoslavia, was presented as the regional equivalent of the western Entente in Central and South-eastern Europe. In the mid-1930s, Nicolae Titulescu (1882–1941), the talented and proud Romanian Foreign Minister, had embarked on a policy almost of great-power dimensions – and beyond the possibilities of his country – seeking to establish a European system of security, and displaying more firmness in the face of Hitler and Mussolini than Romania's French and British allies. All of this came to nothing, however, with the *Anschluss* and the dismemberment of Czechoslovakia in 1938, followed by the joint action of Germany and the Soviet Union (the German-Soviet pact of August 1939, which delimited the two powers' zones of influence) and the dazzling success of Germany in the first year of the war, culminating in France's capitulation in 1940. Romania was now completely isolated, caught once again – as seemed to be its destiny – between Germany and Russia. A few days after the fall of France, the Soviet Union annexed Bessarabia and northern Bukovina, following an ultimatum which Carol II and his government did not dare to oppose. Hitler and Mussolini, meanwhile, who had not forgiven the Romanians for their policy in the preceding years, 'mediated' between Romania, Hungary and Bulgaria. On 30 August 1940, Romania was required by the Vienna 'arbitration' to surrender to Hungary the north-eastern part of its territory over the mountains, in which there was a significant concentration of Hungarians, although the Romanian population was still more numerous. The territory lost amounted to almost half of Transylvania (44,000 sq km out of 102,000). In September, the Quadrilateral, too, was ceded to Bulgaria. Two decades on from the Great Union, Romania had lost a third of its territory.

Carol II was unable to deal with such a massive setback. He abdicated in favour of his son Michael, who was now an adult. However, effective power now came into the hands of General (later Marshal) Ion Antonescu, governing initially in tandem with the Legionaries. Violence spiralled. Carol II had repressed the Legionaries mercilessly, having many of their leaders killed without trial, including the movement's head, Corneliu Zelea Codreanu, to whom its members had a mystical devotion. Now, they took their revenge, butchering the political leaders of the royal dictatorship. In January 1940, Antonescu decided to distance himself from these embarrassing allies. A rebellion of the Legionaries – in fact an attempted *coup d'état* by which they hoped to gain complete control of the state – was liquidated, though not before producing fresh victims, particularly Jews. Until 23 August 1944, Antonescu ruled the country alone. His brand of 'fascism' was different from that of the Legionaries. In contrast to their mystic exaltation and anarchic outbursts, he was a military man who loved order.

It seemed as if quieter times were ahead. Before long, however, Romania entered the war on the side of Germany against the Soviet Union (22 June 1941).

Antonescu did not favour the Germans by nature; in the First World War, he had fought against them. However, his authoritarianism and anti-Semitism brought him closer to the German model (though in a less radical variant) than to the Western democracies. But what else could Romania have done? In the part of Europe where it was situated and in the context of the time, it could only choose between Germany and the Soviet Union. Few Romanians, even among Antonescu's democratic opponents, would have opted for the latter! The Romanians' primary objective was, beyond any doubt, the liberation of Bessarabia and Bukovina. The army did not stop at the Dniester, however, advancing further in what was referred to as a 'crusade against Bolshevism'. On the south flank of the eastern front, it was the Germans' principal ally. The Romanians conquered Odessa, then the Crimea, and advanced as far as Stalingrad and the Caucasus. Then they had to retreat. In April 1944, the Russians entered Moldavia. Concomitantly, the British and Americans carried out a series of air attacks, aimed particularly at the capital and the oil-producing zone around Ploieşti. Most violent of all was the American bombardment of Bucharest on 4 April 1944: 900 houses were destroyed and almost 3,000 people killed.[19]

On 23 August 1944, Antonescu was overthrown by a *coup d'état* organized by the King together with the leaders of the political parties, including the Communists. This was a turning point for Romania, and indeed for the evolution of the war in South-eastern Europe: Germany lost not only the support of the Romanian army but also access to Romanian oil and grain, and saw its whole strategic edifice in the Balkans crumble. The Romanians turned their guns around, went over to the side of the Allies, and advanced, together with the Soviet armies, into Transylvania, then on into Hungary and Czechoslovakia. At the peace conference, however, Romania was treated as a defeated country – three years of war alongside the Germans, not to mention the interests of Moscow, weighed more heavily in the balance than eight months with the Allies. The country had to endure a long Soviet occupation (until 1958), and to pay the Soviets massive reparations. The Romanians regained the part of Transylvania which had been ceded to Hungary in 1940; however, Bessarabia, Northern Bukovina and the Quadrilateral were not returned. The new borders – which remain those of today – enclosed an area of 237,000 sq km, less than Greater Romania by about one-fifth.

THE BALANCE SHEET OF PRE-COMMUNIST ROMANIA

In the first half of the twentieth century, Romania made great and relatively rapid progress. However, it started from a very modest level and still had a long way to go before it could catch up with the West. Industry developed, and the urban population grew. The bourgeoisie began to count for more than the old landowning aristocracy. And yet the country's profile remained rural to a great degree. Barely 20 per cent of Romanians lived in towns in 1930.[20] There can be no doubt that the élite was at a Western level; the interwar period saw a remarkable cultural effervescence. However, the general level of culture was much lower than in the West; in 1930, only 57 per cent of Romanians could read (compared with 60.3 per cent in Bulgaria, 84.8 per cent in Hungary and 92.6 per cent in Czechoslovakia). It is true that most of those who were illiterate belonged to the older generation, and there had been notable progress since 1910–12, when only 39.3 per cent had been able to read. Overall, however, the situation did not look very good. Especially as 85.1 per cent of those who could read had no more than primary education, only 8.6 per cent had completed high school, and a mere 1.6 per cent had studied at universities or similar institutions (men being four times as numerous as women in this last category). The demographic behaviour of the population was also extremely traditional: both birth and death rates were the highest in Europe, and in addition Romania held a sad European record, as the country with the highest rate of infant mortality (another symptom of the precarious living conditions and inadequate education of a large part of the population). Certainly, Romanian peasants of 1930, owning their own land, were no longer the same as the peasants of 1907, at least from the point of view of their material potential (although there were still disadvantaged categories); however, for many, both in rural society and in some urban environments, the conditions of life and level of culture remained very low. Romania continued to be a land of strong social contrasts. The élite was tiny, and the middle class, too, was relatively small. The 1930s were

107

marked by modernization at a sustained rhythm. However, this was too short a period for things to change radically. Romania would have needed another two generations to catch up with the West, not just at the level of the élite but across the whole of society. But history was not going to allow it this chance. Communism was to throw it in a quite different direction.

Another characteristic of the period was the rise of nationalism, particularly its orientation in a more and more autochthonist direction. The nationalism of the nineteenth century had been combined without difficulty with Europeanism, and with admiration for the West in general. Romania wanted to demonstrate that it was a European country – hence the emphasis on Latin origins, and on the Romanians' role in defending European civilization in the Middle Ages. After 1900, without abandoning this orientation, a greater emphasis began to be placed on specifically Romanian values. Many factors contributed to this shift. It was, in the first place, a reaction to the 'abuse' of foreign influence in the previous century. The élite was no longer limited to a handful of individuals educated in the West; as it expanded, it inevitably took on a more Romanian character, particularly as many intellectuals came from a rural background. The confrontation with minorities after 1918 accentuated the manifestations of 'Romanianism'. Finally, the atmosphere throughout most of Europe was similar: it was an age of nationalism, of clear demarcation between 'us' and 'others'.

In March 1906, a violent demonstration against the performance of plays in French took place in front of the National Theatre in Bucharest. This was the moment when the 'Romanianist' offensive took clear shape. Writers were urged to deal with rural and 'specifically Romanian' subjects. The Sămănătorist movement (from the journal *Sămănătorul* – 'The Sower' – founded in 1901: note the 'agrarian' symbolism) brought together the most important writers of the beginning of the century, who were determined to cast off foreign formulas and bring the Romanian landscape and soul into view. In architecture, alongside the Parisian-style buildings of the end of the nineteenth century, a 'Romanian style' emerged in the work of the architect Ion Mincu (1852–1912) and his disciples, a variety *sui generis* of Art Nouveau incorporating elements and motifs from traditional rustic architecture. This tendency continued in the inter-war period, even if opposing points of view were also expressed, in a Romanian culture that was becoming more and more rich and complex.[21] Eugen Lovinescu (1881–1943), the leading literary critic of his generation, strove throughout his life to convince his compatriots that the cosmopolitan city offered a more interesting social and psychological environment than the patriarchal village. The mythology of the village proved tenacious, however, together with that of the 'Romanian soul'. The Romanians, it was said, had a particular spiritual essence, which was preserved in the unmixed, unaltered world of the villages, not in the 'alienated' towns. Even the reign of Carol II, when modernization was in full swing, was marked by an insistent official promotion of the symbolic function of the village. This tendency also gave rise to an interesting development: Dimitrie Gusti (1880–1955) laid the foundations of rural sociology, organizing numerous field investigations with his students. It was also Gusti who, in 1936, founded the Village Museum in Bucharest – a substantial collection of authentic peasant houses, and one of the most important museums of its kind in Europe (comparable with the Scandinavian museums which have become reference points for the reconstruction of the rural habitat).

It is all a question of measure. While a dose of the specifically Romanian might have been welcome, a 'Romanianism' pushed to the extreme constituted the ideological base of the national-extremist tendencies which multiplied in the 1930s, and especially of the Legionary movement. The Legionaries (also known as the Iron Guard) embraced a national mystique combined with a fervent Orthodoxy. Their dream of a 'pure' Romania led inevitably to violence, totalitarianism and hostility towards 'others' (especially towards Jews). Beginning as a veritable religion of national rebirth whose ideal, but obscure and utopian, project attracted some of the most outstanding young intellectuals of the period (among them Mircea Eliade and Emil Cioran), the Legionary movement ended in terror and bloodshed.[22]

Overall, Romania inclined towards the Right. It was a predominantly rural world, both literally and symbolically speaking, and the peasants, with their smallholder mentality, were not easily tempted by left-wing ideologies. Paradoxically, even the Left showed apparently 'rightist' inclinations. This can be seen in the ideologies of Poporanism before the First World War, and Peasantism in the interwar period. The ideal which they proclaimed was a rural, not an urban, one: a Romanian society of smallholders. It was a far cry from the industrial and collectivist project of Communism, but also from

109

modern social democracy. Socialists and Communists had little influence on Romanian society and political life at the time. The Communist Party, founded in 1921 as a branch of the Moscow-based Communist International, was seen as a party of foreignness, treacherous to national interests, and was outlawed in 1924. In fact, it was playing the game of Moscow, proclaiming the multinational character of the state and the right of nationalities to self-determination – in other words, the break-up of Romania and above all the return of Bessarabia to the Russians. Moreover, it had only about a thousand members, and most of them were not ethnic Romanians but Hungarians, Jews, Bulgarians, Russians and Ukrainians (who had, of course, specific reasons to be discontented); this contributed even more to the marginalization of the Party in a society in which 'others' were not seen as fully Romanian.[23]

Who would have imagined that a few years later, Romania would pass through one of the most severe and radical Communist experiments?

iv Romanian Communism

Nothing is easier to see and to explain than the installation of Communism in Central and South-eastern Europe. Regardless of particular national conditions, of cultural and political traditions, and of the effective balance of forces, Communism came to power precisely where the Red Army advanced. The fate of defeated countries like Romania and Germany (the Soviet-occupied zone) was the same as that of countries in the victors' camp like Poland and Czechoslovakia. Communism was a regime imposed by conquerors. However, it would be a mistake to suppose that it was maintained only by oppression and terror. No political system can last so long without commanding, if not general consensus, at least the adherence of some social categories. In operating a radical overturning, building a 'world turned upside down', Communism attracted those who profited (or at least felt they were profiting) from this process: those who 'moved up' while others 'moved down'. The myth of equality which it promoted (and to a certain extent also practised) was, as Tocqueville had shown, an irresistible tendency of the political and social imaginary of the previous two centuries. Equality and liberty are the two great components of democracy. Equality is even more desired than liberty, at least in societies in which there are large disadvantaged categories. In emphasizing equality at the expense of liberty, Communism acquired a democratic aura and succeeded in seducing many with its project of constructing a world without exploiters and great social discrepancies.

The problem of Communism is not whether it was a 'good thing' or a 'bad thing' in itself. The problem is that in the natural order of things, it could not function. It was conceived and put into practice in defiance of elementary human and social laws. How could a system function without property, without competition and without sufficient individual motivation? Perhaps only by creating a 'new man', as was indeed the intention. Communism was kept alive by artificial means (in the first place by constraint) and by deviations from the norm (tolerating a variable sector of private property and free commerce), and its survival was due to a great extent to the inflow of Western credit and assistance. The real miracle was not the collapse of Communism but the fact that it was able to go on so long! It deserved to disappear the moment it was born.

Romania stood out as a country to which Communism was particularly foreign. It was predominantly rural, without a strong left-wing tradition and with no sympathy for anything coming from Moscow. It was, from this point of view, at the opposite pole to Czechoslovakia (especially the Czech part), a highly urbanized and industrialized country with a strong Communist Party and a certain sympathy for the 'great Slav brother' in the east. (Before the war, the Communist Party had had only a thousand members in Romania; in Czechoslovakia there were 80,000, in Hungary 30,000, in Poland 20,000, in Yugoslavia 15,000 and in Bulgaria 8,000.) The paradox is that this society, apparently quite unprepared for Communism, ended up by settling into the most orthodox patterns of the Communist experiment. Communism ended up being maintained precisely by those conditions which had prevented its implantation initially. This was not just a Romanian paradox; it was the great paradox of Communism. According to Marx's economic and historical reasoning, the Communist revolution – a proletarian one – should have taken place in the industrialized West, not in the agrarian and pre-capitalist East: in Britain, not in Russia. In fact, this 'industrial' and 'proletarian' ideology materialized almost exclusively in societies less advanced on the road of capitalism and democratic politics. From this point of view, Romania was quite similar to pre-Communist Russia: a limited élite of Western type, an incipient capitalism (with all the ensuing imbalances and inequalities) and a great rural mass situated at a low economic and cultural level.

What happened was actually quite natural. The élite, which was small in number and formed something of a body apart, was quite simply pulverized; some of its members left the country, others went to prison or descended the social ladder, while others fitted in and were lost in the 'new society'. The peasantry, on the other hand, almost disappeared as such, in as much as peasants may be defined in terms of their relationship, both material and sentimental, with

Blocks of flats for the working class: a view of the Militari district in Bucharest. Until the Communist period, there was a suburban settlement here, with houses of rural type. It is still possible to see a few 'peasant' cottages that have survived among the tower blocks.

the land. Collectivization transformed the peasantry into an agricultural proletariat. Moreover, forced industrialization absorbed a significant mass of the rural population and flung them into the towns, thus creating a large category of 'town-dwellers' cut off from villages but not truly integrated into urban civilization. Thus all structures were overturned. Many Romanians found themselves in a quite different social position to that in which they had started out. Almost overnight, a new political class and intelligentsia were created (largely made up of workers and peasants). In these conditions, tradition crumbled.

Similar things happened throughout this part of Europe, but rarely did they go as far as in Romania. There were multiple causes for this, two of them being acute social discrepancies and the insufficiency of democratic culture. The Romanians showed little solidarity; old motives for enmity rose to the surface. The peasants shot in 1907 were avenged. Those now on top had the satisfaction of seeing how others fell. As for democracy, most Romanians had little idea what it meant. In fact, they had always manifested a sort of respect mixed with fear in the presence of authority. Communism took full advan-

113

tage of this paternalist mentality; moreover, its assault on Romanian society and culture was extraordinarily brutal. To begin with, Romania was treated as a defeated country, with no mitigating circumstances. Then, the Communist leaders who came to power came from quite marginal sectors of society; there was no way they could be expected to feel bound to any tradition. Finally, force was needed to make Romania conform to the Communist ideal – in other words, to transform an agrarian country rapidly into an industrial one, and a society which had hardly heard of Communism into one impregnated with Communist values and attitudes. This was the drama of Romania: an already fragile social body was struck harder than in other countries.

At first, when the Antonescu regime was overthrown, optimistic or naïve observers might have thought that Romania was at last coming under the sign of democracy. But after only a few months, on 6 March 1945, Soviet pressure led to the formation of a government led by Petru Groza, the leader of a small agrarian party, a satellite of the Communist Party. In appearance, this was a broad coalition government, in which there were even some defectors from the historical parties (Liberal and National Peasant). In fact, the key posts (starting with that of Interior Minister) and effective power were in the hands of the Communists. This was already a Communist dictatorship, albeit in democratic disguise. From approximately a thousand members, Party membership rocketed to hundreds of thousands (710,000 in 1947: a more than 700-fold increase!). Among those captured were numerous writers and other influential intellectuals (who had certainly not been Communists prior to 1944!).

The new government immediately implemented an agrarian reform, sharing out among the peasants the limited amount of land that had remained in the hands of the old landowners after the great reform of 1921. (A few years later, however, the government was to take back all that the peasants had been given, not only in 1945 but also in 1921 and 1864!) Voting rights were also extended to women for the first time. Thus, with everyone voting, elections took place in November 1946, and the Communists and their allies won a resounding victory. It is hard to say what the Communists would have achieved in properly conducted elections: certainly well below a majority. The actual result was due to propaganda, intimidation (the opposition was effectually immobilized) and, above all, the falsification of votes. In the period that followed, the historical parties were abolished and their leaders thrown into prison, while 'fellow travellers' were swallowed up by the Communists. A 'fusion' with the Socialists in 1948 led to the creation of the Romanian Workers' Party (in fact the Communist Party under another name; in 1965, it reverted to being the Romanian Communist Party). King Michael tried in vain to stand against this evolution. On 30 December 1947, he was forced to abdicate, and the Romanian People's Republic was proclaimed.

On the road to power, and then in the unrivalled exercise of power, Communism excelled in the combination of democratic discourse and totalitarian practice. Its proclaimed project was the creation of a new world in which there would be no more inequality, oppression or injustice, and of a new humanity, freed from servitude – a free humanity in a free world. In order to destroy the old world and to lay the foundations of the new, there had of course to be a phase (preferably as short as possible) of revolutionary violence. Called the dictatorship of the proletariat, this phase corresponded in the official terminology to the construction of socialism, the phase preceding fully-fledged communism. But since the carefree world of communism stubbornly failed to appear, the project remained in the first, 'socialist' phase (the concept of 'dictatorship' did not sound good and was given up after a while). This was a long, seemingly interminable road. In communism, the state would disappear, along with all constraining institutions. In socialism, on the other hand, the state, or rather the hybrid 'state-party', needed to be consolidated continually, since it was through it that communism was to be constructed. Thus, on the way to the disappearance of the state, you had to pass through the strengthening of the state; on the way to full freedom, you passed through the abolition of freedom. Everything would pass! In fact, everything did indeed pass in the end; however, the transition was to lead not to communism but back to capitalism!

This perverse logic seems characteristic of Communism. Hitler was a criminal, but he spoke sincerely, from the very beginning, in *Mein Kampf*, about what he intended to do. He never promised democracy or respect for the individual. Communism, on the other hand, juxtaposed two registers that did not match. For a long time, the illusion of democracy helped it to maintain a certain respectability – and it still protects its memory. Communism's crimes, with their 'democratic' motivation, seem less terrible than the crimes of the Nazis. As a motive, democracy is clearly respectable and racism abject. In fact, however, Communism was not only responsible for brutal repression, for lives wrecked and for murders which – however motivated they might have been in ideological terms or through the splendour of the 'ideal project' – were still murders, but also for the total breakdown of the social mechanism. The famous words of Talleyrand on the occasion of the execution of the Duc d'Enghien are fitting here: 'It was worse than a crime; it was a mistake!' It is easier to emerge from a dictatorship of fascist type, as in the case of Germany and Italy after the Second World War, or of Spain after Franco. Fascism did not affect social structures to the extent that Communism did. With its 'scientific' and methodical project of constructing a new world from the beginning, Communism replaced 'normal' reality with a parallel reality.[1] The case of the economy is particularly revealing. 'Fascist' dictatorships preserved private property and the market economy. Communism, in contrast, attempted, and to a large extend managed, to abolish these 'capitalist' structures. This is why it is harder to emerge from Communism than from any other type of dictatorship. The 'normal' world has to be remade, reinvented, down to the cellular level. Several generations have paid, and will continue to pay, for Communism and its consequences.

A REPLICA OF THE SOVIET UNION

The Communist model, in its 'ideal' form, was the same for everyone. Inevitably, however, it had to be adapted to pre-existing realities. As a result, there were significant variations, less noticeable in the uniformizing phase of Stalinism but increasingly pronounced as time went on. Romania may claim to have experienced the worst of this.[2] Its insufficient engagement with modernity and the failure of democratic culture to penetrate its society in any depth now made themselves felt. The formless mass of 'working people', cut off from tradition, could easily be 're-educated' and controlled.

The only institution that might have stood up to the state was the Church. But Romania was not Poland. In contrast to the Catholic and Protestant churches, the Orthodox Church has a long tradition of respect for political authority: it had always been more concerned with its theological message than with involvement in the life of the *polis*. Communism and Orthodoxy thus arrived at a *modus vivendi*, curious as this might seem given that the 'struggle against mysticism and superstition' featured prominently in the Party's ideological arsenal. An aggressive atheism was put into practice. In the 1950s, children were kept in school on Easter Night, so that they could not go to church! Many Romanians (especially those 'well placed') were afraid to be seen at church; it would not have been good for their careers. In public, professions of atheist conviction were frequent. And yet the churches remained open and were always full. In the theological seminaries, the number of candidates for the priesthood actually increased. Thus the Orthodox Church was left in peace, on condition that it did not overstep its bounds. It even received a precious gift: the abolition of the Greek Catholic Church in 1948 and the return of the Uniates to the fold. After all, until everyone actually became atheist, a national Orthodox Church was better than a Greek Catholic Church, dependent on the Pope, on Rome, on the West! Such gestures of goodwill were not without a price, however. The Church was not actually asked to promote atheistic propaganda, but it was expected to urge its members to respect authority and the new political order. The Church was enrolled in the 'struggle for peace', one of the cleverest slogans launched by the Communists (and one which caught the imperialist, 'warmongering' West off guard: who would dare to praise war?). Nothing could be more natural than that the Church should have upheld this noble and 'Christian' message! All in all, there were no crises between the Communist regime and the Church. Each gathered its own believers. And between the two categories of believers, in the Party and in God, there was a broader category of practitioners of doublethink and doubletalk: with the Party and also with God. (Orwell, in *1984*, says all there is to say about this kind of thought.) Communism taught people to survive and to lie. This is one of the heaviest of its legacies.

No Communist country ended up resembling the Soviet Union as closely as Romania did, down to small details. In all of the Communist countries, the Party was all-powerful. But in most of the European Communist countries, satellite parties – socialist, Christian Democrat, agrarian etc. – continued to exist. In Romania, however, as in the Soviet Union, the single-party system operated in all its purity.

The driving force of Communist society was considered to be industry, especially heavy industry: steel production, machine construction and so on. What was, in essence, a nineteenth-century

One of the industrial 'temples' of Communism: a cement factory north of
Cîmpulung, disfiguring and polluting a picturesque mountain area.

industrial model was kept alive in the Communist economies almost
to the end of the twentieth century. As a 'production' society,
Communism had no thought to make concessions in favour of
'consumer society'. While everywhere in the developed world the
importance of industry was falling and that of services was
increasing, Communism prided itself on the ever-increasing role of
industry in its overall economic structures. The system had been
conceived as a new world for workers, and so it must remain; to
produce was more important than to consume! Moreover, the accent
was always on traditional industries. As a theory forged in the nineteenth century, Communism never managed to break away from the
strategies of the first phase of the Industrial Revolution. Its great
symbol was steel; it was from steel (*stal*) that Stalin took his name.
Cement was also a potent symbol. Computers and information technology never managed to make much of an impression. They were
even suspect, being on the borderline between the material and the
immaterial. Communism was unable to break away from a heavy,
costly, less and less viable type of industry. And what came first in
economics was ideology, not viability.

However, even this economic model could be applied with
greater or lesser strictness. The Romanians applied it as strictly as

118

they could. Industry was completely nationalized: the principal companies went first, by a decree of 11 June 1948, and the others followed. Heavy industry was consistently given priority over consumer goods. Like the Soviets, the Romanians 'fell in love' with steel, but in their case the aberration was even greater. At least the Russians possessed large deposits of iron and coal; the Romanians did not. Romania ended up importing iron and coal in order to make steel, as much steel as it could! The raw material was brought by sea from India, Australia and Canada, and then transported up the Danube. Hence the great steel plants, above all that of Galați, were built close to the river (far from the old centres of steel production, Reşiţa and Hunedoara in Transylvania). Towards the end of the Communist period, Romania was producing almost 14 million tonnes of steel, while France and the United Kingdom were producing 19 million each. If the relative populations are taken into account, we might say that twice as much steel was being produced for each Romanian as for each citizen of France or Britain.

A hardline approach was also adopted in the collectivization of agriculture. The system recognized two types of organization, known in Soviet terminology as *sovkhoz* and *kholkhoz*. The former was a state agricultural enterprise, while the latter was an association of peasants, holding their land in common. But the property of everyone is the property of no-one, and in fact it was still the property of the Communist state, in a disguised form. The creation of collective agricultural units, later known as Agricultural Production Co-operatives (the Romanian version of the *kholkhoz*), meant that peasants were dispossessed of their land. If state-owned industry worked badly, agriculture of this type hardly worked at all. Russia and Romania had traditionally been the largest grain exporters in Europe. If anything was not in short supply in Romania before Communism, it was food. But food now became Communism's principal problem: how to feed people, given that industry was privileged to the detriment of agriculture, and that the collectivization of property was radically diminishing yield.

Collectivization was carried out at an intense rhythm, using simple and brutal methods. If the peasants could not be 'convinced', then violence was resorted to, and those who opposed the process were denounced as *chiaburi*, or saboteurs. In the Communist imaginary, the *chiabur*, equivalent to the Russian *kulak* – the well-off peasant – became a monstrous figure. But it was precisely such peasants, with their holdings of tens of hectares, who had represented the most dynamic sector of Romanian agriculture. In 1959, the *chiaburi* disappeared by government decree: henceforth, no-one was permitted to make use of waged labour in agriculture. Under Communism, each individual would live by the work of his or her own hands! Finally, in 1962, the completion of collectivization was announced in an atmosphere of national festivity. (Poland and Hungary had already carried out a partial 'de-collectivization' after 1956.) 'Socialism' was triumphant in Romania, in town and village alike! In other words, private property had come to the end of its existence. Some parcels of hill and mountain land remained un-collectivized, and there were also a few small private workshops and shops, but their economic importance was minimal. Socialism had indeed triumphed completely in the towns and villages; all that was left was for the Romanians to pay the bill. They were to continue paying it until 1989. Indeed, if we take all of the consequences into consideration, they are still paying it today, and will go on paying it for some time to come.

FROM REPRESSION TO DÉTENTE

The 1950s were also the years of great repression. Many Romanians went to prison. Some were sentenced for political offences, either real (in terms of Communist legislation) or imaginary, including offences of opinion; others were imprisoned without being sentenced at all, by simple 'administrative' decisions. Alongside the archipelago of prisons, there was also the 'prison canal'. Here, too, the Soviet model was copied. The Russians had embarked on a vast programme of canal construction, which was intended to connect their country's great rivers and seas. This was as much a repressive project as an economic one. 'Enemies of the people' were taken to work on these canals, and to die if they could not survive the inhuman conditions. With characteristic mimicry, the Communist regime in Romania invented its own canal, which was to cut Dobrogea in two, linking the Danube to the Black Sea. Work was begun in 1949 and stopped in 1953, only to be continued later under Ceauşescu. The project was a complete failure in technological and economic terms, but a success for the apparatus of repression.

Who was imprisoned or sent to the canal? In principle, anyone suspected not only of effective anti-Communist acts but of a generally hostile attitude. A denunciation or word out of place was sufficient. An anecdote with an anti-Communist flavour repeated over a drink among friends could result in one's being sentenced to years of hard labour, or even in death; many of those sent to the canal never returned. The important thing was to 'keep your mouth shut'. However, some categories were hit harder than others, starting with the inter-war political élite. In 1950, all of the prominent political leaders were arrested and sent to the terrible prison at Sighet in Maramureş: former ministers, members of parliament, party leaders etc. Few of them came out alive. Among those who died in prison were National-Peasantist leaders Iuliu Maniu (1873–1953) – a key figure in the union of Transylvania with Romania in 1918 and Prime Minister in 1928–30 and 1932–3 – and Ion Mihalache (1882–1963); members of the Brătianu 'dynasty' Constantin I. C. Brătianu (1866–1953), brother of Ionel Brătianu and leader of the National Liberal Party, and Gheorghe I. Brătianu (1898–1953), son of Ionel Brătianu, historian and politician; and Constantin Argetoianu (1872–1955), one of the most influential politicians of inter-war Romania (who left behind him a vast body of memoirs, almost all of which were eventually published after the fall of Communism). The army was similarly decapitated. Many intellectuals were jailed: people who had ideas, who talked too much and around whom nuclei of resistance could be formed were a dangerous species for the regime. A considerable number of peasants also went to prison, those who had opposed the forced collectivization. The hardest-hit community was the Greek Catholic Church. All its bishops and a large number of priests, who refused to 'return' to the Orthodox Church in 1948, were imprisoned; many did not survive. On the whole, however, the society of the Romanian 'gulags', like its Soviet counterpart, was characterized by diversity. It was a meeting place for people of the most varied backgrounds and the most different beliefs, whose paths would never have crossed outside. Some remained in prison for ten or fifteen years. Thus a parallel society was created, in some ways more authentic than the dismembered and fearful society outside. Its life is recalled today in a number of memoirs, the most complete and vivid of which can be found in the prison saga by Ion Ioanid, who was detained from 1953 to 1964.[3]

The prison regime varied within limits from one period to another or according to the goodwill of the jailers, but overall it was extraordinarily tough and humiliating. The aim was the physical and psychological destruction of those who were considered adversaries of the regime. The cells were cold, food was insufficient, there was beating, prisoners' feet were chained etc. Some of the men who suffered these conditions were in their 80s. This explosion of hatred and sadism was also the expression of a conviction that victory (as Communist theory proclaimed) was permanent. No-one would be called to account for their actions! And indeed, far too few have been called to account. In contrast with those responsible for Nazi crimes, who are still being pursued in the courts today, almost no-one has been tried for crimes committed in the time of Communism. There has been no Nürnberg of Communism. As in all cases of massive and secret repression, a statistical assessment of the phenomenon is not easy. As far as Romania is concerned, estimates of the number of those imprisoned or deported vary between 100,00 or 150,000 and a million (or even more). The lower limit is the figure in official records and is probably an underestimate; the true number is likely to lie somewhere between the two extremes.

The Soviet model was not only applied to the concrete structures of political power, society and the economy; it also had to permeate the minds of the Romanians. The single historical and cultural reference point remained Russia; the 'Latin island' was reintegrated into the Slavic sea; history was rewritten. For a decade starting in 1947, the single textbook on Romanian history in circulation, intended for pupils, students and teachers alike, was *History of the R.P.R.* (*Republica Populară Romînă*, or Romanian People's Republic – the new name for Romania), produced under the direction of Mihail Roller, an improvised historian who had became a sort of 'dictator' of Romanian historiography. The 'bourgeois' history hitherto in vogue had emphasized the national idea and links with the West. Now nationalism was prohibited, apart from the Russian variety (disguised as Soviet 'internationalism'). The accent shifted onto 'class struggle' – emphasizing the gulf between the Romanian bourgeois and the Romanian worker – and integration into the Slavic space, with the spotlight on 'fraternal' relations with Russia and, later, the Soviet Union. From the Romanian past and national culture, all that remained was an ideologically oriented selection, in which some of the great names were missing while others were presented in a distorted manner, cast – against their will – in the role of supporters of Communist ideology.

In order to judge Communism correctly, one simple rule has to be grasped. Stated principles are one thing, practice is another. Thus Communist democracy was a dictatorship. But it was not even a dictatorship of the Party, as the theory pretended; it was a dictatorship of restricted groups, maintained in power by a repressive apparatus, in Romania the famous *Securitate*. The Romanian Communists had never given up the conspiratorial spirit of their clandestine youth: the cultivation of secrecy, the settling of scores 'within the family'. The Party was now a mass organization, but it made little difference. The games of power were played in secret, at the top. Things were done in mafia style, complete with killings if necessary. The 'subjects' became aware of a doctored version of what had happened only after the denouement. Those who had lost the match and been eliminated from the sphere of power – establishment figures until the previous day – were presented as 'deviationists', spies and so on. Then they were 'forgotten', removed from the history textbooks and from people's memory. (Here, too, the Soviet model was followed; Stalin had proceeded in the same way, indeed even more harshly, with Trotsky, Bukharin, Zinoviev, Kamenev and almost all of the old Bolshevik élite.)

In 1946, even a former General Secretary of the Party, Ştefan Foriş (deposed in 1944), was killed, without much in the way of formalities, by his comrades; he subsequently went down in history as 'the traitor Foriş', although no-one ever bothered to explain what exactly he was supposed to have betrayed! In 1948, it was the turn of Lucreţiu Pătrăşcanu, then Minister of Justice and a leading player in the events of 23 August 1944. Pătrăşcanu was one of the few intellectuals in the Party leadership; in addition, he had shown himself to be more 'nationalist' than was fitting in a Romania which had become a Soviet annexe. He was removed from all positions of responsibility and arrested; condemned to death a few years later, he was executed in 1954. The turn of the Ana Pauker–Vasile Luca group came in 1952. If Pătrăşcanu was a 'nationalist', their handicap was the opposite: Pauker was Jewish and Luca was Hungarian. In fact, the principles invoked and the accusations formulated counted for little. It was a struggle for power; that was all.

Gradually, the leadership became more Romanian. Initially, the Party was largely controlled by a 'Muscovite' group, comprising those leaders who had spent years close to Stalin in Moscow, many of whom were not ethnic Romanians. However, Party officials from within the country were rising up behind them, and it was in the nature of things that this second group should win in the end. Among them was Gheorghe Gheorghiu-Dej, a former railway worker who had been Secretary General of the Party since 1945. At first, he shared power with the others; at the beginning of the 1950s, the Party secretariat, which held effective power, consisted of one Romanian, Gheorghiu-Dej, and three 'non-Romanians'. However, the anti-Jewish tendency manifested in the last years of Stalin's rule clearly worked against the Pauker group. Gheorghiu-Dej got rid of his rivals and remained uncontested at the head of the Party till his death in 1965 (eliminating a few 'awkward' comrades along the way).

The Party also embarked on a policy of emphasizing national identity, which had been almost completely erased around 1950. Stalin's death in 1953, followed by a period of openness but also by the inconsistencies of Khruschev, eased the ascent and projects of Gheorghiu-Dej. He was a Machiavellian character; by a mixture of skill and unscrupulousness he triumphed at home and won himself a degree of freedom of movement in foreign affairs. His master stroke came in 1958, when he managed to persuade Khruschev to withdraw Soviet troops from Romania. From then onwards, the 'Romanian' orientation became intensified. I remember – I was at secondary school at the time – how we celebrated, for the first time under Communism, the anniversary of the Union of the Principalities on 24 January 1959. This was the recovery of a founding moment of national history. (Previously, more had been made of 7 November, the date of the Bolshevik revolution in Russia!)

The motivation behind this evolution was twofold. On the one hand, a return of 'Romanianism' was understandable, as neither Gheorghiu-Dej nor the other leaders in his entourage had much connection with Russian or Soviet culture (nor for that matter did they have much connection with Romanian culture!), and in any case they could not go on ignoring the population's national sentiments for ever. On the other hand, they were also rejecting the timid but nonetheless effective liberalization sketched out by Khruschev (the denunciation of Stalin's crimes in 1957, the first publication of Solzhenitsyn's writings a few years later etc.). Gheorghiu-Dej had no intention of going that far. He was unsettled by the Russian 'liberalization', the denunciation of the 'personality cult', and the changing, almost everywhere, of the Stalinist old guard. His distancing from the Soviet Union can be explained not only by 'patriotic' motives but also by his fear of losing his position if he allowed himself to be caught up in the movement unleashed by Khruschev. He played the two-sided card of patriotism and personal rule. In contrast to all of the other European Communist countries except Albania, there was no de-Stalinization in Romania. In place of a dose of liberty, the people were offered a dose of nationalism – which, of course, they found pleasing after the anti-national offensive of the preceding years. This also explains the intensification of repression after several years in which it had been relaxed. The years 1958 and 1959 saw great political trials, with intellectuals in particular as the victims. The message was twofold: to Moscow ('We are capable of maintaining Communist orthodoxy on our own') and to the Romanian people themselves ('Keep toeing the line; the dictatorship is not over yet!'). The events of 1956 – the revolution in Hungary and unrest in Poland – had been a warning signal: nothing of this kind must be allowed to happen in Romania!

The culmination of the process occurred in 1964, Gheorghiu-Dej's year of glory. By the 'April Declaration' of that year, the Communist Party – and implicitly the country – proclaimed its independence from Moscow. A bitter ideological and political conflict (which threatened to degenerate into armed confrontation) had just broken out between the Soviet Union and China. Instead of standing by Moscow, like its other European partners in the Warsaw Pact, Romania took a middle position, setting the principles of independence and non-interference at the heart of its relations with other Communist parties and states.

It was a spectacular gesture, and one that seemed promising. At the time, I was a student in the History Faculty of the University of Bucharest. We were assembled in a large lecture theatre and given a talk about the new orientation: about the abusive demands of the Soviets, about a Romanian tradition that needed to be recovered, about our links with Western culture and so on. As a first stage, rapprochement with the West meant Paris. On the one hand, there was an old tradition to be revived; on the other, there was the special attitude, likewise independent, which De Gaulle displayed within the Atlantic alliance; the shift in Romanian relations with Moscow seemed somewhat symmetrical with the Gaullist position regarding Washington. And so the Prime Minister of Romania, Ion Gheorghe Maurer, visited Paris. French newspapers and magazines appeared in Bucharest, something my generation had never before seen; for a few years, until the ideological hardening of the early 1970s, we could buy *Le Monde* and *Le Figaro* (a few days late, of course, since they were subjected to careful reading before being released for sale, and with some issues missing, as their content was deemed unsuitable).

In the same year, 1964, the prisons were opened. All political prisoners were released, some of them after almost two decades in detention. Once again, the motive was twofold. The regime felt itself to be so strong that it no longer had anything to fear from a few individuals who were half crushed anyway; at the same time, the message to the West was clear: 'The repression is over; Romania is becoming a free country!'

DYNASTIC COMMUNISM?

By this time, Gheorghiu-Dej had cancer. He died in March 1965. His replacement – by another 'conspiratorial' decision at the highest level – was the man he had been preparing to succeed him, Nicolae Ceauşescu, then aged 47.[4] Later, the Romanians would have every reason to wonder what would have happened without Ceauşescu, if Gheorghiu-Dej had lived longer or been replaced by someone else. For Ceauşescu was not a Communist leader like any other. Under his leadership, Romanian Communism took a surreal turn. Gheorghiu-Dej, or any of the other possible successors, would probably have ruled in a more balanced way (in comparison with Ceauşescu, this would not have been difficult). However, it is a long way from this to imagining, as some sympathizers of Gheorghiu-Dej like to suggest, that Romania would gradually have advanced towards greater liberty, democracy and a market economy. The Party and the *Securitate* never let go of the reins; they may have relaxed them from time to time, out of tactical motives, but they never gave up, and never intended to give up, their control of Romanian society. Without Ceauşescu, things would probably have been better at the level of details – and it is true that life is largely made up of details – but we may question whether the system itself would have evolved to any significant degree.

The period between 1964 and 1971 was the best in the history of Communist Romania (by 'best' I do not mean 'good', but 'good in relation to the rest'). Some Romanians began to travel in the West; it was not easy to get an exit visa, but at least it was possible. The greater part of the national culture was recovered. History began to be written with an increasing emphasis on Romanian values.

126

Censorship continued however. You were free to be a nationalist, just as you had been free to be pro-Soviet in 1950! But you were certainly not free to think and to express yourself as you pleased. It was certainly more pleasant to think nationally than to think anti-nationally, but thinking itself remained a risky business. The risk of ending up in prison was considerably reduced, but that was partly because people had learned to take care. At the height of the great repression of the early 1950s, Romanians opposed to Communism had still not completely stopped behaving as free individuals. Moreover, they believed that the regime would not last long, that the Americans would come (a tenacious myth). Communism proved durable, however, and the Americans never came (indeed, they never had any intention of coming). If repression under Ceauşescu was softer than under Gheorghiu-Dej, this was due in the first place to the fact that society itself had become quieter, settling into the mould prepared by the Communists. Deviations were now individual, easy to track down and punish. In these same years, people's standard of living also rose perceptibly. Consumer goods came to occupy a more significant place in the Romanian economy. Some of the Western credit which had been taken advantage of on a massive scale for years, principally for the development of heavy industry, began to trickle down to the level of everyday life. You could eat and dress rather better than before, and even see American movies at the cinema (carefully selected, of course).

Ceauşescu's problem was his extremely modest background. He had been born in Scornicești, an insignificant village in the west of Muntenia, in a house on the edge of the village. So he was a marginal person from a family of marginal people. His proletarian activity – indispensable, symbolically speaking, for a Communist leader – was limited to apprenticeship in a shoemaking workshop. His education did not extend beyond four years of primary school; to the end of his life, he had difficulty reading. With the coming of the Communists to power, none of this was a handicap: quite the opposite. His wife, Elena, had started at the same level. Her studies, too, had been limited to primary school. However, she was eventually to become (it does not matter how) a chemical engineer, a doctor in chemistry and, finally, an academician. At the height of her intellectual ascension, she was always referred to as 'Academician Doctor Engineer Elena Ceauşescu'. Such an ascent from such lowly beginnings turned both the Ceauşescus' heads; their frustrations were trans-

A painting from the 'Golden Age': *She* and *He*, under the flag of Romania, surrounded by children wearing red neck-scarves.

formed into megalomania, which they fed and stimulated in each other. It was not enough for them to dominate Romania; *their* Romania had to become a great power, and they themselves had to be recognized as leading figures not just of the country but of the whole world. Buildings had to be constructed in Pharaonic style. The largest palace in the world, which they erected for themselves in Bucharest, was certainly revenge for the humble cottages in which they had been born. Alongside their own phantasms, however, they also cultivated national pride. Romania was a land of peasants, a land in which everything had been built on a small scale for a long time; even its churches are of modest dimensions. Now, it was to become a land of town-dwellers, with great industries and monumental constructions. Beyond the individual madness, the Ceauşescu project corresponded to a wider desire to leave patriarchal Romania behind. It was a bet on modernity, but an extravagant and ultimately disastrous bet.

Gheorghiu-Dej had concentrated power in a relatively discreet manner (as leader of the Party and, from 1961, as President of the Council of State, the 'collegial' presidency of Romania). The fact that one of his daughters, completely lacking in talent and nothing much to look at, aspired to be a movie star and interpreted leading roles in a number of films was no more than a minor and anecdotal departure from the Communist rule of personal power manifested impersonally. Officially, the Party remained the supreme authority. With Ceauşescu, the supreme authority became the family, which was placed, even officially, before the Party. At first, Ceauşescu inherited only the position of Party leader. In 1967, he added that of President of the Council of State. In 1971, he became the first President of Romania (the collective presidency having been transformed into a personal presidency). As President, he appeared like a monarch, with a sceptre in his hand (to the enthusiasm of Salvador Dalì, who sent him a congratulatory telegram – the whole thing was surrealistic indeed!). Then, Elena Ceauşescu climbed the ladder of power, to become number two in the Party. The couple shared out responsibilities, with the First Lady taking charge of staff policy, science, technology and culture (she was an academician, after all!). Their son, Nicu Ceauşescu, a playboy more inclined to drink and womanizing than to politics, was to ensure the succession. In their last years, he appeared more and more often alongside his parents in official contexts, and his name was heard with increasing frequency. Otherwise, not many names were heard. Members of the 'Political Executive Committee' of the Party or of the government were reduced to the rank of mere servants of the Ceauşescu couple, and were continually changed or 'rotated' so as not to acquire too much importance in a particular post (or as the penalty – since someone had to pay – for failure). At the very moment of the fall, in December 1989, a sensation was caused by the subservient gesture of a former Prime Minister, who actually kissed the dictator's hand!

The Romanian model ended up close to that of North Korea: dynastic Communism. Though this seems a complete aberration, it was actually true to the logic of the system. In its interpretation of history and in the justification for its political actions, Communism puts the *masses* in the foreground: everything happens through the people and for the people. But in fact, the masses are represented by the *Party*; and the Party by its *leaders*. Everywhere, the Communist leadership became personalized to an appreciable, though of course varying, degree. (Even 'collegial' rule meant a small group of no more than a handful of leaders.) All the Romanians and the North Koreans did was to take the final step. A closed system in which decisions were taken at the top by a restricted group permitted, and indeed almost encouraged, such a shift. In Romania, an attitude older than Communism also contributed: a paternalist mentality, a seemingly self-evident respect for someone placed above others. To this may be added the fact that all autonomous structures had been crushed, more harshly than anywhere else, and the people amalgamated into a mass without an independent will.

THE CEAUŞESCU STYLE

Nothing worked better and more easily – incredibly easily! – than the Ceauşescus' desire to play a major role in the world. The distancing from Moscow in 1964 had already made Romania an interesting country. In August 1968, when the Soviets, along with their Warsaw Pact allies, invaded Czechoslovakia and put an end to the 'Prague spring', Ceauşescu stood up against the aggression. This was something out of the ordinary in Communist Europe: from the balcony of the monumental building that housed the Central Committee of the Party, in front of a square full of people, a Communist leader condemned the policy of Moscow and expressed his firm resolve to meet any similar aggression with armed resistance. It was Ceauşescu's finest hour. With a single gesture, he seemed to have won independence from the Soviet Union, the respect of the West and the general admiration of his own people. In fact, he feared for his own position, and the situations of Czechoslovakia and Romania were not at all similar. In Czechoslovakia, a liberalizing process had been launched which could only end in the loss of the Communists' political monopoly. That was why the Russians intervened in force. There was no other solution for them – except to lose! In Romania, nothing like this was happening: the Party was fully in control. If anything was going to bother the Soviets, it was not internal policy (which was no more liberal than their own) but Romanian foreign policy in some of its manifestations. These could give rise to irritation from time to time, but they did not pose a threat to the Communist system. Hence the Russians did not intervene.

The site of the great Communist gatherings: the square between the Central
Committee building and the former royal palace. Ceauşescu (not visible) is speaking
from the balcony of the Central Committee building. A sea of people hold up his
portrait, slogans and flags. To the left, part of the royal palace can be seen; opposite is
the University Library (the former Carol I Foundation). This was the scene of
Ceauşescu's triumph in August 1968, but also of his downfall in December 1989.

It is not easy to weigh up the extent to which the claimed independence of Romania between 1964 and 1989 was real or only
apparent. Romania remained to the end a member of the Warsaw
Pact and of the Communist states' economic organization, and the
Soviet Union was its principal trading partner. It was a troublesome
member of the family, but it never left the fold. Ceauşescu liked to
believe that he was more independent than he really was. But the
West liked to believe the same thing. (As Caesar said, 'People will
easily believe what they want to believe.') An independent Romania
would indeed have made a breach in the Communist system. What
was more serious, however, was that on the basis of Romania's
distancing from Moscow, Westerners were prepared to credit
Ceauşescu with openness in internal policy too. Comparisons were
bandied about with Tito's Yugoslavia, a Communist regime more
flexible both outside and within. And so Ceauşescu became
respectable and indeed acceptable company. The reality was quite
the opposite, however. The Romanians did not benefit from this
foreign policy: they paid for it. In order to have his hands free on the

131

For decades, the centre of Communist power was here. The building (begun at the end of the 1930s and finished in the following decade) first housed the Interior Ministry, and then the Central Committee of the Romanian Communist Party. Above the entrance can be seen the balcony from which Ceauşescu spoke and, in the upper right, the terrace from which he fled by helicopter in December 1989.

outside, Ceauşescu stopped the process of liberalization within his country. It was clear that it was not out of sympathy with the Czechoslovak experiment that he had become so heated in 1968. On the contrary, he feared the contagious force of such a model every bit as much as he feared Soviet intervention. With the 'Prague spring', Romania's timid liberalization came to an end; Ceauşescu would now be the most consistent defender of Communist orthodoxy.

The West pretended not to see or understand, and so Ceauşescu enjoyed favourable treatment for years. He travelled all over the world, to Communist countries, the West and the Third World. He was on friendly terms with everyone. From Washington to Pyongyang, doors were wide open for him. Kings and queens, presidents and prime ministers received him ceremoniously, or were received by him in Bucharest; hardly a single political personality of the period was missing from the list. Ceauşescu pursued grand politics, and not only in appearance. His foreign policy was that of a great power. In a world polarized along a multiple system of faults – the Soviet Union and the United States, NATO and the Warsaw Pact, the Soviet Union and China, Israel and the Arab nations, the developed

132

world and the Third World – he managed to present himself every-where as the linking element, the conciliatory factor, the ideal mediator. Thus Ceauşescu was able to play an effective role in the negotiations between Israel and the Arab nations (Romania being the only Communist country that did not break diplomatic relations with Israel after the war of 1967). As things went so well for him, he natu-rally began to aspire to more: a 'new political and economic order' which Romania, through him, would propose to the whole world!

What Romania still lacked if it was to be a true world power was economic and human weight. Here, too, Ceauşescu set to work. In the economy, he displayed a voluntarism and a megalomania every bit as intense as in international politics. However, it was easier to talk about the destiny of the world than to make the economy work (especially a Communist economy, which by its nature did not work well!). Ceauşescu carried to its extreme the economic voluntarism specific to Communism. Industry must be 'obliged' to develop at a heightened rhythm (especially heavy industry), and the consumer needs of the population must be sacrificed as a consequence. Steel production and machine manufacturing, not to mention the chem-ical industry (Elena Ceauşescu's speciality), took first place. There was a frenzy of production, of greater and greater production, production understood as an end in itself. Romania imported huge quantities of raw materials (including oil, which it had formerly exported) in order to make finite products, often of mediocre quality, which brought it little profit or even loss. Moreover, Ceauşescu imagined a self-sufficient Romania, capable of producing every-thing. In a world of interdependency and specialization, in which even large countries with an industrial tradition no longer manufac-tured the whole range of products, Romania seemed set to cover all branches of production. From steel bars to cars and planes, Romania could make anything, and with a technology that was going to be above the world average!

An interesting problem with Communism concerns the rhythm of economic development. From one year to the next, in all of the Communist countries, the economy, and especially industry, grew several times faster than in the West. The ideology required it: Communism was superior! For capitalism, an annual growth in industrial production of 2 or 3 per cent is satisfactory, and 5 per cent is excellent; the Communists attained, as a rule, a rate of over 10 per cent! How did they do it? Partly by 'inflating' the statistics, but also

133

to a certain extent by really producing, but without taking account of market demand. (What counted was the value 'in itself' of the product, not its market value. Marx defines *value* as the quantity of work materialized. Value is distinct from price. Whether a product is needed or not, whether it sells or not, is not so important. After the fall of Communism, the same mythology was perpetuated in the evaluation of enterprises for privatization at a 'value' far above what they were actually worth. In fact, their value was below zero, because they were only producing loss!)

Even among the Communist countries, Romania stood out by its exceptionally high rhythm of growth: on average, over almost the entire period of Communism, it was 12 to 13 per cent annually. In the 1970s, the 'Romanian miracle' was proclaimed, by analogy with the 'Japanese miracle', at a time when Japan came first in the world in terms of the rhythm of development, and Romania second. The difference between the two is that the Japanese miracle was real. The true Romanian miracle would appear to be the fact that after half a century of impetuous development, the country is one of the poorest countries in Europe. Whatever method we choose to calculate gross production per head of population, the difference between Romania and the West today is considerably larger than it was on the eve of the Second World War. Indeed, former Communist Europe as a whole has lost ground in comparison with the West (a remarkable result in view of those much higher growth rates!). A statistic from Ceaușescu's last year sheds some light on how the calculations were made. The order had been given from above that agricultural production per hectare must overtake the Western yield. And so the figures fell obediently into line, giving an annual production of 60 million tonnes. After the fall of Communism, there was a recalculation. The result: 16 million, four times less!

The Romanians were also rather few in number. A 'great' Romania had to have more inhabitants, especially more young people. In October 1966, the Communist regime offered the Romanians a present which was to ruin the lives of many of them for over two decades. Abortion was forbidden by decree. The decision – a 180-degree turn – took people by surprise. The Communists had come to power under the banner of women's liberation and their complete equality with men. Consequently, abortion was made freely available at very 'attractive' prices. (An average monthly salary would have paid for some tens of abortions.) Sex education and family planning were out of the question. (Under Communism, nothing official was said about sex; dictatorships are prudish as a rule, and sex is an area of liberty which they can only try to cover up or limit.)

As women came to work alongside men, and styles of behaviour became freer, the consequences are easy to guess. Romania experienced a veritable epidemic of abortions. Then suddenly, without warning and without any alternative programme being offered (since contraception was almost unknown), something which had seemed a natural right suddenly became a criminal offence, punishable by years of imprisonment (both for the practitioner who carried out the operation and for the woman on whom it was performed). Countless dramas ensued: improvised operations, deaths, convictions; women interrogated by public prosecutors while their lives were still in danger; unwanted children; children born with abnormalities because of the empirical methods used in the attempt to abort them. More than anything else, the policy created a state of permanent irritation in family life, in the day-to-day relations between men and women, and it was an immense insult to people, and especially to women, who were treated as breeding animals. At first, as might be expected, the number of births rose abruptly. Then, since people always find a way of coping, it began to fall again. The phases of falling birth rate were countered by fresh campaigns of repression: the birth rate would rise, then fall again, and so on. For years, a silent war was waged between the regime and the people. This was one of the Romanians' great frustrations and concentrated part of the violence unleashed in December 1989.[5]

The 'systematization' of the villages was the signal that began to awaken Westerners to the reality of Romania. It is curious that they had not previously noticed the even greater 'systematization' of the towns. The reason is probably that the village has a mythical significance: it is there that we find our roots. In this respect, too, Ceauşescu went very far, but still along the lines of Communist mythology. Communism announced the coming of a new world; this inevitably meant the radical transformation of the landscape and the human habitat. Entire areas of the towns were flattened, without sparing historical buildings or even tiny segments of the traditional urban landscape.[6] The district of tower blocks became the great symbol of Communist modernization. Of course, all over the world, part of the population has been squeezed into tower blocks: this is the price of

135

The demolition of old Bucharest in the 1980s: the end of the early 18th-century Văcăreşti Monastery. Only the tower blocks remain!

industrialization and urbanization. In Romania, however, the transformation of the towns was presented as the ideal solution, a *summum* of modern civilization. What could be more uplifting than living in a tower block! Propaganda images highlighted the splendour of the new districts. And so the Romanians' life changed radically. Whether in town or in the country, most people had lived in individual houses, modest though they may have been. As a consequence of Communism, the great majority of townspeople came to live in blocks of flats. This was another blow struck against individualism: Communism meant communal living! The rooms in these blocks were, and still are, small and badly finished. There are no garages (which would have been too great a luxury), play areas for children, churches (of course) or cinemas. These are places where people simply 'stay': eat, sleep – in short, exist.

Next came the turn of the villages. Here, it is true, Ceauşescu's approach was extreme even by Communist standards. The villages had to disappear – nothing more, nothing less! According to the territorial systematization programme prepared in the 1980s, each group of villages was to be replaced by a small centre of urban type (with blocks of flats, of course). A number of targets would be attained at the same time: the extension of agricultural land, the complete 'urbanization' of Romania, the 'collectivization' of the people and the homogenization of their way of life. This project, which indeed seemed to be the work of a madman, aroused indignant protests in the West and contributed to a large extent to the ending of the long (far too long) honeymoon period which Ceauşescu had enjoyed in his relations with Western governments. He only had time to destroy a handful of villages; these were replaced by blocks of flats of poor quality, without so much as running water. Among them wandered the courtyard animals that the peasants had brought with them!

Ceauşescu did not like churches at all. (In this respect, too, his ideology was consistent with the atheism of Communism. In the end, what was wrong with Ceauşescu was that he took Communism too seriously!) He took advantage of the systematization of the towns to have many churches, including historical monuments, demolished. Some of the churches which were spared were 'hidden' by tower blocks erected in front of or around them, or even shifted to less visible locations. In Bucharest, this strategy was put into practice on a large scale. The objective was, of course, to create an urban landscape without churches. The episode is not one of the most glorious pages in the history of the Orthodox Church, which put up no effective resistance. One wonders what would have happened if the Communist regime in Poland had started to demolish churches.

On the other hand, again in line with Communist mythology and the Soviet model, Ceauşescu loved canals and artificial lakes. He resumed, and indeed completed, work on the Danube–Black Sea canal, which the Gheorghiu-Dej regime had been unable to bring to a conclusion. He began the digging of other canals as well. The idea was that Bucharest should also be linked to the Danube, and so become a port. Villages were destroyed in order to 'install' lakes in their place, some of them vast. Today, a number of 'false lakes' – abandoned craters without water – can still be seen around Bucharest, where people used to live. There can be no doubt that waterways preoccupied Ceauşescu more than conventional roads. While they waited to be able to travel by canal, the Romanians found it harder and harder to travel on land, as the roads fell into an

Nicolae, Elena and Nicu Ceauşescu at the opening of the Danube–Black Sea Canal in
1984. The picture is doubly symbolic, illustrating both dynastic Communism (*He, She*
and the 'heir to the throne') and the regime's great works, especially the 'aquatic'
preoccupation of Ceauşescu's last years.

advanced state of decay. (Romania had only 100 km of motorway,
and even that more in name than in reality.) Ceauşescu's games with
water also included the draining of the Danube lakes (to extend the
land available for agriculture) and even a project (fortunately never
finalized) for the partial draining of the Danube delta! Clearly, he
had never heard of ecology.

Communism promoted engineering; its programme of transformation called for more and more engineers. About half of all
graduates of Soviet higher education were engineers. Here, the
Romanians outdid even the Russians; out of every three Romanian
students, two studied engineering – an indisputable world record.
Nowadays, the Romanian professional class is largely made up of
engineers, many of whom are trying to find work in other areas.

Ideology and culture also took on the Ceauşescu imprint.[7] The
year 1971 saw the launch of a 'little cultural revolution', Romanian
style. Ceauşescu proclaimed the end of ideological relaxation. No
more concessions would be made; deviations and bourgeois influence would no longer be accepted. The feeble liberalization which

had begun in 1964 now came to an end. Until 1989, people's liberty of expression and movement (in particular, travel abroad) would become more and more restricted. After a few years of cultural 'discipline', the regime could even allow itself the luxury of abolishing censorship (in the form of the 'Press Directorate', the institution which had been responsible for this activity). Again, the message to the West was confusing. In fact, censorship actually became harsher after it had officially been abolished; editors and anyone else responsible for publications had to take their role as 'unofficial' censors very seriously. Relations with foreigners, which had never been viewed favourably, began to be supervised with greater vigilance. Romania was slowly becoming a closed society at just the time when its foreign policy was becoming more open.

Professionalism was no longer the order of the day in culture. Everyone was called on to produce culture, or at least to sing and dance. This was the aim of the *Cîntarea României* ('Song of Romania') festival, which was held for the first time in 1977. Hundreds of thousands of amateurs were taken from factories, from the fields or from schools, and urged, or if necessary forced, to improvise all sorts of performances. This was a way of pushing intellectualism to the background ('Look, anyone can do it!') and of submerging the increasingly serious problems of Romanian society beneath a wave of artificial optimism.

National symbols were everywhere; in fact, nationalism ended up being manifested as virulently as anti-nationalism had been in the 1950s. The key ideas of historical discourse were now *unity* and *continuity*. A fragmented history – such as Romania's in fact was – was now presented as the perfect model of unitary history. As ancient Dacia fully corresponded to modern Romania, 1980 saw the celebration of 2,050 years (according to an utterly approximate calculation) since the founding of Burebista's 'centralized and independent Dacian state'. Speeches, symposia, scholarly meetings and press articles followed one after the other, culminating in a 'grand spectacle', in Ceauşescu's presence, in the largest stadium in Bucharest. Through such historical recreations, the leader of Communist Romania met, 'in effect', the heroes of national history. Gone were the days when the pantheon had been made up almost exclusively of revolutionaries and Communist fighters for a new world. Now, these withdrew discreetly to clear the front-of-stage for Dacian kings and medieval *voivodes*. Ceauşescu was reflected in them all, and was a synthesis of them all. Burebista effectively entered Romanian consciousness in 1980; previously, only specialists had known anything about him, and even they had known little. Michael the Brave, the 'unifier', was Ceauşescu's favourite hero. He had united the Romanians and fallen victim to foreigners: a twofold lesson to be remembered.

As nationalism became accentuated, not only did the Romanians' merits grow, so did the 'sins' of others. 'Others' bore the guilt for all Romanian failures or latecomings; Romanians had not been allowed to make full use of their own qualities. Under Stalin, almost all of the world's science and technology had been presented as the work of Russians. The Romanians now experienced a similar fever, known as 'protochronism', a theory aimed at bringing Romanian priority to light in the most diverse fields. This frenetic nationalism, which did not even speak its name (the word *nationalism* was repudiated, since Communism was defined as 'internationalist' – yet another illustration of doublethink and double discourse), was Ceauşescu's trump card for a long time. Nationalist discourse is the simplest and cheapest way of keeping people united and making them forget the 'prosaic' misfortunes of life. Almost everywhere, Communist regimes slid from internationalism towards nationalism, but few went as far as in Romania. Even intellectuals of the old school allowed themselves to be attracted, seeing in nationalism a revenge for the pro-Soviet anti-nationalism of the 1950s. The extremes seemed more practicable than the middle way. The question was how long nationalism could take the place of bread.

THE DISASTER

Bread was beginning to be in short supply. From around 1980, nothing seemed to work anymore, and the situation worsened from one year to the next. The outsize Romanian industries did not give the expected yields; they had cost more than they were producing. Obsessed with production (it was a production society, not a consumer society), Communism went on producing even at a loss. The credits which had been swallowed up brought nothing but debts. In an excess of pride, Ceauşescu (leader of an independent country which could manage on its own) decided to pay off Romania's foreign debt down to the last dollar. Now, the ordeal really began. Exports were forced up. As industry alone could not

A queue in front of a food shop in the centre of Bucharest in the 1980s; perhaps there had been a delivery of meet, eggs or cheese. The photographer's courage is worth noting; it was not prudent to take such pictures!

cope, the traditional export of agricultural produce was resorted to, in a country barely able to satisfy its own food needs. The people were left without food. The Romanians may not actually have died of hunger, but increasing numbers suffered the effects of malnutrition, and the hunt for food became their principal preoccupation. The food shops were empty. When a delivery came, regardless of what it was (there was no choice anyway!), huge queues formed. Often, there were queues in front of empty shops, in expectation. People sat down in the street in the evening and spent the whole night there, or waited by shifts, in the hope (since there was no certainty) that the next day they might be able to buy a piece of meat or cheese. An interesting queue culture developed in Romania. The queue was a space of sociability (something which otherwise tended not to exist in Romanian culture), where people – many of them pensioners, who had more time – met day by day and spent long hours together. Goods, especially foodstuffs, also circulated underground, evading the 'state'. As in the Middle Ages, barter was practised: produce for produce, or produce for services. You had to pay somehow even for things that were supposed to be free. Medical care, for example, was free, but everyone knew that they had to bring something for the doctor – money, produce or the inevitable 'Kent' cigarettes, which became the country's hard currency. Doctors would take them, and might in turn pass them on to someone else: they had to pay other people too!

It was cold in the homes of Romanians, those famous blocks of flats of which the regime was so proud. For six months of the year, from autumn to spring – winters are severe in Romania – people kept their overcoats on in their flats and slept fully dressed. To complete the spectacle, lighting was interrupted as well. In Bucharest, each district had its hour in the evening when the electricity was cut and candles were lit. Bucharest was privileged; other towns had more hours of darkness, and villages had more darkness than light – not to mention the hundreds of villages which did not yet have electricity, despite the Communist project of 'electrification of the whole country'.

When the electricity was on, you could watch television. Programming (on the one and only channel) was initially reduced to three hours, then to two. It began with a news broadcast, largely devoted to the visits and other pastimes of the Ceauşescus or to the achievements of industry and agriculture. This might be followed by a patriotic show or even a film (but not a whole film, since there was not enough time: the second part would have to wait for the next day). Then it would be time for the 'night news', which repeated the items that had been announced two hours previously. Romanians near the edges of the country considered themselves lucky, especially those who could pick up Yugoslav or Hungarian stations. In Iaşi, they had to be content with broadcasts from Chişinău, in the Soviet Republic of Moldova, and in Bucharest with Bulgarian television. Many Romanians, however, listened – sometimes obsessively, for hours on end – to foreign radio stations broadcasting in Romanian: Voice of America, BBC, but above all Radio Free Europe, which transmitted the greatest number of hours and provided a wealth of detail which was concealed by the information and propaganda apparatus of the regime.

Nowhere were the Romanians left in peace. The working programme was extended beyond legal limits, to include not only Saturday (which was a working day) but also, sometimes, Sunday. On top of that, there was so-called 'patriotic work'. For a worker who had laboured all week in a factory, the 'relaxation' on offer was a few extra hours of 'patriotic work'. In the villages, and in towns too, pupils and teachers began school not in September but at best in October and often in November; until then, they were at work in the fields. There was a shortage of peasants! The army became an army of slaves: private soldiers and officers alike worked on the great construction projects or in agriculture. The free time that remained was filled up with all sorts of meetings and assemblies for ideological indoctrination. Even the most minor freedoms were restricted. The banal typewriter had become suspect (in the computer age!); once a year, those who possessed one had to take it to the police station to give a sample of type – a precaution against the spread of clandestine texts and manifestos.

In the 1950s, access to higher education had been limited or even forbidden to 'unhealthy' social elements (those with a 'bad file', with parents who were bourgeois, *chiaburi*, political prisoners or simply intellectuals). Then discrimination had been given up for a while. In the mid-1970s, however, the practice was resumed in many faculties with an ideological or political profile: law, history, philosophy, economics etc. Entry to these institutions was no longer open to anyone at all. All of the teachers had to be Party members, and the students had at the very least to be members of Communist Youth. Young people with relatives abroad, with political prisoners in the family, or with the misfortune of being the children of priests were no longer admitted.

The Party had swollen its ranks. It now numbered almost 4 million members (a huge number in a country the size of Romania), which meant that the status of Party member no longer had much value. Romania had no way of supporting a privileged class of 4 million! However, it was a further way of enrolling and controlling people. A Party member had to be more circumspect than an ordinary Romanian; mistakes could cost him or her more dearly.

In the minds of many, an idea took root which was to become an obsession: to flee the country. However, it was becoming harder and harder to get out. In contrast to the Czechs, the Poles and the East Germans, the Romanians found it hard to travel not only in the West, but even in 'fraternal' Communist countries. Some, however, managed to obtain the much-desired visa, and often they did not come back. Members of their families who remained behind were subjected to all sorts of harassment. After years of insistence (sometimes aided by Western intervention, or payment, which was the most certain method), the person who had left would be able to take their wife or husband and children too. Some crossed the border clandestinely, into Yugoslavia or Hungary. Some died there, shot by border guards. For someone who wanted to leave, the ideal situation was to have relatives abroad who could insistently call for them, or buy them. The Ceauşescu regime made a speciality out of trading in people, which became a precious source of hard currency. Romanian emigrants spread throughout the world, from Western Europe to America and Australia. All the more easy to understand is the massive emigration of minorities to join their co-nationals in the free world. The Romanian Jewish community, one of the largest in the world, disappeared. At the end of the Second World War, in 1945, there were still 355,000 Jews living in Romania. In 1956, 146,000 were left; in 1966, 43,000; in 1977, 25,000; and in 1992, less than 9,000. The Germans left especially in the 1970s and '80s, bought by their co-nationals in the West. In 1956, there were 384,000 Germans in Romania; in 1977, there were still 359,000; but by 1992, there were only 119,000. I was in Sighişoara, an old German burg in the heart of Transylvania, towards the end of the 1980s. In the cemetery, there are only German names, but I did not hear a single word of German in the street. The houses abandoned by Germans had been taken over by families of Gypsies.

REVOLT

Did the Romanians oppose Communism? And if they did, how and to what extent? Nowadays, the opposition is highlighted. Every society that has lived under an oppressive regime amplifies the image of its own resistance. (Something similar happened in the West with the resistance to Nazism.) In fact, those who give in, accommodate themselves or even profit are everywhere more numerous than those who resist. And those who resist 'passively' are more numerous than those who actually stand up in opposition. In Romania, there was an effective resistance in the first years of Communism, but even then the opponents of the regime did not manage to carry their compatriots along with them. Society as a whole gave in or accepted the new rules. Armed bands took refuge in the mountains, where some of them survived until the end of the 1950s. Their story makes a heroic epic, but it is the story of a small number of people, who had no chance of success. (They died in clashes with the *Securitate*, or were captured, condemned to death and executed.) Many peasants were opposed to collectivization; peasant rebellions even broke out, but they were localized and quickly put down. A large proportion of intellectuals could not reconcile themselves to Communism either. But few tried to take effective action. People waited, longing for a change, but how many would be ready to sacrifice themselves for it? A thrill was felt in Romania, too, especially in the western part of the country, when the Hungarian revolution erupted in 1956. However, there was nothing more. The actions of individuals or small groups can be added up, but overall Romania was quieter than Hungary, Poland or Czechoslovakia. Society had not evolved to the point where there could be an efficient response to abuses of power, so any anti-Communist action remained isolated and without consequences.

The Gheorghiu-Dej period was the time of repression (until the relaxation marking his last years). Under Ceauşescu, few people went to prison for political reasons. Ceauşescu himself criticized the excesses of his predecessor's time, presenting himself as the exponent of a 'Communism of humanity' in which there was no repression and people no longer had reason to be afraid. The truth is that either people had become resigned, or they no longer dared to move. There was now hardly any repression because there was no longer anything to repress. The *Securitate* – a reality, but also an obsession, a myth – was watching. Perhaps its archives will reveal the extent to which it really was omnipresent and omniscient, and how far it simply managed to create the impression that it was. In any event, people were afraid to speak. They might be heard by an informer or recorded by hidden microphones, real or imagined. In many situations, parents avoided telling children what they thought. The only manifestation of freedom consisted in an impressive collection of political jokes. They constituted a psychological valve, a sort of folklore which was ulti-mately tolerated. In the 1950s, a political joke could have led to years in prison; now they probably seemed to be the means of releasing tension that was least dangerous to the regime.

There is much talk nowadays of 'resistance through culture'. In fact, the role of intellectuals, in particular of writers, was equivocal. In the 1950s, things were clear: for the Party or against it. Some writers kept silent, while others, including some of the leading names, aligned themselves, from the beginning or along the way, with 'socialist-realist' literature. Under Ceauşescu, however, propa-ganda literature was left to second-rate writers. Moreover, writers broke away from the 'socialist-realist' model, trying to take their freedom to the ultimate permitted limit, but no further. Their criticisms were aimed at abuses, not at the system itself. And as a rule they focussed on abuses from the time of Gheorghiu-Dej rather than under Ceauşescu. No literary work in those years rivalled the fame of Marin Preda's 1980 novel *The Most Loved of All Mortals*. It was a political novel, but the injustices it hit out at were those of the 1950s (and even then not the worst of these, and certainly not Communism as a system). Preda was most critical of the things that Ceauşescu had criticized too. Many readers were impressed at the time. Today, it is hard to read the book without a certain feeling of embarrassment; it does not say the things that should have been said.

Other writers took refuge in pure aestheticism. This would have been a mortal sin in the 1950s, but now the regime permitted it: better this than expressing unpleasant things in a way that everyone could understand. The Romanians became expert in the technique of 'reading between the lines'. They looked for the 'key', the words left unspoken but suggested. Sometimes, the allusions became transparent. The poet Ana Blandiana managed to publish a book of verses for children in which the hero, a conceited tom-cat, was clearly recognizable as Ceauşescu. After getting past the censors, or being allowed past, the book was rapidly withdrawn from the bookshops. The Romanians became great readers of poetry among other things, not for the sake of the poetry itself (hardly anyone reads poetry nowadays!), but for the pleasure of deciphering the presumed coded messages. They were looking for a confirmation of their own anxieties and hopes.

The writers had made a sort of wager with the authorities: who could trick whom? The authorities allowed them to go quite far, but *no further*. And they were content with this equivocal situation – which also offered them certain advantages, including material ones, and assured them of a central position in society: in Communism, the writer was significant, precisely by virtue of his or her function as mediator between the authorities and society. The result of this compromise was that in Romania there was no *samizdat* phenomenon, no clandestine publishing (as there was in the Soviet Union and the other Communist countries). All writers published their books through the publishing houses of the Communist state; anti-Communist literature was limited to émigré writers. In 1977, when the novelist Paul Goma took a stand against Ceauşescu, he found himself alone; he was arrested and subsequently expelled. All in all, the period produced some interesting literature, but the Romanians have no Solzhenitsyn or Havel.

A dissidence took shape in the 1980s, as the crisis of Communism intensified. However, the dissidents were few in number, treated with contempt by the authorities and isolated from the mass of the population. This was a far cry from the model of Solidarity or Charter '77. In the end, it was not the dissidents who stirred people up to fight, but Ceauşescu himself and their exasperation with him. It was not a matter of the regime against an 'opposition', but, more brutally, of the regime against Romania.

The Communist regime in Romania ended in a bloodbath, and it is hard to imagine how it could have been otherwise, given the accumulated tensions and frustrations, and the impossibility of dialogue. In the other East European countries, the foundations of a transition had been laid in the 1980s. Gorbachev did not, of course, want to bury Communism. He thought, naïvely, that he was reinvigorating it by infusing it with a dose of liberty. But how can a dictatorship be consolidated by liberty? Ceauşescu was more logical, after his own fashion. In the Soviet Union, and even more so in Hungary and Poland, the premises of post-Communism were created while Romania was heading in the opposite direction, back to a pure, hard Communism. Ceauşescu, the champion of non-intervention in 1968, was now the one who called for intervention in Poland. Communism of any kind was doomed; the problem was how to get out of the system, and Romania made the worst exit of all. While neighbouring countries were seeing the sketching out of a civil society, which was to play a fundamental role, and the outlining of a market economy, in Romania ideological and political control of society and the economy was hardening. The reason the revolution was bloody was that there was no-one to negotiate with. For the same reason, its results were disappointing: in Romania, practically nothing existed apart from the Communist structures.

The revolt broke out in Timişoara on 16 December 1989. The army opened fire, killing some tens of people. In order to restore calm, on 21 December Ceauşescu attempted a repeat of the balcony scene which had been so successful in August 1968. This was a serious error of judgement: it only needed someone to gather the people of Bucharest together, and that person turned out to be himself! The place was the same as in 1968, and a similar immense mass of people

147

assembled. Two decades had passed, however. The crowd was promised a meagre pay increase; the dictator was trying to buy off a revolution! It responded with catcalls. Nothing like this had ever been heard in Communist Romania. 'Do you want to be unemployed?' Ceauşescu shouted. It was his final argument. That night, blood was shed in Bucharest too. The next day, surrounded by a million people, the dictatorial couple had no choice but to flee. A helicopter lifted them from the terrace of the Central Committee building. They were caught, held in a barracks in Tîrgovişte, judged by an improvised tribunal, condemned to death and shot on Christmas Day. The trial was grotesque, defying legality and decency, with the defence lawyers accusing their clients as vehemently as the prosecutors. Perhaps no other end would have been fitting. For years, the couple had mocked millions of people. The parody of their trial concluded the 25-year parody that was the 'Ceauşescu era'.

The Romanians do not yet agree (and probably never will) on the events of December. Was it a revolt, a revolution, a *coup d'état*? It was all of these at the same time. There was the spontaneous revolt, without any well-defined programme, of thousands of people, many of whom had no philosophical objection to Communism but simply could no longer endure a life which had become an endless series of deprivations and humiliations. But there was also a *coup d'état*, since this unorganized mass alone could never have produced a new regime and a new leader. Power was seized by a group of Communists who had been marginalized by Ceauşescu for various reasons (some of them were actually former members of Gheorghiu-Dej's circle or had been considered too pro-Soviet). The leader, Ion Iliescu, had followed a completely orthodox career – studies in Moscow, membershp in the Central Committee, appointment as First Secretary of the Communist youth organization, then as minister — before being relegated to the second rank by Ceauşescu. Iliescu's horizons did not then extend beyond a reform of the Gorbachev type. His accusation against Ceauşescu was that the latter had defiled the 'noble ideals of Communism'! A revolt, a *coup d'état*? And yet it was indeed a revolution. Regardless of the motivations of the protagonists, history had been set loose on 22 December 1989, and nothing could keep it in check. Slowly and hesitantly, held back by its new leaders more than it was stimulated, Romania set out in the direction of democracy and a market economy – towards the West.

148

The Romania that emerged from Communism hardly resembled pre-Communist Romania at all.[8] Communism had buried patriarchal Romania for ever. The effective and symbolic reference points had shifted from the village to the town. In 1930, 21.4 per cent of the inhabitants of present-day Romania lived in towns. In 1948, the percentage had risen to 23.4: despite the economic progress of the 1930s, the situation had not changed very much. In 1956, however, a jump to 31.3 per cent was recorded. By 1966, the figure was 38.2 per cent; in 1977, 43.6 per cent; and in 1992, 54.4 per cent. Part of this increase can be accounted for by urbanization 'on paper', whereby modest localities were declared to be 'towns' for the sake of statistics. But many people whose homes were in the country, especially young people, were also 'commuting' to work in the towns. Many villages were depopulated, with only the elderly remaining. Communism had won its bet: it had urbanized Romania. It may have meant unviable industries, precarious conditions of urban life and the sacrifice of agriculture, but Romania had been urbanized.

A process of social levelling also took place. Working in the service of the state, educated in a uniform manner, earning similar salaries, gathered in districts of almost identical blocks of flats and enjoying access to the same reduced range of products and services, people ended up living in much the same way. The regions of Romania also lost much of their former identities. Before Communism, as we have seen, they had displayed a remarkable ethnic, religious and cultural variety. Even today, they are not identical, but their distinguishing features have been considerably attenuated. Communism levelled and homogenized everywhere (without ever succeeding completely: only Utopia is absolutely homogeneous). Romania is more Romanian nowadays than it was in the past. This Romanianization was in line with the logic of the national state anyway, but Communism accentuated it. Industrialization and urbanization caused the predominantly Romanian population of the villages to move into the towns; there were also movements from one region to another, particularly from less-developed Moldavia towards Transylvania and the Banat. On top of this, emigration emptied Romania of certain ethnic communities, above all of Jews and Germans. The weight of the minorities was reduced, people were mixed, and Romania became more ethnically and culturally homogeneous.

In 1930, Romanians accounted for 77.9 per cent of the population of the present-day territory of Romania. By 1992, the percentage had risen to 89.5. In Transylvania (counting also the Banat, Crişana and Maramureş), the proportion of Romanians rose in the same period from 57.8 to 73.6 per cent, while that of Hungarians fell from 24.4 to 21 per cent. Dobrogea, formerly the multi-ethnic region *par excellence*, is nowadays over 90 per cent Romanian (after the departure of the Greeks and part of the Turkish population, and an exchange of population with Bulgaria already in 1940). Almost all of the towns, which were once so cosmopolitan, now have a substantial Romanian majority (the exceptions being in Harghita and Covasna, the two predominantly Hungarian counties of eastern Transylvania). In 1930, the population of Cluj, the capital of Transylvania, was 47.5 per cent Hungarian, 35 per cent Romanian and 13 per cent Jewish. By 1992, the Romanians had risen to 76 per cent and the Hungarians had fallen to 23 per cent. In Timişoara, the capital of the Banat, the population in 1930 was 30 per cent German, 30 per cent Hungarian and 26.5 per cent Romanian. In 1992, it was 82 per cent Romanian, 9.5 per cent Hungarian and 4 per cent German. The confessional structure of Transylvania also underwent modification. Between the two world wars, only a third of the population of the province were Orthodox, as a large proportion of the Romanians were Greek Catholics. Nowadays, as a result of ethnic and religious changes, three-quarters of the Transylvanians are Orthodox. (The Greek Catholic Church was re-established after 1989, but it no longer has the strength that it had before Communism: slightly over 200,000 Greek Catholics were recorded in 1992, compared with almost a million and a half in 1930.) Romania today is more tightly bound together, more unitary, than before Communism. A collection of provinces, each with its own particular synthesis, has blended into one synthesis. Is this a gain or a loss? It depends on what we prefer: a uniform colour, with variations of tone here and there, or a variety of different colours.

Was Communism a solution to the problem of modernization? That was its aim, but the results proved to be perverse and contrary to the spirit of the time. The number of industrial workers rose immensely, but this is no longer the mark of modernity that it once was. The number of university graduates was far higher than in pre-Communist Romania; however, they were prepared for a closed society and for projects which in many cases no longer had any value (the abuse of engineering and ideology). Since the fall of

Communism, the best of them have adapted to an open society and the new challenges it brings; however, that is to their own credit, not that of the system in which they were trained.

Communism turned Romanian society almost completely upside-down. Almost all Romanians either rose or fell. Few families have kept a tradition. The townspeople of today were peasants not so long ago. The intellectuals come from families of peasants and workers. It is a society of 'new people', whom Communism made what they are today. The present élite is overwhelmingly a recent creation. Despite their discontent at the abuses of Communism, the majority of Romanians have found it hard to break with the only system that gave them a point of reference.

The most serious inheritance is the complete upsetting of structures and mentalities: an economy almost completely state-controlled or 'collectivized', with reduced yield and a profile that does not match market needs; the invasion of political authority into all areas of life; a society accustomed to the authorities giving and taking as and when they see fit. The 'second entry into Europe' looks set to be harder for the Romanians than the first one was in the nineteenth century. It might have been easier starting from zero. Instead, they have to build on a ground where much has already been built, but built wrongly.

Communism preached and practised collectivism but left people lonely. Just as the property of everyone is the property of no-one, so a general solidarity is no solidarity at all. In gathering all the members of society into an undifferentiated mass, Communism only ended up separating them. The system continually attacked any intermediary form of sociability. People lost the habit of coming together. Between the authorities and the people, nothing was to exist. Everyone played the collectivist game and looked after their own personal interests. Collectivism gave rise to individualism, and, more generally, to a lack of concern for anything involving common interests. The Romanians learned how to adapt and to get by as well as they could, all on their own. As a result of long experience, they had not had much trust in history anyway. They now had even less. Principles and rules work in stable societies, where evolutions are predictable. Otherwise, all that counts is survival. When the Communist regime fell, Romania found itself faced with a huge void: the fabric of society was vague, and the social organism non-functional.

No other country entered post-Communism as spectacularly as Romania, but no other country entered it so badly prepared either.

v Between the Past and the Future

On 22 December 1989, the Romanians experienced a moment of euphoria. They had won their freedom, and it seemed that freedom would solve everything.[1] The next day, however, they awoke to the sounds of civil war. More people died in the days that followed Ceaușescu's fall than had lost their lives as a result of the repression he had ordered. Who had the guns, now that the Ceaușescu regime had fallen, and the army and even the *Securitate* had gone over to the side of the new authorities? And what was their aim? There was talk of 'terrorists', but who were they? They were present everywhere, but they were invisible: no-one ever saw them face to face, alive or dead. The post-Communist history of Romania began with a mystery. Suspicion has been voiced that the terrorists never existed, that everything was staged in order to scare people and legitimize the newly installed regime: this is certainly one possible interpretation, though it is hard to say how true it might be. It is a disturbing fact that, despite being 'assaulted' by 'terrorists', the former Central Committee and Television buildings, the revolutionary authorities' two command posts, were not even scratched, while buildings around them were riddled with bullets and set on fire. In Romania and all over the world, people followed events on their television screens with their hearts in their mouths. This was a world premiere: the first revolution transmitted live! At the time, it seemed so authentic. We know now that it was a manipulation.

In any revolution, the problem of power is essential: who loses and who gains it. It is clear in this case who lost power – Ceaușescu and those close to him – and who gained it – the Iliescu faction. But in a broader sense, if we consider the ruling élite as a whole, it can hardly be said that a real transfer of power took place in December 1989. The nomenklatura, and the privileged beneficiaries of Communism in general, did all they could to preserve their privileges, and they may

During the Revolution (the last days of December 1989): tanks on Calea Victoriei, and the University Library gutted by fire. In the centre left can be seen a wing of the Central Committee building.

The cemetery of the heroes of the Revolution: the young people who gave their lives so that Romania could escape from Communism.

be considered to have won the contest. The fall of the pre-Communist system had also meant the fall of its élite; the fall of Communism did not affect the élite it had created (an observation that is valid not just for Romania but for all of the former Communist countries).

Already from the first moments of the revolution, the Romanians gained a number of freedoms whose taste they had forgotten. Among these were the right to travel abroad without restriction and the liberalization of abortion: the two great obsessions of the Ceauşescu period. Fundamental democratic freedoms were proclaimed: of speech, of the press, of assembly, of association and so on. But the new leaders did not seem ready to apply democracy all the way, at least not as far as the holding and exercise of power were concerned. The National Salvation Front (FSN) which now headed the country was conceived at first as an umbrella organization, leaving very little outside it. The concept of 'original democracy' was launched – an expression that would soon raise ironic smiles. Having invented so much in the Ceauşescu period, the Romanians – or some of them at least – now claimed the luxury of launching a new political concept. 'Original democracy' was intended to mean a sort of national solidarity under the aegis of the Front. At the same time, the dissolving of the Communist Party was a stroke of genius (something no-one thought of in the other former Communist countries). All at once, Communism ceased to exist, and so no-one was Communist any more: there was no longer any way that they could be. A former official of the Ceauşescu regime became every bit as non-Communist as a former political prisoner. The past no longer counted; a new history was beginning.

In these conditions, the 'others' had little chance of success. In any case, they were too few in number and too scattered. A few survivors of the Communist prisons, men already over 70, with Corneliu Coposu at their head, re-established the National Peasant Party (PNŢ) and added to its name the words 'Christian and Democratic' (PNŢCD) (already before 1989, Coposu had secretly affiliated to the European Christian Democratic family). The National Liberal Party (PNL) likewise re-emerged. Perhaps a better solution than the somewhat artificial resurrection of these historical parties would have been the formation of truly new parties, as happened in Poland, Hungary and Czechoslovakia. However, in those countries the foundations of the new political movements had been laid before 1989, in a way that had been impossible in Ceauşescu's Romania; here, the opposition was starting from nothing. Thus dozens of parties were founded, taking advantage of very permissive laws. This, too, was a tactic of the authorities: on the one side, there was the National Salvation Front, which had given itself half the seats in the temporary parliament, the Provisional Council of National Unity (CPUN); on the other, there was a scattering of parties, all of them treated as equals, and not a few of them mere annexes of the Front, among which the Peasantists and Liberals could play no more than a secondary role.

Property goes hand in hand with *power*. Normally, whoever holds one holds the other too. It is not surprising that those who came to power in December 1989 were not in a hurry to change the property situation. The issue of restoring nationalized enterprises to their original owners was not even raised. Nor was that of the houses which had been confiscated by the Communist regime. (The rights of tenants were upheld against those of former owners or their heirs. Indeed, this was perfectly logical: the new aristocracy lived in the finest of the houses which had previously belonged to others. But since tenants are generally more numerous than owners, this attitude corresponded to the interests of quite a large category of people.) The peasants were given back part of the land they had lost, but only up to a limit of ten hectares. In industry, a new law permitted the founding of private enterprises with up to twenty employees. All in all, the philosophy was more 'perestroikist' than capitalist and democratic. It was evident that the economic élite associated with the large-scale industry and agriculture of the Communist state was going to keep its control of the country's wealth.

Nor was foreign capital received with the enthusiasm that might have been expected, although this would certainly have been in the country's interests. 'We won't sell our country' was the slogan shouted by thousands of workers who supported Iliescu in his project of slow and limited reform in the first months of 1990. Romania took up a position in complete contrast to the shock therapy practised in Poland. Even Romanians who returned from exile were regarded with suspicion. 'You didn't eat soya salami like us,' they were told (referring to the food shortages of the 1980s, which they had been lucky enough to escape). The press rapidly won complete freedom. But television – the single national television channel – was to remain a monopoly of the authorities for some years. 'With television you lied to the people,' chanted the opposition. And in fact, television contributed on a large scale to the

155

discrediting of the opposition and of alternative projects, especially in rural areas and among people of limited education. However, what people were being told was what many of them wanted to hear. They were afraid of the uncertainty of an open society, and, educated as they had been in a paternalist, autochthonist spirit, they regarded the Western model with suspicion.

The struggle for power took on a dramatic aspect. Faced with an opposition that was a minority anyway, the government did not hesitate to resort to brutal methods, appropriate more to the Bolshevik arsenal of class struggle than to that of democracy, whether 'original' or not. It was a curious choice: the forces of law and order would have been sufficient to disperse a few unauthorized demonstrations. However, the new leaders felt the need to legitimize themselves at the same time as they disqualified the 'others', and this could only be done through the 'people'. According to the Communist conception (which still applied), the 'people' meant the 'working class'. Thus Bucharest became a field of conflict between anti-government demonstrators and working-class shock troops summoned from the factories. Miners from the coal-fields of the Jiu valley (400 km from Bucharest) also put in an appearance, providing a foretaste of the disgraceful and bloody episodes that were soon to follow. Surrounded by a threatening crowd, Corneliu Coposu was evacuated from the offices of his party under the supervision of the Prime Minister himself, Petre Roman. 'They have been unmasked,' announced Roman in a short address to the besiegers. The 'unmasking' of class enemies was exactly the formula used in the 1950s! Another episode of the same sort, but this time with an ethnic colouring, took place in March, in Tîrgu Mureş, a Transylvanian city with a half-Romanian, half-Hungarian population. Romanian peasants from the surrounding villages clashed with Hungarian demonstrators: people were killed and injured. The incident might easily have sparked a large-scale Romanian-Hungarian conflict: fortunately, it did not.

In April 1990, protesters occupied University Square in Bucharest. For almost two months, the square was the scene of a marathon demonstration; speeches were made and songs sung against the Iliescu regime. All sorts of people were there, though prominent among them were intellectuals and students. The television was careful to broadcast the least favourable images (groups of Gypsies, for example), giving the impression that this was a gathering of the dregs of Romanian society: *golani* (louts) was what Iliescu called

Terror on the streets of Bucharest: the miners hand in hand with the police in June 1990.

them. The label was adopted with pride by the protesters themselves. University Square became 'Golania', 'land of the *golani*'. A *golan* hymn was composed, and it resounded endlessly. The chorus contained the lines 'Better a *golan* than an activist' (an allusion to the Communist, activist past of Iliescu and his comrades) and 'better dead than a Communist'.

On 13 June, the square was evacuated by the forces of order. Disturbances followed in Bucharest, including an invasion of the Television building. (It is hard to say how far these were actually the work of the demonstrators, and how far they were provocations by the authorities.) Once again, Iliescu called on the 'people', and so on 14 June, thousands of miners from the Jiu valley arrived in Bucharest, dressed in black overalls and armed with clubs. Among them, giving directions and encouragement, there were also 'false miners'. For two days, terror reigned in Bucharest. The headquarters of the opposition parties, the University and the Institute of Architecture were ransacked. Intellectuals in particular were singled out, or those who looked to the miners like intellectuals or people of dubious habits: men with glasses, women with short skirts and so on. They were ferociously beaten with clubs, to the cheers of a fanaticized population, and bundled into vans by the police, who on this occasion became the miners' auxiliaries. Outside Bucharest, an improvised concentration camp became the site of appalling scenes of torture and humiliation. Finally, Iliescu officially thanked the miners and sent them home. Now that they knew the way to Bucharest, they promised to come again. They were to keep their word.

Of course, the opposition had not kept strictly within the law either (in fact, legal channels had been blocked by the authorities), and it had deluded itself as to its own strength in a society which the elections had shown to be substantially behind Iliescu. However, the government, and above all Iliescu himself, were morally disqualified by their recourse to strategies that could have brought on civil war. The West watched the events with astonishment. At first, the Romanian revolution had aroused a wave of international sympathy. So the disappointment was all the greater when false notes began to multiply. The miners' invasion in June put a seal on everything. By the will of its leaders – more preoccupied with their own future than that of the country – Romania had isolated itself.

Naturally, the rulers could say that most Romanians were behind them. And so they were. However, it would have been better, and more moral, in a country which had been deprived for so long of any experience of democracy, if the democratic tone had been set by the authorities themselves. But this may have been too much to ask; given the chance, any government tends to consolidate and perpetuate its power. In May 1990, both parliamentary and presidential elections were held; there were some irregularities, but not enough for the effective result of the ballot to be called into question. Iliescu won the popular mandate, with 85 per cent of the vote, far ahead of the Liberal Radu Câmpeanu, with 10 per cent, and the Peasantist Ion Rațiu, with only 4. In the parliamentary elections, the National Salvation Front obtained two-thirds of the vote, compared with between 6 and 7 per cent for the Liberals and 2.5 per cent for the Peasantists. For the Iliescu regime, this was a triumph. But not – as can now be seen clearly – for Romania. The country became bogged down on a path of slow and partial reform; in addition, it was regarded with suspicion by the West and avoided by Western capital. (Poland, Hungary and the Czech Republic meanwhile proceeded with radical reforms and attracted almost all of the Western investment in the region.)

The Iliescu regime continued until 1996. These were years in which Romania moved forward slowly, though, by force of circumstance, things did change. Disputes tended to shift from the streets into the political arena, although the potential for violence remained, symbolized above all by the Jiu valley, where the trade-union leader Miron Cozma, a man with an apparently hypnotic hold on the miners and an utter disregard for the law, created a sort of state within the state. Cracks began to appear in the 'almost single' party of the National Salvation Front. A young wing, more modern and dynamic, began to take shape around Petre Roman, who was two decades younger than Iliescu. Two men, partly bound together by a common history, but yet very different, now confronted each other: Iliescu, a Communist leader of proletarian origins, who had studied in Moscow, and Roman, whose father had been a high-ranking member of the 'old guard', the representative of a new generation, more open to the 'bourgeois' values of the West (significantly, he had studied not in Moscow but in France, at Toulouse). The gap widened between Iliescu's conservative grouping and Roman's reformists. It was time for the miners to intervene again! In September 1991, they occupied Bucharest once more, this time calling for Roman's head. And they were not disappointed. A new government was formed, headed by an 'independent' financial specialist, Theodor Stolojan, and including a number of Liberals (in a largely decorative role). Its principal mission was to prepare for the elections of 1992 while managing the country as convincingly as possible in a state of Iliescu-style relative immobility.

The National Salvation Front broke up. Its name was kept at first by the Roman faction, which later became the Democratic Party (PD). The Iliescu faction initially called itself the Democratic National Salvation Front (FDSN), and later became the Romanian Party of Social Democracy (PDSR). The opposition was united in the Democratic Convention, which consisted of a number of parties grouped around the Peasantists and Liberals, together with citizens' organizations (the Civic Alliance). The elections of 1992 took place on the basis of a new constitution, which had been ratified by a referendum at the end of the previous year. Inspired to a certain extent by the French constitutional model, it conferred far from negligible powers on a President elected by popular ballot. (These powers were, and still are, somewhat less extensive than in France, however: the problem was clearly how to give Iliescu as much power as possible while at the same time not pushing things too far in a Romania which had not yet forgotten the Ceauşescu tyranny.) Along with the President, the Romanians also elect a bicameral parliament, comprising a Chamber of Deputies and a Senate (which, curiously, have almost identical roles).

While Iliescu and Roman represented two of the principal types of the post-1989 Romanian political class, the Democratic Convention offered two others. The first was symbolized by the Peasantist leader, Coposu, who had spent almost all of his youth (seventeen years!) in Communist prisons; unflinching in his anti-Communism, he was the principal artisan of the Convention and its guiding inspiration. Emil Constantinescu, Professor in the Faculty of Geology and Rector of the University of Bucharest from 1992 to 1996, emerged as the second symbolic figure. Before 1989, he had, like millions of Romanians, been a member of the Communist Party, in which he occupied minor positions at faculty level; he had been one of those 'passive' Party members who neither resisted nor served the regime with any enthusiasm. In 1990, as Pro-rector, he had declared his solidarity with the University Square demonstrators.

Without threatening the Iliescu regime, the elections of 1992 produced interesting results quite different from those of 1990. In the first round, Iliescu was unable to gain an outright majority, obtaining 47 per cent of the votes compared with 85 per cent two years previously. The Democratic Convention candidate, Constantinescu, obtained 31 per cent, not enough, but still a remarkable result for an opposition which had started out from almost nothing. Naturally enough, Iliescu won the second round, with slightly more than 60 per cent against slightly less than 40 per cent for Constantinescu. The parliamentary landscape was also modified, the rough percentages obtained being as follows: Iliescu's FDSN (the future PDSR) – 27 per cent; the Democratic Convention – 20 per cent; Roman's FSN (the future PD) – 10 per cent; and the Democratic Union of Hungarians in Romania (UDMR) – 7 per cent. Three ultra-nationalist parties also won parliamentary seats: the Party of Romanian National Unity (PUNR, a sort of Romanian answer to the UDMR, with its main strength in Transylvania) – 8 per cent; the Greater Romania Party (PRM) – 4 per cent; and the Socialist Party of Labour (PSM) – 3 per cent.

In the course of two years, Romanian society had matured. The logic of the 'great party' and the uncontested leader had been left behind. In Transylvania, which is somewhat closer to the West in feeling as well as geographically, the election was won by Constantinescu. However, Iliescu won in Muntenia and on a massive scale in Moldavia, the poorest province and the one least integrated into modernity. The map of the presidential election results divided quite clearly along the pre-1918 border between Romania and Austria-Hungary: Constantinescu to the west, Iliescu to the east! In Bucharest, the scores were almost equal, with a slight advantage to Iliescu. However, he had lost the dynamic categories of voters. Those who voted for him and for his party tended to be the elderly rather than the young, peasants rather than townspeople, and those with a modest level of education. In contrast, those who voted for Constantinescu and the Convention were above all the young, townspeople and intellectuals. Roman's party fell somewhere between the two extremes. This pattern had already been seen in the local elections held a few months previously: the Convention had won in most of the large cities (including Bucharest), the Democratic Party had obtained good results in the medium-sized cities and towns, and the PDSR in the small towns and villages.

Having lost its absolute majority, the PDSR shared power between 1992 and 1996 with the three parties of the nationalist Left: the PUNR, the PRM and the PSM. The resulting coalition was nicknamed the 'red quadrilateral'. The government led by Nicolae Văcăroiu pursued a policy of small steps, though it is true that these moved in the direction of a market economy and the West. Indeed, there was no other option available. The Iliescu regime embarked on an obligatory course; it is to its credit that it recognized that there was no other way, but it remains guilty of having continually put brakes on a process that should have been much more dynamic. The process of privatization was set in motion, but slowly, too slowly. The agony of the great industrial establishments, the pride of the Ceauşescu regime (like the famous steel industry), was prolonged, while they greedily devoured the Romanians' money. Production growth was recorded, but it was production in the old, Communist style: unviable products which accumulated in stockpiles rather than revitalizing the market. No privatization took place in agriculture. Investments of Western capital rose somewhat but remained at a very modest level. The West had lost its confidence in Romania, and confidence is much harder to regain than it is to lose. Fortunately, a private sector developed independently, but in an atmosphere of complicated and unstimulating legislation.

Some Romanians dreamt up unconventional business ideas. Thus it was that dozens of private universities sprang up overnight (probably more than in the entire rest of Europe). Having been set up initially as commercial organizations, some are now going through a process of academic accreditation. On the whole, however, they have been more generative of profit than of academic competence.

Externally, as the indignation provoked by the miners' invasions of 1990 and 1991 faded, relations with the West began to relax. But Iliescu never became completely respectable for Westerners. The door was kept half-open for Romania, while for others it was opened wide. In April 1991, Iliescu had been quick to sign a treaty with the Soviet Union, at a time when no-one else was staking anything on the future of a moribund empire. (The treaty was never ratified, as the Soviet Union disintegrated in the meantime.) Gradually, however, the Bucharest regime came to put more emphasis on rapprochement with the European Union and with NATO. In 1994, Romania became a member of the Partnership for Peace (NATO's waiting room). In 1994–5, it joined the embargo imposed on Yugoslavia by the West. It is suspected, however, that the Romanian authorities were playing a double game here, tolerating or even supervising the breaking of the embargo with shipments of petroleum products. All in all, the rapprochement with the West seemed to lack conviction and to be strictly determined by circumstances. There was no sign of any great love for the West or for Western values.

The Iliescu regime gradually lost ground at home too. The stagnation of reform might have given some people the illusion that they were escaping something worse – unemployment, uncertainty about tomorrow etc. But it could only result in continuing poverty. Most Romanians distanced themselves from Iliescu much as they had distanced themselves from Ceauşescu, not out of ideological motives, but because they were dissatisfied with their precarious living conditions. Better information also helped. In its last years, the regime lost its television monopoly. A number of private stations began to communicate a different message to that given out by the official channel. It was time for a change.

Presidential and parliamentary elections were held in November 1996. A few months previously, local elections had already pointed to the defeat of the PDSR. In the first round, Iliescu won 32 per cent of the vote, giving him a slight lead over Constantinescu, with 28 per cent. Roman, who had attracted 20 per cent of the electorate in the first round, recommended that his voters support Constantinescu in the second. Finally, Constantinescu obtained 54 per cent, nearly 9 per cent more than Iliescu. It was a significant change: an intellectual had taken the place of a former Party activist. In the parliamentary elections, the Democratic Convention took first place, though with 30 per cent of votes for the Chamber of Deputies and 31 for the Senate, it was still far from an absolute majority; the PDSR took 22 and 23 per cent of votes, respectively. Consequently, the new government, with Victor Ciorbea (from the PNŢCD) as Prime Minister, was formed by the Convention in coalition with the Social Democratic Union (whose principal component was Roman's PD, and which had won approximately 13 per cent of the vote for both houses) and the UDMR (with slightly less than 7 per cent for both houses). The involvement of the Hungarian minority in government was something new, the more so as the 'red quadrilateral' had fed to a considerable extent on hostility to the Hungarians' demands.

The hopes aroused by the change were immense, even if it has to be said that the votes of a large number of Romanians had expressed disappointment with the PDSR rather than sympathy with the Convention. Romania was now setting out on a new road, the opposite of that followed up until 1996. This meant unreserved adherence to Western values and to alliance with the West; integration as fast as possible in NATO and the European Union; the re-establishment of private property by accelerating privatization and putting right the injustices of the Communist regime (the restoration of land and nationalized houses to their rightful owners); the attraction of foreign capital to Romania on a massive scale; and, not least, moral cleansing and a ruthless war against corruption, which had flourished under the Iliescu regime. There were to be no more sacrifices imposed on the many for the sake of the privileges of the ruling class. 'From now on it is the leaders who will sacrifice themselves,' Constantinescu had promised. There was also to be a renewal of personnel. From the economy and administration to diplomacy, far too many Communist officials still occupied the posts they had held under Ceauşescu. The Convention announced that it had 15,000 specialists in reserve, all of them well trained in the spirit of modern culture and democracy.

Everyone knows that in politics, achievements never match up to electoral promises. It is easier to make calculations on paper than to implement effective reforms. It is dangerous to nourish illusions: you risk being even more disappointed than you would have been otherwise. Unfortunately, the government of the Convention and its allies ended up generating even more disappointment than the Iliescu regime had done, given that the hopes placed in it were even greater and that the Romanians' patience had already been tried for too long. It would be unfair to say that things got worse. In some respects, they went rather better than before 1996. But it was still a far cry from the radical change that had been announced! The pace of privatization was stepped up, but it remained slow and inadequate; the Romanians still support the cost of a host of unviable and hard-to-privatize enterprises. Foreign capital began to appear, and there were even a few spectacular transactions (like the purchase of the Dacia automobile plant in Piteşti by the Renault group), but this hardly added up to the expected, and promised, 'invasion'. A lack of confidence accumulated over the years, poor economic performance, and dense, contradictory and unstable legislation, which looked as if it might have been made to deter Romanian and foreign entrepreneurs alike, not to mention the regular demand for backhanders, combined to make Romania a less than attractive country for investors. In the first three years of the new government, the economy showed negative rates of growth; a slight recovery – still to be confirmed – was registered in the fourth year. Even the essential reforms supported by the Convention were set in motion with great difficulty. A new land law finally increased the areas that could be recovered by former owners or their heirs, from the 10 hectares permitted by the Iliescu regime to 50 hectares of arable land and 10 of forest.

But the debate over the law on the restitution of nationalized houses dragged on until the end of the parliament, as did that on the privatization of state agricultural enterprises. Ten years after a revolution which was at least proclaimed to be anti-Communist, and after four years of government by the Democratic Convention, much remains in state ownership, and not even houses have been returned to their former owners. The law on the restitution of nationalized houses eventually reached its completed form, but its progress was held up in a final vote, and it was not actually passed until January 2001, by the new parliament elected in November 2000. As the coalition had lost its majority in the Senate (and as it was feared that, once back in power, the PDSR would modify a law with which it did not agree), a compromise was reached with Iliescu's party. Houses that had already been bought by their tenants would no longer be restored to their original owners. Nor would buildings occupied by institutions (including political parties) – which were, of course, the largest and grandest. Their owners would only receive compensation (it remains to be seen how much!). It might be noted that many politicians, including the senators and deputies (of all parties) who contributed to the law's final form, live in houses that were not originally theirs. In the end, the rightful owners will not receive very much. Such restitution looks more like dispossession: a characteristic story for the Romania of the last decade!

'Moral reform' did not go very far either. At least an anti-corruption initiative was launched (something which had not existed in Iliescu's time). There were a few arrests, and there are trials in progress. But as with everything in Romania, progress was slow and incomplete. Accusations of corruption and nepotism hung over some participants in the government installed in 1996. Romania is perceived by Romanians and foreigners alike to be a society profoundly affected by corruption. Perhaps what evolved farthest in the right direction was the 'intellectual atmosphere': democratic reflexes became more sure; the Romanians became accustomed to a plurality of ideas and options; and nationalist demagogy at least lost the direct (or indirect) official support which it had enjoyed under the Iliescu regime. Overall, there was some progress, but it did not live up to expectations and, most importantly, it made little difference in people's everyday lives (which many Romanians actually felt to be worse in 2000 than in 1996).

Relations with the West developed in a much more relaxed atmosphere. Given the choice between Iliescu and Constantinescu, the West had never concealed its preference for the latter. Romania's ambition (almost a national obsession) had become to be accepted into NATO. It lost (only just, but it still lost) in 1997, when the Alliance added Poland, Hungary and the Czech Republic to its membership. Romania was promised that its turn would come next time; it remains to be seen what will happen. Even President Clinton went to Bucharest to sweeten the bitter pill. Though he may have expected catcalls, in fact he received an ovation. In 1999, negotiations also started for membership of the European Union. And with the crisis in the Balkans, Romania once again became an interesting country for the West, as the region's most important observation and control post. From a political point of view, democracy was working relatively well (with elections run correctly, diversified and influential mass media etc.). But from an economic point of view, there is still a great gulf between Romania and the West. Westerners are frightened, too, of a Romanian 'invasion', and thus, in spite of the beginning of negotiations for EU membership, they have been in no hurry to give up their insistence on visas for Romanian citizens (a restriction which has long since ceased to apply to the ex-Communist countries of Central Europe).

What is happening to Romania? The causes of its present state are, of course, multiple. The disruptions caused by Communism were extremely serious, and the break with Communism has been slow. Iliescu's government was, in its own way, more coherent than that of 1996–2000. It represented those who did not want a sudden and radical break with Communist structures: from the leaders, many of whom were former nomenklaturists (or their relatives) and administrators of the centralized economy, to workers in state-owned factories, who wanted stability and feared unemployment. The opposition, which came to power in 1996, had no such coherence. At the top, the leaders of the revived historical parties were former political prisoners (a category of people one might seek in vain in the PDSR). But this 'old guard' was quite insufficient on its own and naturally called on the support of younger people; some of these came from families with a Liberal or Peasantist tradition, others probably joined out of ideological conviction, but not a few came out of sheer opportunism, seeking a party that would accept them. The Convention was a conglomerate, with notable differences between its component parties, as well as between generations and between the paths followed by their members. It was a broad spectrum, from the elderly former political detainees, for whom anti-Communism remained the key word and whose objective was to reconstitute Romanian society as close as possible to its inter-war form, to younger people who had followed satisfactory careers before 1989, who were motivated more by present-day interests than by inter-war or anti-Communist symbols.

The alliance with the Democratic Party complicated things even more, in as much as this party in many ways occupied an intermediary position between the Convention and the PDSR. (For example, on the issue of restitution, it tried to satisfy both the owners and the tenants of houses, showing an inclination towards the latter, while the Convention upheld the primacy of owners' rights.) There is no question that Petre Roman has evolved considerably since 1990, when he 'unmasked' Coposu and declared himself to be a partisan of 'original democracy'. He has come to represent a party of social democratic type, dominated by relatively young and pragmatic people, free of complexes and without too many scruples. The presence of the UDMR in government was an advantage (contributing to Romanian-Hungarian 'historical reconciliation' and improving the image of Romania), but it also created an additional problem, given that the Hungarians were determined to promote their own objectives (decentralization to the highest degree possible, the use of the mother tongue in local administration, a Hungarian university) at the risk of placing the government in a delicate position in relation to the country's Romanian majority.

All of this led to a disordered and largely inefficient movement. The parliament passed laws with great difficulty, adopting only a part of the legislation so necessary for reform. (This sluggishness was aggravated by the identical attributions of the two chambers; laws have to go through the same process twice, then again for mediation.) Within the government, misunderstandings and crises came one after the other, not only between the Convention and the PD but also within the Convention, between the Peasantists and Liberals, and even within each party. Resignations from parties and migrations from one party to another are large-scale phenomena in Romanian politics. The political game is highly personalized, and all too seldom faithful to the principles proclaimed. The Convention's first Prime Minister was Victor Ciorbea, a lawyer by training, who had been a magistrate before 1989 and a trade-union leader since 1990. He had supported Iliescu in the first elections, but in 1996 he had joined the PNȚCD and been elected Mayor of Bucharest. He left this post a few months later to become Prime Minister; when he lost the premiership at the start of 1998, he left the PNȚCD too and founded his own party. He was followed by another Peasantist, Radu Vasile, who was Prime Minister until December 1999. When confidence in him was withdrawn, he, too, left the party! The two men hardly seem to have been dyed-in-the-wool Peasantists! In any case, the PNŢCD, reconstituted thanks to Corneliu Coposu (who died in 1995, before he could see the triumph, but also the decline, of the Convention's pilot party), suffered from a lack of identity. Its electorate was hardly a peasant one, as it had been in the past: on the contrary, the party scored higher in the towns and among intellectuals.

Having failed with two prime ministers, the Peasantists no longer had ambitions to try a third. The man called to lead the government in December 1999 was Mugur Isărescu, a technician without political colouring who had been Governor of the National Bank since 1990. This was a solution calculated to please the Romanians, who were disillusioned with professional politicians and looking around for a 'saviour'. Indeed, the 'saviour' myth had been in operation since 1989, to the benefit first of Iliescu, then of Constantinescu. Who could say – perhaps a specialist in finance would finally do something for the economy. And indeed – as if by suggestion! – the economy started to recover. For the moment, Mugur Isărescu appeared to be the only person capable of saving the coalition, and President Constantinescu, from shipwreck. It was nonetheless embarrassing that the 'providential figure' had had to be sought outside politics (and, implicitly, outside the Convention).

The local elections of June 2000 showed the scale of the disaster. The Convention fell apart, with the Liberals splitting from the Peasantists (who, fairly or unfairly, were blamed for everything that had gone wrong). Since 1992, the Convention had held Bucharest. Now, it lost it; the PDSR came back in force and won control of the town halls in all six sectors of the capital, while in a closely fought contest with the PDSR, Traian Băsescu, the Minister of Transport and number two in the PD after Roman, was elected general mayor. On a national level, the Convention (now almost exclusively comprising the Peasantists) and the Liberals obtained around 7 per cent each, while the PDSR easily won over 25 per cent (compared with 16 per cent in 1996), followed by the PD with 10 per cent.

The Romanians were returning to the Left. In fact, the 1996–2000 government had not been particularly rightist anyway. A truly right-wing policy would have meant rapid privatization (even at the risk of social tensions) and a general removal of the structures inherited from Communism, something which had not happened to any great extent. (For example, in four years it was not even possible to demilitarize the police force, which retains a hierarchy of ranks as in the army, according to the old Soviet model. This will probably be reformed in the near future, but why so slowly?) Today, Romanian society leans strongly towards the Left, in a complete reversal of the situation before Communism. Then, as a country of greater or lesser property owners (especially peasants), it inclined towards the Right. Communism smashed property and taught people to depend on the state. And today, state assistance is still preferred to the risks of free initiative. Even the increase of rural properties to 50 hectares did not arouse the expected enthusiasm. The village population is ageing, and even if people have obtained land, they have neither money nor agricultural machinery. Most Romanians are content to be assisted, or are obliged by poverty to accept the situation, and so vote for the Left – for a state that keeps its hands on the economy and guarantees them a minimum level of subsistence.

There is no need to point out that this Left – represented by the PDSR (at least as it manifested itself prior to 1996) and even more by the PRM – is not a modern Left, but one that feeds on authoritarian and nationalist inclinations. Many Romanians lament the dissolution of authority. Indeed, it is true that there is rather too much anarchy in Romanian society. The Romanians have never been particularly good at rigour and discipline; they are better at improvising and sorting things out as they go. The uncertain transition in which they have found themselves since the fall of Communism has accentuated this characteristic. There is a high degree of disorder, which suits a few people but hurts the majority. Laws contradict one another, people run from one office to another to resolve the simplest of problems, public officials behave as if citizens existed for them and not the other way round ... Ordinary people feel abandoned; many of them have lost their savings, having been attracted into dubious financial schemes. (The latest scandal of this nature centred on the National Investment Fund, which attracted huge sums by offering suspiciously high interest rates; of course, all the money evaporated in the end!) Criminality, too, is on the increase; the level is no higher than in other countries (in this respect, Romania is probably about average), but thanks to the diffusion of sensational stories in the mass media (things which were not even mentioned under Communism), murders and robberies have begun to worry people, giving them the feeling that they are unprotected. Hence many dream of authority, of a ruler who will put things in order and reestablish justice. In fact, no-one could say that the Romanian state is not present. In some respects, it is too present, and centralization is excessive; in other respects, there does seem to be a void. It is a state which lacks authority, despite its authoritarian reflexes. The two tendencies feed one another: authoritarianism gives birth, by reaction, to anarchy, and anarchy leads to authoritarian solutions.

And so we come to the parliamentary and presidential elections of 26 November 2000. In July, Constantinescu (aware that he no longer had any chance of success) had announced his decision not to seek another mandate. At first, his tactic had been to lean on Isărescu: now Isărescu remained alone as the exponent of the 'Constantinescu regime'. Despite an initial show of reluctance, Isărescu finally registered his candidature for the presidency, standing as an independent, but supported by what was left of the Democratic Convention. The Liberals definitively broke with the Convention and persuaded Theodor Stolojan (who had been Prime Minister in 1991–2) to stand as their candidate. Thus the standard portrait of the 'saviour' with no clear political colour, expert in economics and finance, was duplicated in the form of Isărescu plus Stolojan. Weary of politicians, the country might be tempted to elect a technocrat. The Hungarians had their own candidate, György Frunda. Roman, in his turn, registered as a candidate again. Thus there were four candidates from the side of the governing coalition – as if that coalition could count on at least three-quarters of the popular vote, which they might then have safely shared! This was not the most intelligent of political moves. The PDSR, of course, put forward Iliescu, and the PRM's candidate was its leader, Corneliu Vadim Tudor.

I must pause to say something about this last candidate. Corneliu Vadim Tudor – known as 'Vadim' – is a highly picturesque and aggressive figure, with something of the second-rate actor about him. He is also a poet (again, second-rate at best), the author, among other things, of poems in honour of the Ceauşescus, and the source of an endless stream of verbiage and insult. A sort of Romanian version of Zhirinovsky, he also has close connections to Jean-Marie Le Pen, the leader of the National Front in France. In the West, what he stands for would be called the 'extreme Right'; however, in the Romanian context it is more of an 'extreme Left', as both its members (many of whom are connected with the former *Securitate*) and its ideas (authoritarianism, nationalism, a state-run economy) have their origins in the Ceauşescu era.

The results of the parliamentary election were as follows: PDSR – around 37 per cent for both the Chamber of Deputies and the Senate; PRM – 19 and 21 per cent, respectively; PD – 7 and 8 per cent; PNL and UDMR – both around 7 per cent. In other words, the PDSR won the election, but without obtaining an absolute majority, while the Greater Romania Party made an astounding leap from less than 5 per cent in the previous parliament to around 20 per cent! The Liberals obtained less than they had hoped for. However, the greatest shock was reserved for the Convention (and its principal party, the Peasantists), which had utterly collapsed, gaining only 5 per cent of the vote and so failing to enter the parliament (for which it would have needed 10 per cent; the new 'electoral threshold' is 5 per cent for parties and up to 10 per cent for coalitions, according to the number of their component groups). The Right was crushed!

In the race for the presidency, neither Isărescu nor Stolojan managed to realize the hopes which had been placed in them: in addition, they were competing for more or less the same segment of the electorate. Isărescu won slightly less than 10 per cent of the vote, and Stolojan just over 11 per cent. Frunda obtained the usual Hungarian score, with 6 per cent, while Roman dropped to a sorry 3 per cent. The candidates who remained in the second round were Iliescu, with 36 per cent, and Vadim, with 28 per cent. The myth of the 'technocrat saviour' had only worked for 20 per cent of the population. A larger number had opted for another type of saviour, one who came not with an economic programme but with the promise to 'clean up' the country and put it in order, regardless of the means.

A moment of shock ensued; Romanians and Westerners alike could hardly believe what had happened. The mass media proclaimed the greatest success of the extreme Right since the Second World War (the Romanians would say 'extreme Left', but ultimately what matters is the thing itself rather than the terminology). What if Vadim, who had risen in popularity week by week as the elections approached, were to continued his ascent and become President by winning the second round? The Milošević regime in Serbia had just fallen; was it Romania's turn to repeat the unfortunate Serbian experience? Vadim had promised government by machine-gun and public executions in stadiums, and one of his associates had threatened journalists 'bought by the West' that they would end up in labour camps. (Such words were subsequently denied by those who had uttered them, or presented as jokes and rhetorical figures.) In fact, what came next was almost surreal: a considerable number of Romanians – politicians, journalists, intellectuals – many of whom had hitherto been Iliescu's bitterest opponents, began to campaign for his election. According to their logic, the choice was between 'bad' and 'very bad', and they went to the polls to help the lesser evil triumph over the greater. In fact, if things were looked at more coldly, Vadim had no chance of winning substantially more votes than in the first round. Iliescu was already eight percentage points ahead, and the greater part of the votes of the other candidates (who were to his right, while Vadim was to his left) would naturally flow in his direction. All the same, half of Isărescu's voters preferred not to vote in the second round. The others' fear of Vadim offered Iliescu much more than he would have won in normal conditions. He was re-elected President of Romania with almost 67 per cent of votes cast, compared with 33 per cent for his opponent.

Once again, Romania had astonished the West by behaving out of character. In the end, Westerners and Romanians alike are glad that Iliescu has returned to power and nothing worse has happened. The Vadim phenomenon is less a matter of policies (his programme is quite summary) than of emotional states. It is an expression of exasperation, a 'cocktail' made up of poverty, frustration, indignation at corruption, unease provoked by the insecure conditions of life, a culture of paternalism (a powerful state and a providential leader) and so on. The 'Greater Romania' voters are typically relatively young townspeople with education to secondary level, the dynamic categories who feel unfairly disadvantaged by social dysfunction, unemployment etc. (Meanwhile, Iliescu continues to be favoured by country people and the elderly, categories who are less tempted by Vadim's revolutionary rhetoric.)

Iliescu should not be too proud of the victory he has won. This time (unlike the previous two occasions), he was elected less for his own sake than out of dissatisfaction with the Constantinescu regime and fear of a possible Vadim regime. Mythologically speaking, he is no longer a 'saviour'; he is a *former* 'saviour'. At the same time, his discourse has become more European. And so has his party, on the whole. But is it still his party? The new Prime Minister is Adrian

Năstase, an exponent of the younger, more open and more pro-Western wing of the party. Up until 1996, Iliescu was effectively in control, or at least his influence was decisive. There is no certainty that this will be the case from now on. Moreover, by absorbing the small Social Democratic Party – at first a member of the Convention and later an ally of the Democratic Party – the PDSR is preparing to acquire a new European respectability and a new name; it will become the Social Democratic Party, PSD.

It may be that the PDSR, having learned something over the years and shed at least part of its statist and nationalist baggage (which has been picked up by the PRM), will manage to push forward the process of reform and European integration. This is not certain, or even probable, but it is possible. It would be ironic, and another Romanian paradox, if the PDSR were to succeed where the 'European' Convention failed. In any case, formal collaboration with the PRM has been ruled out. Under such circumstances, it would seem that the government has no option but to make deals with the democratic opposition parties, and this is likely to consolidate the reformist and European line. This is something different from the 'red quadrilateral', whatever anyone says. The road to Europe is obligatory if Romania is to have any chance at all. Already its performance places it last among candidates for membership (especially in economic terms, as was highlighted by a European Union report in the autumn of 2000). Romania has no option, whatever the government, other than to try to do something about this, or to accept defeat.

The new government has the advantage of a coherence such as the previous coalition, with its heterogeneous character, never enjoyed. But there are also plenty of obstacles in its way. Romanian society is tired: tired before it has brought the task confronting it to completion. The Romanians have just about had enough of reform (and such reform as they have known has been incomplete and defective anyway). Many of them may theoretically accept privatization, while in fact they fear it and want social protection before anything else. The PDSR's electorate largely belongs to this category. This situation explains (at least partially) the slow pace of reform in Romania: there is always the fear of large-scale workers' protests. The government's room for manoeuvre is thus limited. If it accelerates the pace of privatization, it risks alienating its own electorate. In trying to reconcile economic and social demands, it risks doing nothing properly: both privatizing and maintaining social assistance by half-measures.

Meanwhile, the Greater Romania Party is ready to pounce. Even if it lost the final race for the presidency, Greater Romania remains a massive presence in the parliament (with a quarter of the seats) and on the Romanian political stage in general. This will mark Romania, both in its internal affairs and in its European relations. To the extent that the PDSR government generates dissatisfaction, it may be that the PRM will gain in strength. The democratic game has become unbalanced. On one side is a single large party, the PDSR, and on the other a number of smaller parties with different objectives. The weight of the 'historical parties' has fallen almost to the level of 1990: a return to the situation ten years ago! Will the democratic opposition become an important political force again in the next few years? What will become of the Peasantists, who are in danger of quite simply disappearing? Will a new grouping, more modern and more coherent, come into being? The years ahead are full of uncertainties.

NATIONALISM AND ORTHODOXISM

Are the Romanians nationalist? Albeit in differing degrees, they do feel an attachment to the national idea. This is how Romania was made, and how it has lasted. Moreover, for decades Communist nationalism educated them to believe in their own uniqueness and to distrust others – above all to be suspicious of Western values. Something of all this remains in people's minds and behaviour. Even today, the conception of the nation that many Romanians have is the traditional one, out-of-date in the West but still alive in Central and Eastern Europe. It can be summed up in the phrase 'the nation before everything'. Nowadays, the nation cannot be placed before European solidarity, or the principles of democracy, or the rights of minorities, or indeed of every individual. In Romania, as in the region as a whole, there is still a strong emphasis on the nation and the national state (just as there was in the West until not so very long ago).

Romania is proclaimed by its constitution to be a unitary national state; the idea of federalism is viewed with suspicion. Federalization would be the first step towards the dismemberment of the country; above all – and this is a national obsession – it could lead to the loss of Transylvania to Hungary (in spite of the fact that Romanians now outnumber Hungarians there by more than three to one). The reality is that, thanks to the uniformity promoted by Communism, the Romanian provinces have become quite similar to one another, and there are only a few isolated voices calling for federalization; it may be the dream of some Transylvanian Hungarians and of a few Transylvanian Romanians disgusted by the 'Byzantinism' of the 'Old Kingdom' (like the journalist Sabin Gherman, who provoked a scandal with his article entitled 'I have had enough of Romania'). There is now also a 'Party of the Moldavians', but it has no well-defined programme in favour of autonomy, and its electoral significance is minimal. So far, federalism is not even under discussion. All the more telling, therefore, is the fear of federalization, a fear manifested even in the absence of an effective 'threat'. The dismemberment of Yugoslavia has rung alarm bells for some (complete with talk of foreign conspiracies). But Romania is not Yugoslavia; it is a much more coherent state, which has proved its capacity to endure.

For the time being, not even a limited autonomy for the provinces has any chance of being discussed, although this is the European model which is currently taking shape. In Romania, the 'French model' still applies in its nineteenth-century form: a centralized system with an administrative division into 'counties' (Romanian *judeţe*; in fact, they correspond more to French *départements* than to English counties), each of which is the responsibility of a prefect appointed by the central government. In the meantime, even France has reconstituted its regions, and among the ex-Communist countries Poland has reorganized its territory on a regional basis. Romania has gone no further than a vague administrative decentralization, leaving the power of the centre almost intact.

Pure, hard-line nationalism has largely been absorbed by those parties which have emerged to a greater or lesser extent from the old Communist structures. Although it cannot be defined as primarily a nationalist party, the PDSR has a nationalist component, and at certain moments (especially around election times) has not hesitated to play on anti-Hungarian or anti-Western reflexes. However, it seems that this inclination is now becoming attenuated. The PUNR justified its existence in terms of resistance to the pretensions of the Transylvanian Hungarians, but it has now almost disappeared, having obtained an insignificant share of the vote in the November 2000 elections. Extreme nationalism has been absorbed almost entirely by the Greater Romania Party (and this is what has stimulated its electoral ascent; previously, the ultra-nationalists were divided between several parties). This is a party that does not hesitate to proclaim openly its hostility towards Jews, Gypsies and Hungarians, and also towards the West. (For all that, in the recent elections Vadim proclaimed, in a less than logical manner – but logic was never his strong point – that he was a partisan of European integration: all that is needed now is for Europe to want him!) The Romanian-Hungarian nationalist polarization has placed Cluj, the capital of Transylvania, in a shameful situation. There, the vote of a majority of Romanians (notwithstanding the hostility of others, and of the Hungarian minority) has repeatedly given the post of Mayor to Gheorghe Funar, initially the President of the PUNR, now Vice-President of the Greater Romania Party, a politician with a rudimentary and extravagantly nationalist discourse. Thus a university city with a remarkable intellectual life, European in character and tradition, has become an embarrassment for Romania, in complete contrast to Timişoara, the capital of the Banat, a city open to the West and a model of the cohabitation of different ethnic groups and cultures.

Asked for which institutions of the state they have the highest regard, Romanians invariably select the Church (80–90 per cent) and the army (70–80 per cent). This is a remarkable illustration of the inclinations towards authority and national cohesion which I have been discussing. Indeed, it is interesting that the Church – the Orthodox Church, it goes without saying – is considered to be an 'institution of the state'; a somewhat vaguely defined religious ideology has taken the place vacated by Communist ideology. Of course, the Church and Communism do not share the same values, but some of the reflexes and attitudes they encourage are similar: Communism, too, was a religion. In both cases, people are gathered together around revealed truths, which are considered to be above discussion. The values of the community are placed above free and individual choice. Again and again, we are told that the Romanian nation is an 'Orthodox nation' – in spite of the existence of other confessions, and of the fact that the nation is a political, not a religious, concept. (According to 1992 figures, the Romanian population is 86.8 percent Orthodox, compared with 72.6 per cent in 1930; despite this dominant position, the Orthodox clergy are frightened by the revival of the Greek Catholics, to whom they are in no hurry to return the church buildings that were made Orthodox after 1948, and by the relative success which neo-Protestant churches have enjoyed in recent years.)

Before 1989, a great many Romanians pretended to be atheist. Nowadays, almost everybody claims to be a believer. Having been well educated in the Communist spirit, Ion Iliescu persevered for some time after the revolution in defining himself as a 'free thinker'. 'Mr Iliescu, do you believe in God?' was the unexpected final question which Emil Constantinescu asked him in their televised confrontation on the eve of the presidential elections in 1996. Caught off guard, Iliescu did not know how to reply. He tried, rather unconvincingly, to argue that 'free thinker' does not exactly mean 'atheist'. It would have been more honest – albeit impolitic – simply to say that he did not believe in God. There is no crime in being an atheist! But this is not an available option in today's Romania, at least not for a politician. After losing the election, Iliescu adopted a new line (in the hope that he might win the next time): he began to cross himself! In any case, all political leaders, including, of course, the President, now piously attend all sorts of religious manifestations. A huge Cathedral of the Salvation of the Romanian People is to be erected in the centre of Bucharest. (It remains to be seen whether it will actually be built; in Romania, not all that is planned actually happens.) And when the miners set out to march on Bucharest yet again, in January 1999, Prime Minister Radu Vasile could find no better place to negotiate with them than the Cozia monastery, with the Church in the role of mediator.

However, Romania is far from being under fundamentalist assault. What can be seen is more a blend of traditionalism, conventionalism and political demagogy. In traditional environments, relgious belief is still very much alive. But otherwise, I find it hard to say how many Romanians are believers and how many simply perpetuate, out of attachment to tradition, a mass of rules, rituals and even superstitious practices. There are plenty of people, especially women, who respect the long and rigorous Orthodox fasts, while baptism and burial remain the two obligatory religious acts (as they were under Communism, though practised with a certain discretion by Party activists). The Orthodox Church is above all a symbol of Romanian identity. That is why the militant ideology of Orthodoxism (not to be confused with Orthodoxy itself) is the natural ally of nationalism. It is also a sign of non-adherence, or at least reserve, in relation to Western values. Gone are the days when the tone was set by a thoroughly pro-Western élite (Orthodox, of course, but able to separate their religion from their political and cultural projects). Nowadays, the approach to the West is more pragmatic than sentimental. When conflict broke out in Kosovo and the bombardment of Yugoslavia began, opinion polls showed that NATO's standing dropped by some tens of percentage points. The government, firmly respecting its pro-Western options, was harshly criticized for 'excess of zeal'. In sentimental terms, the Romanians seemed closer to their neighbours than to the West – in complete contrast to the situation a hundred years ago – and many of them preferred Orthodox, nationalist and authoritarian Serbia to the democratic and cosmopolitan West.

WORSE OR BETTER?

Obstructions and failures notwithstanding, the Romanian economy and Romanian society have not stood still. The Romanians have many reasons to complain, but perhaps they complain a little too loudly, forgetting or softening the memory of the disaster before 1989. I have just seen a sequence from a film made in the Communist period: a view of a boulevard in the centre of Bucharest. Although I have lived there all my life, the image struck me as strange. The street was almost empty, with just a few cars here and there, and everything seemed 'calm' and colourless. Nowadays, there is life everywhere, indeed perhaps too much life and too much disorder. There is continuous bustle on the streets (one wonders if anyone is actually working). The large, empty state shops of former days are now full, and beginning to resemble Western shops. There are stalls along the pavements. Everyone is buying and selling. I come downstairs from my flat and find that peasants and street-traders have spread their produce on the ground right in front of the block. It may not be very hygienic, but you can always wash the vegetables! Before 1989, nothing could be found in the market; people who had cars went to the country and bought direct. All of these things now seem normal, because *they are*; they can even be annoying, because they are not quite as they should be. Under Communism, they did not exist at all: it was simpler then!

The picture on the television screen has changed too. Having been deprived of information for so long, Romanians are now great tele-

A street scene in Bucharest in the summer of 2000. Along the pavement can be seen improvised 'boutiques' stocking all sorts of goods, and peasant women selling greens.

vision viewers. They can choose between half a dozen national channels (not to mention local ones) and numerous foreign stations (German, French and Italian television, CNN, Euronews etc). This too seems normal.

The past hurts less and less: it is always the present that people are discontented with. Before 1989, the Romanians had some money, but there was not much they could do with it. Nowadays, you can get anything for money, from food to luxury villas or travel anywhere in the world. Unfortunately, there is not a lot of money available anymore. The average monthly salary today is worth appreciably less than before 1989, but how relevant is such a calculation? Then it was around 3,000 lei. Nowadays, thanks to inflation, it has risen to over 3 million; the Romanians are all millionaires. While fewer things can be bought with those 3 million lei, at least they can now be bought, while previously you were more likely to search for them than to buy them. Additionally, they are now bought at the market price, whereas previously you had to resort to the black market or to all sorts of combinations which consumed your time, nerves and money. Then, the Communist salary was fixed, but nowadays many

Romanians earn more than their basic salary, by working extra hours or taking another job. Of course, for most people, the situation is not good; those 3 million lei of the average net salary correspond to about a hundred dollars. Pay is about fifteen times lower than in the West, and three or four times lower than in Hungary or Poland. Goods and services are on average rather cheaper than in the West, but some things, especially imported products, are more expensive. And many products are imported, since the Romanian economy produces so little. Even the present standard of living, low as it is, is beyond the country's real means.

In the West, there is a relatively shallow layer of poor people, and an even shallower layer of rich people. Between these extremes, most Westerners belong to the middle class; this ensures the smooth functioning and stability of the social and political system. In Romania, there is a shallow layer of rich people, a middle-class layer that is also relatively shallow, and a very large category of people living in various degrees of poverty. For many of them, having enough to eat every day is a problem, not to mention paying domestic bills. The condition for Romania to succeed will be the development of the middle class. Its present social structures are closer to those of Latin America or the Third World than to those of the First World.

At the same time, large fortunes have been amassed, not a few of them in dubious circumstances. The new capitalists are to a considerable degree people who occupied key posts in the economic or information structures of the old regime: *Securitate* members (a large category), commercial representatives and Party activists. The facts are not very pleasant, but how else could a class of capitalists be created in the space of a few years?

Year by year, the United Nations Development Programme publishes a list of countries ranked according to an index which combines per-capita gross domestic product, life expectancy and conditions of education. According to this 'human development indicator', Romania was in 64th place in the year 1998; the only countries in Europe with a lower ranking were Macedonia (69), Albania (94) and Turkey (85), to the extent that the last of these can be considered a European country. Even Bulgaria (60) was a few places ahead of Romania, disagreeable as this may have been for Romanians, who are accustomed to looking across the Danube with a feeling of superiority. Russia, too, was slightly higher (62), while the ex-Communist countries of Central Europe were appreciably better placed: Poland – 44, Hungary – 43, the Czech Republic – 34 and Slovenia – 29. The comparison with Greece (25) is edifying. Before Communism, Greece was no better off than Romania; nowadays, the difference between them says all there is to say about the effects of Communism. Romania was also behind the West before the Second World War. Now it is even further behind, much further behind.

While the West has been modernized rapidly and profoundly in the course of the last half-century, Communism has left behind an unexpectedly large number of areas which have scarcely been touched by modernity, despite its intense industrialization programme (or perhaps precisely because of this programme, which resulted in an artificial industrial sector unable to bring the rest of society along with it). The country's complete electrification was proclaimed a priority (and of course to have been successfully carried out). After the fall of Communism, we all found out that there were still hundreds of villages without electricity! Running water is almost non-existent in rural areas. And even marginal districts of towns (where they have not been replaced by blocks of flats), including whole streets of Bucharest, lack sewage systems. Outside the capital and a few large cities, hot water is a rarity in blocks of flats. Streets and roads are in appalling condition – there have been some improvements in the last few years, but these are far from sufficient. The trains move with difficulty. But all this does not mean that Romania has not seen a multiplication of computers, and – more than anything else! – mobile phones. While some Romanians still get their light from gas lamps, others are navigating the internet. Romania seems to be made up of distinct parts: a mixture of traditionalism, nineteenth-century modernity, Communist modernity and postmodernity.

On the whole, the levels of education and intellectual achievement in Romania are higher than the material conditions of society. This gives rise to all sorts of frustrations, and even an element of despair. Can you make a career in Romania? There are Romanians who believe that they deserve more but are not convinced that they will ever be able to get it. Romania has become a country of emigration, something it was not in the past. Communism determined many Romanians to leave the country, or at least to dream of doing so. The flow intensified after 1990. Hundreds of thousands of people have gone out into the world, legally or illegally, to destinations ranging from Western Europe to Canada and Australia. Most of them are young people, who, as Sabin Gherman put it, have 'had enough of Romania'. Some of them cross clandestinely into Germany, Italy or Greece. If they are caught and deported, they try again; perhaps they will be luckier the next time. In any case, they can earn much more on the black market in the West than they could ever earn at home. In addition, many young people who have left Romania to study, with qualifications acceptable anywhere, prefer not to return to a country where there is no certainty that they will find work corresponding to their abilities.

At the beginning of 2000, Romania had a population of some 22,455,000 people. In 1989, it was around 23,200,000. Thus in ten years it had dropped by 750,000. This is partly due to emigration and partly to a falling birth rate (both of which are themselves the results of precarious living conditions and a negative spiritual state). Having been champions in the birth-rate league before Communism (due to the predominantly rural environment) and for a time under Communism, thanks to Ceauşescu, the Romanians now have fewer and fewer children. The fertility index is among the lowest in Europe at 1.17 (compared with 1.71 in France and 1.72 in Great Britain). The country is emptying little by little, and those who are left are getting older. Already, the number of pensioners is higher than that of wage earners (and the rate of unemployment is also high: 10 per cent).

Romania is also experiencing a moral crisis. The lack of confidence is becoming more and more pronounced; society is disoriented. What can people believe in? The political class has disappointed them; the economy is marking time; living conditions are not getting better. Meanwhile, the West says fine words but does very little. All too often, Romania is treated as a second-rate country, as is shown by the continuation of the visa requirement (which does not achieve much, as the 'undesirable' element will get through without visas anyway, but which gives Romanians the impression that they are subject to unfair discrimination).

While some leave the country, others have come to be nostalgic for Communism. More than half of the population consider that their lives were better then. How can one explain to them that the present upheavals are due precisely to Communism, without which their lives would be better today?

Immediately after December 1989, the eyes of a number of Romanians turned towards King Michael, who had been in exile for almost half a century and was living at Versoix in Switzerland. Born in 1921, he had already reigned twice, first as a minor between 1927 and 1930, and again from 1940 to 1947. The arguments in favour of monarchy were not without substance. The republic had been born illegitimate, as the outcome of a Communist *coup d'état*. The abolition of Communism should also have meant the abolition of the republic which it had created. Moreover, monarchy seemed better able to arbitrate internal disputes and to boost Romania's credibility in the West. Spain was singled out as an example of the role which could be played by a King in the evolution from dictatorship to democracy. It was also argued that King Michael had the sort of balanced personality that an unbalanced Romania needed so badly.

However, the Romanians, having been monarchist until 1947, had become firmly republican in the meantime. And no wonder: Communism had turned everything upside down! A referendum would probably have shown no more than 10 to 15 per cent in favour of monarchy. For this reason, Iliescu's reaction seemed excessive; faced with a simple private visit by the King, he seemed to go into a state of panic. In the first years, King Michael was systematically refused an entry visa, and even the right to regain his Romanian citizenship (which had been taken from him by the Communist regime). When the King did manage to get as far as Otopeni Airport, and the border police, intimidated by the situation, allowed him through, what followed was like something out of an adventure movie: a motorway chase, the King's car turned around in its tracks, the former sovereign forced to take the plane back again. He finally was allowed to enter the country to celebrate Easter in April 1992. For a time, Iliescu was eclipsed; on Easter Sunday, King Michael truly reigned over the capital, surrounded by a sea of cheering people. It was an incredible triumph. For a moment, it seemed as if history was turning again.

This was an illusion, however. The majority of Romanians wanted a republic, even a republic headed by Iliescu! The King was supported by a section of the opposition, not even the whole opposition. Corneliu Coposu made no secret of his monarchist option. In the anti-Iliescu demonstrations, the slogan 'Monarchy saves Romania' was frequently chanted. But the democratic opposition could not bind its entire future to the King's uncertain future; a firmly monarchist attitude would have risked alienating part of the electorate. Before being elected President, Emil Constantinescu rather imprudently made declarations favourable to the King which very nearly backfired. After becoming President, he received the King at Cotroceni Palace, but nothing more. Having been reproached by some for his pro-monarchy position, he was now accused by others of abandoning the King. But what else could he have done?

Paradoxically, the King was better served by Iliescu than by Constantinescu; many saw him as an antidote to Iliescu. Once the latter was out of the way, the King was no longer of such interest (except, of course, to the hard core of monarchists, who are not very numerous). For Michael I, there followed a slow decline. His age (he is almost 80) became a handicap. So did the fact that his marriage to Anne of Bourbon-Parma produced five daughters. The crown can be transmitted only in the male line; a woman on the throne would be something unheard of in Romania. A decade after the fall of Communism, it is clear that King Michael has lost the race. It is hard to say how Romania would look if it had been re-established as a kingdom: it might not have been the worst of solutions!

A FEW PECULIARITIES

Westerners who come to Romania observe with amazement that in certain respects Romanians think and behave 'differently'. This amazement is only partially justified. Many of the Romanians' curious attitudes were characteristic of the West until not so long ago. As far as 'politically incorrect' attitudes are concerned, the Romanians have invented nothing: they are just a little behind.

Many Romanians still do not know that it is not correct nowadays to manifest yourself vehemently against minority groups. Less than pleasant things are often said about Hungarians, sometimes also about Jews, and above all about Gypsies. Even on the national television channel, the Gypsy is treated as a Gypsy. When a Gypsy is implicated in a crime of any sort, we are sure to be told that he is a Gypsy (something which does not happen with other groups).

Romania is still a man's country (just as the West was until recently – and still is to some extent!). While women are active and present in almost all fields, they remain somewhat in the shadow of

184

men. Plenty of men still consider that a woman's place is 'over the cooking pot'. The fact that they work just as hard as men do does not exempt them from the 'cooking pot' and all the rest of the housework. There are very few women 'at the top', and I would find it difficult to name a great feminine 'model' in Romanian public or intellectual life. Few women *lead*; one could count the women in the parliament on one's fingers; for years, there was not a single woman in government. Out of a total of 26 ministers in the Năstase government formed at the end of 2000, as many as five are women; who says that Romania is not progressing? The composition of the Romanian delegation to a world women's congress attracted ironic comment: the head of the delegation was a man! A woman President or Prime Minister would seem like a joke. While the younger generation will probably engender a new mentality, the Romanian male bastion will not surrender overnight!

Among the categories with the highest percentage of disadvantaged members are children and the elderly (exactly the groups a civilized society should take the greatest care of). Far too many families abandon their children because of poverty. There have also been cases of children sold or 'adopted' in dubious circumstances; who knows what happens to them once they are over the border? Some end up in 'children's homes' where the conditions (insufficient food and the absence of any human warmth) have shocked Western visitors. Others live under the open sky: these are the 'street children' who wander the cities in rags, sheltering in manholes and living by begging. Often, they end up in prostitution; there are 'tourists' who come especially to Romania in search of young boys. A separate category are children with AIDS, who are more numerous than in any other European country. These should have been a priority of all governments, but sadly they have not been. The European Union has advised Romania that it must take care of its own children. It is possible to detect a slow process of improvement, largely due to Western assistance. There seem to be fewer children living in the streets, and some children's homes are now more welcoming places. However, there is still a great deal to be done. Above all, there is a duty to be recognized. Should it be necessary for Europe to point it out?

The elderly are not pampered in Romanian society either. Pensions are small, quite insufficient for a decent life. Homes for the elderly look no better than those for children. There is also a problem of vocabulary. While euphemisms like 'troisième age' and 'senior citizens' have been generally adopted in the West, Romanians talk bluntly about *bătrînii*, 'the old'. This is the official term, even on television – an equivocal word, in which it is hard to separate the respect accorded to age in traditional societies from a slight contempt for those who are 'out of the race'. And since journalists and news-readers are often very young, they can be heard talking of 'old women' and 'old men' who are scarcely past 50! No-one has told them it is not nice to do so.

Curiously, the Romanians do not seem very concerned about their health. Here again, they are at the opposite pole to the West, where recent decades have seen the rise of a veritable cult of health and prolonged youth. The majority of Romanians do not worry very much about the quality of their lives. They are too little bothered about the environment in which they live or about what they eat, drink and smoke. There are also women who continue to have abortions with nonchalance, although they could use contraception: abortion remains the principal means of limiting births. Everyday life, too, is unhealthy, as a consequence of the dysfunctional character of Romanian society: hurrying from place to place, stress, irritation and so on. And when all this happens in the freezing winter or under the torrid sun of summer (for the climate does not favour the Romanians either), things become even more unhealthy. Meanwhile, the dirty environment is responsible for illnesses such as hepatitis, typhoid fever and meningitis. The important thing for a Romanian is not to end up in hospital. Hospitals (with certain outstanding exceptions, of course) are among the least attractive of the country's institutions; they are overcrowded and hardly shine as far as hygiene is concerned. You may get better in hospital, but you may also come out worse than when you went in.

Consequently, the life expectancy of the Romanians is among the lowest in Europe: approximately 66 years for men and 74 for women (compared with an average of 74 years for men and over 80 for women in the West). The Romanians also hold the record for infant mortality (as indeed they did in the inter-war period): according to statistics published at the end of the 1990s, 21 children out of every thousand live births die before the age of one year. (In the West, the figure varies between five and seven; in Hungary, it is ten, and in Bulgaria fourteen.) Such a deplorable situation calls for a greater effort, both financially and in terms of organization and information.

However, health does not seem to be the government's first priority any more than it is for Romanians in general.

Homosexuals, on the other hand, are a priority. The Romanians have been talking about them for years. The guilty party – as so often! – is the West, which has been putting pressure on the parliament to modify the famous Article 200 of the Criminal Code, which makes homosexuality an offence. Deputies and senators, encouraged by the Church, have resisted all the way. As the West continues to insist, the story goes on interminably, leaving some Romanians with the impression that homosexuals are the West's chief preoccupation! In fact, they have ended up becoming a major preoccupation, in the opposite direction, for the Romanians; it is claimed among other things that Romanian tradition and Orthodox values do not admit homosexuality. The article in question has nevertheless been 'softened', without giving up its discriminatory provisions completely. (Thus legal sanctions still apply in situations in which homosexual relations may give rise to 'public scandal' – an expression open to interpretation.) The final battle is still raging for the full decriminalization of this 'offence'.

The Romanians do not have a very good record on ecological awareness either; this applies at all levels, from everyday life to the activities of major industries. People happily throw whatever they have finished with into the street and so end up living among heaps of refuse. Communism did not have the slightest idea of ecology – indeed, its programme of industrialization at any price was anti-ecological par excellence – so mining and industrial establishments took no account of environmental norms. Apart from a few modest improvements, things have continued in much the same direction (with the complicity, indeed, of a number of foreign businesses: why should they pay if the Romanians themselves cannot be bothered?). An incident that received much media coverage, though it was far from isolated, took place recently at a gold-extracting plant in Maramureş. A large quantity of cyanide leaked into the river system and reached the Tisza, to the indignation of the Hungarians, through whose country the river flows from one end to the other. Not only did their fish die, but a national symbol was defiled!

What is perhaps most needed in Romania is a change of mentality, as well as material conditions.

The Romanians' relationship with the Communist past remains troubled and equivocal. A formal condemnation of Communism is woven together with all sorts of only partly acknowledged nostalgias. Repudiated as a system, Communism is rehabilitated in segments, which add up to an overall rehabilitation.

There has been no trial of Communism (although such a thing has been called for insistently by some intellectuals). Even individuals whose hands are stained with blood, the torturers of the 1950s, have not been brought to judgement. Only those implicated in the repression of December 1989 have been sentenced, and they all came out of prison quickly enough, generally on medical grounds – since when they seem to have enjoyed excellent health (with a few exceptions, like Nicu Ceauşescu, the dictator's son, who died of cirrhosis of the liver). Former Party leaders and their close relatives (including Ceauşescu's family) are doing very well for themselves; they are involved in all sorts of lucrative ventures and have every reason to look down with a condescending smile on the former political detainees with their modest pensions. They certainly have no intention of giving up the villas in which they are living to their rightful owners. In Timişoara, the city where the revolution first broke out and the most anti-Communist and Westernized corner of Romania, a proclamation was launched in 1990 calling for former Communist officials to be excluded for a time from political life. It is hardly surprising that the Iliescu regime did not take the idea on board. Even the West discreetly advised the 'ex-Communists' not to embark on a 'witch-hunt'. Unhunted, the witches have got on with their own affairs. In the Czech Republic such a law was adopted, but the Czechs had Havel, while the Romanians had Iliescu. The current tactic is to talk of collective guilt or, preferably, collective innocence. Everyone was a Party member or was implicated in the Communist regime in some way or other. When Iliescu is taken to task about the high function he held in the Party, he likes to put Emil Constantinescu in the same boat: he was a Communist too! And if everyone was, then no-one is.

Securitate officers, too, are everywhere, though how much in reality and how much in the imaginary it is hard to say. There was and continues to be an obsession with the *Securitate*. The older members of the Romanian Information Service (SRI), who also hold the highest posts, do come from the former *Securitate*. This explains certain leaks of information, especially towards the Greater Romania Party. Many former *Securitate* officers are well placed in the economic and financial system. Disturbing questions inevitably arise. Do they still make up an operational network? Are the present leaders of Romania, including former political detainees who became informers, being blackmailed? Such questions lead easily – perhaps too easily – towards a conspiracy theory according to which the *Securitate* continues to play a key role in Romanian society and political life. The image of a Romania which continues to be led by *Securitate* officers seems rather mythological, but groups exerting pressure and influence undoubtedly exist.

The figure of the *Securitate* officer is doubled in the Romanian imaginary by that of the informer. Here, too, there is a high degree of uncertainty. How many Romanians were informers? And, above all, how many are still 'dependent' as a consequence? Only a few, more courageous, more honest or more cynical than the rest, have confessed of their own accord that they were informers; they can be counted on one's fingers. Otherwise, no-one is willing to accept that they had anything to do with the *Securitate*. If we were to go just by confessions, the subject could be laid to rest once and for all. It remains to be seen what the files will say. A member of the Senate, Constantin Ticu Dumitrescu, initiated a proposal for a law on the East German model – in other words, an independent commission to take over all of the files, and complete transparency. The way in which this initiative was obstructed (by all parties) raises serious doubts about the innocence of the political class. After all sorts of delays and modifications, the law was passed, but in such a form that the initiator says he no longer recognizes his original project. The Commission has been constituted and has begun to function. However, state secrecy and all sorts of vested interests seem to be preventing the full recovery of the archives. And is all this not in fact coming rather late? It would have been more appropriate if the moral cleansing of society and the exclusion of compromised individuals from the political game had taken place in 1990. Now, it is difficult for anything to change. The question then arises as to whether precisely the most sensitive or compromising files may not have disappeared. And it is not entirely clear what is meant by 'informer'. Former political detainees were obliged to give declarations. At what point did someone become an 'informer'? It is possible that it will be the victims, those blackmailed by the Communist regime, who will fall into the net rather than those who are really guilty. For example, it was said of Coposu that he had been an informer, on the basis of his 'declarations' to the *Securitate* (which, in his case as in others, easily leaked out of the archives: who was guarding them?). But what need did Communist officials have to be informers? And of course, *Securitate* officers did not 'collaborate with the *Securitate*' either: they *were* the *Securitate*! It is strange that in the imaginary of the Romanians, the informer appears more guilty than the *Securitate* officer!

The inevitable finally happened. On the eve of the elections of November 2000, the commission made public the names of those candidates for the parliament who had collaborated with the *Securitate*. Most were Peasantists and Liberals; there were hardly any from the Greater Romania Party. *Quod erat demonstrandum!*

Communism has left behind it a sick society, a thoroughly disturbed country. As the years pass, the Communism/anti-Communism opposition is gradually losing its relevance. Growing numbers of pragmatic Romanians have cut themselves loose from history and care about efficiency more than ideology. The elections of 2000 showed that the theme of anti-Communism (as upheld particularly by the Democratic Convention) no longer counts for much with the electorate (or at least can no longer take precedence over the problems of the present). However, the shadows of Communism will only disappear completely with the natural succession of generations.

VI Romanians and Foreigners

Few European peoples have had to deal with foreigners as much as the Romanians have done. As regional dominance passed from one power to another, one model of civilization succeeded another, and populations of an extreme diversity settled in the territory where Romanians made up the majority. The fundamental contradiction lies in the fact that this uninterrupted onslaught of foreignness came up against a society which was until recently predominantly rural and inclined to close in on itself. Relations with foreigners and the importing of foreign civilization remained the preserve of an élite which in this way set itself farther and farther apart from the mass of the population. Opening towards 'others' went hand in hand with a permanent inertia coming from the deeper layers of Romanian civilization: hence the internally contradictory character of an endless process of acceptance and rejection.

The Romanians are convinced that they have a positive attitude towards foreigners. They will claim that no-one shows more goodwill or is more friendly and welcoming than they are. And there is much truth in this characterization. However, such an attitude is not exclusive to them; it is characteristic of traditional communities in general. Wherever you go, the peasant is more hospitable than the town-dweller. A foreigner (or even a Romanian) who goes into a village in Moldavia or Maramureş will be received with more warmth and attention than when he or she goes to Bucharest and is lost in the anonymous mass. (Yet even there, something remains of traditional and oriental kindness; there is every chance that a Western visitor will be given a better welcome and surrounded by more attention in the capital of Romania than he or she would be accustomed to offer a foreigner at home.)

However, the 'favoured' treatment reserved for foreigners means above all that they are treated as foreign. A traditional community

191

regards the 'other' with goodwill but still keeps its distance. In the Romanian imaginary, foreigners, with all their qualities and defects (especially defects!), are invested with a high degree of otherness. When the need arises, they will be found guilty of all the evils that have befallen the Romanians. According to this view, the country's present condition and historical delays are largely due to foreigners; had it not been for so many invasions – Turks, Russians, Hungarians and all the rest – Romania would have flourished. (The good things which have been borrowed from foreigners are passed over rapidly, as is the fact that the Romanians have done plenty of harm to themselves without necessarily needing any foreign 'assistance'.)

Communism accentuated the Romanian-foreign opposition, cutting off the Romanians first of all from the West, and then from the rest of the world. 'Foreignness' took on a mythical dimension, as positive in ordinary Romanians' dreams of prosperity as it was negative in official propaganda. Before Communism, relations with the West had been restricted to an élite with secure reference points (Paris!) and refined tastes. Under Communism, as a result on the one hand of propagandist intoxication and on the other of general dissatisfaction, the imaginary of foreignness was democratized and became a national obsession. Everything foreign was bundled together; even foreign students, most of whom came from Third World countries (including many Arabs, but not from the richer Arab states), appeared with their handfuls of dollars in the guise of messengers from a mysterious and forbidden world. And so the concept became degraded. Romanians were happy when they received 'packages' from abroad, generally assorted items of second-hand clothing (but still better than the shabby and monotonous Communist output). Coffee, cigarettes and soap were other foreign products that were much sought after. For the majority of Romanians – with the exception of a handful of intellectuals of the 'old school' – such bits and pieces (which, it is true, helped make life bearable) came before the essential values of the West.

Since the exit from Communism, contacts with foreignness have become more direct and much more frequent, but there has been no diminution of their dramatic intensity. The Romanians feel pushed aside because of their poverty. Their current state of mind is best defined as frustration, an immense frustration. And thus the West continues both to attract and to repel. There is still a long way to go before the Romanians will be able to regard Westerners with the same detachment (or indifference) with which Westerners regard them. In the meantime, the psycho-drama of foreignness continues.

'Foreigners from outside' are doubled by another category, that of 'foreigners within'. Romania is a country that has had little success in assimilating, or even integrating, its minorities, and indeed it has hardly had the time and the means to do so. How could it assimilate the Hungarians, who not so long ago were a dominant social element? How could it assimilate the Jews, themselves a closed community, and one with a cultural level above the Romanian average? How could it assimilate the Gypsies, who live in a world of their own? Romania is not France! It is not even Hungary, which has integrated its Jews very well and has even managed to assimilate its Germans. The member of a minority has tended to be seen first of all as foreign, before being considered a member of the Romanian nation and a Romanian citizen. This confrontation was particularly acute in the inter-war period, when Romania, having doubled its territory, suddenly found itself with an almost endless collection of minorities. But even today, when the weight of the minorities is smaller and a few steps have been taken in the direction of integration, the member of a minority is not yet considered by the Romanian majority to be truly Romanian. How could one say of a Hungarian that he is Romanian? Or of a Gypsy? The Hungarian is Hungarian and the Gypsy is Gypsy!

Romania is a country encircled by foreigners, and this gives rise to all sorts of complexes and sensitivities.

THE 'BELGIUM OF THE EAST'

The great gamble taken by the Romanians, almost two centuries ago, was their break from the East and their consequent embarkation on a complicated history with uncertain chances of success: the Westernization of a society which in its deeper structures belonged to another type of civilization, and of a country which, at least on the map, belongs to the East!

On the whole, the Romanian élite succeeded up to a point in its aim of copying the Western model in general and the French model in particular.[1] For several generations, France was the Romanians' great love. With the exception of the monarchy, almost the entire political, judicial, administrative and cultural framework had Paris as its main source of inspiration. What would Romania not have given to become a little France of the East! And if that was too ambitious a project, then at least a 'Belgium of the East', to use an expression which appeared frequently towards the end of the nineteenth century. Belgium was a small country, just like Romania, and likewise had a Francophone élite. Its regime was monarchical (in this respect, the Belgian model was more appropriate than the French), and it had an advanced constitution, which the Romanians had imitated, in letter if not very faithfully in spirit; it enjoyed a European status guaranteed by the great powers, and, not least, an economic dynamism and impressive prosperity. (Scarcely visible on the world map, it had become one of the great economic powers of the nineteenth century.) Belgium had all the requisite characteristics to make the Romanians dream. 'Belgium of the East' and 'Little Paris': these two formulations symbolized Romania's desire to be attached to the West, and especially to the Francophone community.

For almost a hundred years, the obligatory road of the Romanian intellectual led to Paris. Until the advent of Communism, French was the language which every Romanian with any degree of culture had to know. (It was studied throughout the seven or eight classes of secondary school.) Cultivated Romanians preferred to read French literature and even read non-French authors in French translation. Not a few of them came to see the world through French eyes, judging the British and the Germans, for example, in a very 'French' manner!

But France was far away! Being farther away than Germany, it relied in Romania on its cultural prestige and on the irresistible (and, as with any great passion, almost inexplicable) attraction which the Romanians felt towards it. Germany, however, had always been much more present in this part of Europe. From the Middle Ages to the nineteenth century, successive waves of German colonists had settled from Hungary, Transylvania and the Baltic shores to Bessarabia, Dobrogea and even the Volga. Commercial relations with the German space had been much closer than with far-off France. With the unification of Germany around Prussia, the project of German expansion toward the East (the traditional *Drang nach Osten*) was renewed with particular energy; on the eve of the First World War, even the Ottoman Empire came into the German sphere of influence. From a sentimental point of view, France enjoyed a more favourable position in Romania, but geopolitical and economic factors were on Germany's side.

The medieval centre of Braşov (in German, Kronstadt). In the foreground is the Gothic-style Black Church, while the Council House is in the centre of the square. This is a typical view of a Saxon town (though nowadays it is predominantly Romanian).

Moreover, the Germans provided the second model invoked by the Romanians after that of France. The intellectual training of the Romanians of Austria-Hungary (Transylvania, the Banat, Bukovina etc.) was of German (Austrian) type, an aspect in which they differed from the Kingdom's Romanian élite. But even within the Romanian state, an influential minority of intellectuals and politicians had more faith in Germany than in France. Such an attitude can be traced in *Junimea*, the cultural association which had the greatest impact on Romanian intellectual life in the last decades of the nineteenth century. The supporters of the German model highlighted the order, rigour and stability which characterized German society; France, on the other hand, was the very image of instability, mingled perhaps with a dose of superficiality. Romania had emerged from its revolutionary phase and now had to quieten down, to settle on secure foundations; from this point of view, the German model seemed more convincing. And the King was German! From 1883 to 1914, Romania was Germany's ally; around 1900, many young Romanians were studying in Germany – fewer than in France, but their number was increasing. In 1864, when the University of Bucharest was

195

founded, sixteen of its professors had been trained in France and only three in Germany; in 1892, 42 were French-trained, compared with eight German-trained. By 1914, the gap had narrowed and the ratio was 62 to 29. France still had the advantage, but Germany was catching up rapidly.

And so it was that the Franco-German duel, the most dramatic manifestation at the time of a divided Europe, was fought out on Romanian territory too. What would have happened if the First World War had not intervened? Germany went to war with mistaken confidence and lost. But for the war, or if it had won the war, its influence in Central and South-eastern Europe would have become predominant; perhaps Romanian intellectuals would have ended up speaking German rather than French!

For almost a century, these two models, French (with its Belgian subsidiary) and German (with its Austrian variant), almost completely filled the Romanians' political and cultural imaginary. Not that the Romanians did not have ideas of a broader Latin solidarity, but in the end this, too, was absorbed by France. Romanians went to Rome to admire Trajan's Column (their birth certificate recorded in stone), but until after the First World War they did not show much inclination to develop special relations with Italy. There was even less interest in Spain, Portugal and Latin America. 'Pan-Latinism' had its attractions for some Romanian intellectuals towards the end of the nineteenth century. As a small Latin country lost in a Slavic sea, such a formula of solidarity would have been to Romania's advantage. But in contrast to pan-Slavism and -Germanism, doctrines which coincided for a time with the projects of two great powers and thus took on a well-defined political sense, 'pan-Latinism' remained a merely sentimental attitude. France, the least Latin of the Latin countries, did not orient its policies according to any such criterion; Italy, frustrated in its relations with France, turned towards the latter's adversaries, Germany and Austria-Hungary; Spain always stood apart; Romania, faced with the Slavic peril, likewise chose to ally itself with Germany and Austria-Hungary. It is true that the First World War saw the Latin countries (with the exception of Spain) fighting on the same side, but this had less to do with sentiment than with interests specific to each country. (The inter-war period and the Second World War were to separate the 'Latins' once again.) The theme of Latin solidarity at one point brought together the Romanians and the Provençals, who, stimulated by the poet Frédéric Mistral and the *Félibrige* movement, were trying to reaffirm their identity. Vasile Alecsandri (1821–1890), the leading Romanian poet of his generation, won a prize at Montpellier in 1878 for his 'Song of the Latin Race': 'The Latin race is queen / among the great races of the world ...' claims the poem; 'She goes at the head of other races, / Pouring light wherever she goes.' The Romanians did indeed believe in the superiority of the Latin genius, not only that of the ancient Romans but also that of their modern heirs. But a poem and a literary prize do not add up to much!

Following the First World War, Germany lost ground in Romania, and France gained ground. All the same, the situation was relative and fluid, since Germany remained a nursery for Romanian intellectuals, and towards the end of the inter-war period the Third Reich was to return in force in the economic, military and political spheres. Moreover, the French cultural model was increasingly counterbalanced by the affirmation of autochthonous values. Italy, too, was gaining ground; something of what Berlin and Vienna had lost went to Rome. (Between the two wars, the Romanian School of Rome was, like the similar institution at Fontenay-aux-Roses, close to Paris, an important centre for training in the human sciences.) The Italian Fascist regime (initially perceived as authoritarian rather than dictatorial) also had its admirers in Romania. As for the Romanian extreme Right – and its most advanced and aggressive embodiment, the Legionary movement – it drew, after a fashion, on a number of foreign models, as well as on indigenous sources. French nationalism, especially Charles Maurras' *Action Française*, Italian Fascism and German Nazism, each made a contribution. But they were combined with a blend of Romanian autochthonism, traditionalism and Orthodoxism. Even if the Legionaries, or Iron Guard, can be seen as having belonged to the 'family' of European fascism, they nevertheless represented a distinctive synthesis. Their Orthodox mysticism differentiated them clearly from the Western variants. (Nazism and Italian fascism manifested independence from, or even hostility towards, the Church.) Their anti-Semitism brought them close to Nazism, but it was the specific anti-Semitism of a traditional society unwilling to accept the leaven of modernity represented by Jews (and foreign elements in general).

If I have not yet mentioned Britain and British culture among the lands and cultures which meant something to Romania, this is because Britain long remained a very distant island for the Romanians. If they got as far as Paris, they rarely went any further. All the same, one or two did manage to cross the English Channel. In 1865, Ion Codru-Drăguşanu (1818–1884), a Transylvanian, published his impressions of travel in a number of European countries under the title *The Transylvanian Pilgrim*. The book includes three 'letters' from London, dated September 1840 and November 1843. Despite being primarily a Francophile (although he reproached the French for their frivolity: a commonly encountered stereotype!), the author was able to appreciate the British: 'Without a doubt Great Britain is the most civilized state in the world.' He likewise admired their seriousness and perseverance (in contrast to the French). France and Britain combined, each after its own fashion, the characteristics of the ancient Greeks and Romans: 'In alliance together, these two nations are destined to lead the world, and for ever to decide on the fate of other peoples.' (More perspicaciously, Tocqueville announced around the same time that the future belonged to America and Russia.) Codru-Drăguşanu admired museums and technological achievements, but was astounded at the large number of bald men (perhaps due to the climate!) and horrified by the violence he encountered at a boxing match. The English language offended his ears: he believed that the shortness of its words made it good for nothing but naval orders![2]

Dimitrie Brătianu (1818–1890), the brother of I. C. Brătianu and a member of the foremost 'political dynasty' that contributed to the construction of modern Romania, also spent a few years in London. In the period after the revolution of 1848, and on the eve of the Union of the Principalities, he represented the Romanians there on the European Democratic Committee founded by Giuseppe Mazzini. Between 1881 and 1890, the post of Romanian Minister Plenipotentiary in London was held by Ion Ghica (1816–1897), one of the most interesting Romanian politicians and intellectuals of the time, and moreover an 'Anglophile', a rare breed in a period filled with Francophiles and occasional Germanophiles.

There were also Britons who travelled in Romania; some even settled there. Among them was a certain Effingham Grant, who

Constantin Daniel Rosenthal, *Revolutionary Romania*, 1850, oil on canvas. Apart from its symbolic meaning and its significance as a portrait of Mary Rosetti, this painting illustrates two elements of peasant costume: the *ie* (a richly embroidered blouse) and the *salbă* (a necklace of gold coins).

worked at the British consulate in Bucharest at the time of the revolution of 1848. Nowadays, he himself may be completely forgotten, but his name is preserved, though no-one makes the connection, in the 'Grant Bridge' that crosses the railway on the site of his former property at the edge of Bucharest. Effingham Grant's sister, Mary

199

(1820–1893), married Constantin A. Rosetti (1816–1885), a leader, alongside I. C. Brătianu, of the Liberal Party, and one of the emblematic figures of modern Romania. Mary Rosetti was an energetic woman who not only supported her husband but was herself prominent in various social and cultural activities (at a time when Romanian women generally limited themselves to the roles of wife and mother). In 1850, the painter Constantin Daniel Rosenthal (1820–1851), by origin a Jew from Hungary but attached to the Romanian cause, painted a symbolic representation of 'Revolutionary Romania'. It shows a beautiful woman with a determined look on her face, dressed in peasant costume with a golden necklace at her throat. In fact, this is a portrait of Mary Rosetti. An Englishwoman, painted by a Hungarian Jew, became the symbol of Romania! It is an amusing anecdote, no less significant for the European spirit of the moment.

These were isolated cases, however. To return to the professors of the University of Bucharest, prior to the First World War none of them had studied in Britain (although a few had studied in countries other than France and Germany: namely Austria, Italy, Russia, Switzerland and Belgium). Few Romanians could read English literature in the original, and even in translation they did not read it very much – with the obvious exception of Shakespeare (perhaps more universal than English!), whose plays were published in a number of editions and endlessly performed in Romanian theatres. I have made a count of the translations published in Romanian periodicals between 1859 and 1918, which illustrates very well the cultural reference points of the period:

COUNTRY	LITERARY HISTORY AND CRITICISM	POETRY	DRAMA	PROSE
FRANCE	1,463	1,726	688	5,438
GERMANY	539	1,576	134	1,001
RUSSIA	552	100	26	1,350
ITALY	428	358	30	595
BRITAIN	420	277	51	408
UNITED STATES	100	81	-	408
AUSTRIA	72	233	8	224
HUNGARY	57	246	14	167
NORWAY	184	18	17	109
SPAIN	95	20	4	101

France, of course, leads by a long way, while Germany is in second place, coming close behind France in the realm of poetry. Russia comes third, largely due to its great novelists. English-language literature (British and American) is in a modest position. If we turn to translations published in book form, English literature, with the exception of Shakespeare, is striking in its absence. Some Romanians read Dickens in French or German (more rarely in the original), but until the First World War only a few of his stories and a single novel in instalments were translated into Romanian; only after the war did his novels appear in book form. As for Thackeray, the Romanians had scarcely heard of him. (By way of comparison, between 1895 and 1918, sixteen works by Balzac and five by Hugo were translated, not to mention the fact that they were also read in the original. The same period also saw the publication of books of tales by the Americans Mark Twain and Edgar Allan Poe.)

In the inter-war period, things moved on a little. Britain had come closer, at least in political and military terms, as a result of the common struggle in the First World War, and in as much as it remained, together with France, one of Romania's principal Western allies. And there was a significant British involvement in the Romanian oil industry. Here and there, English began to be taught in schools (to about the same extent as Italian, and far less than French and German). It was only in 1936 that the University of Bucharest acquired a chair of English language and literature: the first professor, Dragoş Protopopescu (author of the 1936 volume of essays *The English Phenomenon*), was among the first popularizers of British culture. A certain leaning towards Britain began to be apparent among young people of well-off families. Translations multiplied, including the long-overdue works of Dickens, but above all fashionable contemporary writers like Somerset Maugham and A. J. Cronin, whose works appeared in considerable print-runs.

America, too, was far away, but perhaps not as far away as Britain. While Romanian intellectuals were looking towards France and Germany, around 1900 the US was becoming a magnet for the Romanian peasants of Transylvania. About 100,000 Transylvanian Romanians settled on the other side of the Atlantic in the first two decades of the twentieth century. (Their emigration, part of a larger flow out of the Austro-Hungarian Empire, was the only notable Romanian experience of this kind. Prior to Communism, the Romanians – mostly peasants with close ties to the land – were not much tempted to set out into the wider world.) Having worked the land at home, these Transylvanians became unskilled workers in the great factories of the northern US (Cleveland, Detroit etc.), turning into Americans without noticing what was happening to them. Their initial intention was to amass money and return to their villages; however, most of them stayed and formed the nucleus of the principal group of Romanians settled outside the Romanian space.[3]

A second bridge between Romania and America was provided by Hollywood. American films conquered the Romanians in the 1930s; it might be said that this was when they began to hear English spoken, albeit with an American accent. The magazines of the time are full of photographs and news of cinema stars. When war broke out, an additional hardship was the disappearance of American films, which were replaced by German productions (utterly ghastly!) or Italian ones (somewhat more acceptable). At the end of the war, cinema-lovers rejoiced in vain: they expected the return of American movies, but instead they had to put up with a prolonged dose of Soviet cinema. (Western, principally American, films reappeared in the 1960s, but they were carefully selected, and 'unsuitable' sequences were cut.)

The Americans also left the Romanians with two less pleasant memories. First, there were the terrible American (and British) air raids of the war years. Then, there was the illusory 'waiting for the Americans' which kept a ray of hope alive for the opponents of the Communist regime. People end up believing what they want to be true; they could go on believing that 'the Americans were coming' even when the Americans had no intention of doing anything of the kind (although they were not above cynically exploiting this hope in the early 1950s, when they dropped manifestos from aeroplanes, urging the Romanians to resist Russian domination).

BACK TO THE EAST

The reorientation towards the East came as a shock to the Romanian élite (though less so, it has to be said, for the mass of the population, who had never been much involved in the Westernizing process anyway; for those who were only now starting to climb the cultural ladder, there was nothing shocking in Eastern reference points).

For cultivated Romanians, the only reference points for over a century had been Western, in combination, of course, with traditions and values that were considered specifically Romanian. After centuries of religious, cultural and political integration in the Eastern space, the East had suffered a sudden devalorization. A curious hostility towards the Greeks can be traced through almost the whole of the nineteenth century (after the two cultures had been closely bound together in the eighteenth). The Romanians had come to look down on the Bulgarians with a very superior gaze: the neighbours on the other side of the Danube had no aristocracy or intellectual class to compare with those of the Romanians, who liked to observe that Bulgarians came to Bucharest in the same spirit as they themselves went to Paris. As for the Russians, rejection of their civilization was mixed, naturally enough, with a sense of fear. All the more so after the installation of Communism in Russia. The Russians had already repeatedly invaded the Romanian lands; at first, they had been seen as 'saviours', but such salvation was no longer needed. When would the next invasion occur?

As everyone knows, it did occur. Even more abruptly than they had left the East, the Romanians were reintegrated in it. In its first phase, when absolute fidelity to Moscow was the order of the day, the Communist regime embarked on an intense campaign of brainwashing, designed to wipe both Western and national-traditional reference points from the Romanians' minds. Friendship was cultivated with the small 'fraternal countries' in the vicinity (Bulgaria and Hungary), with whom relations had never been very warm, but above all with the Soviet (i.e. Russian) 'big brother'. In Romanian education, the Russian language took the place of French; it was the only compulsory language, taught from the fourth year of primary, and all through secondary, school. But in fact, everyone, not just children but adults too, was encouraged, and often obliged, to learn Russian. The radio broadcast a programme entitled 'Let's Learn Russian by Singing', in which Soviet songs were first sung and then deciphered word by word: this was an artistic, linguistic and political exercise at one and the same time. In the training of élites, there was a change of direction from Paris, Berlin or Rome to Moscow. Battalions of students from all fields (carefully selected according to clearly defined social and political criteria) were sent to study in the homeland of Communism. There, they acquired everything they needed: further qualifications, political convictions and, of course, the Russian language – and a fair number of them returned with Russian spouses too. They were then assigned to key posts in all sectors of activity.

In anticipation of the day when everyone would speak and read Russian, translations from Russian invaded the market. Anything and everything was translated, from the great classics to propaganda brochures, books for children or works of popular science. A book on aviation began with the sentence: 'The aeroplane is a Russian invention.' Everything of any significance in culture, science and technology was the work of Russians: the Romanians had to be convinced of this. But other cultures were not completely sacrificed. I remember reading very good translations of Charles Dickens and Mark Twain in the 1950s. They appeared, in attractive editions, in a collection entitled 'Classics of World Literature'. (It was in the same collection that the complete plays of Shakespeare were published in Romania for the first time.) The 'classics' were skilfully manipulated by the Communist cultural administrators. They represented what was called 'critical-realist' literature and, as such, offered a harsh critique of bourgeois society – and that was fine! On the other hand, almost no contemporary Western literature was translated. However critical it might have been, it was criticizing a society which, of course, looked much better than Communist society. The Romanian reader was meant to retain the impression that bourgeois society was just as Dickens had described it around 1840, and could not be any better!

There was a change of direction in 1964: Russian culture ceased to be superior to others, and the Russian language lost its monopoly, being demoted to the status of a mere option in secondary school, alongside French, English and German (and in fact rapidly falling behind the first two). Translations from Russian became thinner on the ground, while more and more Western literature was translated, including recent books: fiction, history and science (carefully selected, of course, censured where necessary and accompanied by introductory studies which explained to the reader how things ought to be interpreted). A similar evolution could be seen in the theatres and cinemas. As for the training of young Romanians, the road to Moscow was practically abandoned, but roads to the West were not opened very wide either. A restricted number of privileged individuals managed to go to the 'free world' to study. Cultural opening towards the West was only sufficient to attenuate Soviet influence. The model invoked was neither Soviet nor Western: it was the *Romanian model*! The Moscow-trained 'élite' had to pass through some unpleasant moments; having gone straight to the top, they were now regarded with suspicion and removed from sensitive posts. Those with 'Soviet' wives found themselves in an even more delicate situation. From the point of view of the Communist regime, having 'relatives abroad' made one suspect from the start. Initially, this applied to Western relatives, but in the phase of national Communism the concept became generalized: it was no longer good to have relatives anywhere! It is interesting to note that this Russian-trained élite, having been marginalized under Ceauşescu (they were not exactly persecuted, but they considered themselves to be treated unfairly), contributed to the overthrow of the regime and supported the Iliescu version of post-Communism.

The Russian attempt to re-install Romania in the East was partly successful and partly unsuccessful. Where it succeeded beyond reasonable expectations was in the implantation of the Soviet system, which the Romanians are now finding difficult to cast off. Romania is still further from the West than it was when Communism was installed. Thus while the Russians succeeded in Sovietizing Romania, they did not manage to Russify it. Even in the 1950s, when Russian was studied intensively, few Romanians really learned it. Many just 'pretended': it was a sign of non-adherence, a form of passive resistance. Nowadays, with the exception of the survivors of the Muscovite generation, hardly anyone can speak a word of Russian. Even less did the Romanians come to love the Russians; not even Romanian Communists loved them. So Communism had the paradoxical effect of separating Romania from the West without ulti-mately bringing it closer to Russia. At present, too, the Romanians look upon Russia as a rather murky, not very respectable place somewhere to the east (the more so as Romania no longer has a border with Russia but with Ukraine). More prudently, some point out that Russia is still a great power, with which normal and the friendliest possible relations should be cultivated. But this seems to be the Romanians' last concern.

AND BACK TO THE WEST

Since 1989, the Romanians have turned their faces to the West once again. But the idyll is no longer as straightforward as in the nine-teenth century; there is suspicion and reserve on both sides. Moreover, the country's material condition anchors the Romanians in the region to which they belong; 're-Westernization' is progressing hand in hand with 're-orientalization'. Turks, Iraqis and other Eastern people (including Chinese) are quite at home in Romania. Here and there in commercial districts, one is struck by the atmosphere of an Eastern bazaar – different from the solemnity of Communist trade but also from the more discreet and orderly aspect of Western commerce. The Turkish presence has returned in force throughout much of the former Soviet empire, from Romania to Central Asia; having been dismembered bit by bit by the Russians, the Ottoman Empire looks set to be resurrected with a vengeance. The fact that Turkey, a modestly developed country by Western standards, is proving successful in establishing a significant economic presence in a country like Romania (which was appreciably more developed than Turkey before the Communist takeover) demonstrates yet again the real meaning of Communism, and how much has been lost by countries that took the road of state-run economy rather than free enterprise.

As for the West, as a reference point in matters of culture and prestige, America has taken first place. The Americans have been forgiven for the bombing, and for abandoning Romania. They are quite simply the symbol of a free and prosperous world. Of course, there is no unanimity about this: those Romanians who are less attracted by the West opted recently for Serbia against America. But out of all the countries of the world, America is the one that inspires the most admiration. Even everyday life is becoming Americanized in Romania. The films Romanians see in the cinema, on television or on video are American to an overwhelming degree; likewise the music they hear. McDonald's have multiplied at a dizzying rate, while Coca-Cola has become a national drink. There is nothing peculiar in this: it is how the world is today! NATO, the internet and so many other things all point towards America. In an opinion poll in October 1999, a sampling of Romanians were asked 'For which country do you have the highest regard?' Twenty-seven per cent opted for the US. Germany came second with 19 per cent, while France barely made third place with 9 per cent. Next in line came Italy (7), Switzerland (5) and Britain (3).[4]

Among European countries, Germany is well on the way to reconsolidating what was for a long time (with partial eclipses always followed by recovery) its traditional position in Central and South-eastern Europe. However, few members of the Romanian élite are immersed in German culture any longer. Not many speak German (and there are few Germans left in Transylvania). Half-joking, half in earnest, it could be said that there is more Romanian spoken in Germany than German in Romania. In fact, today Germany is home to the largest Romanian community in the West, numbering hundreds of thousands and including Germans who have left Romania. Romanians who set out for Germany are attracted less by German culture than by the opportunities to earn money there; thus Romanian-German relations have a predomi-nantly economic base. When it comes to investment, America is far away; it is predictable that Germany will play the principal role.

Immediately after 1989, French people who went to Romania were astonished and delighted to discover how many people could get by in French. (They no longer knew that Romania had formerly been a great Francophone country; while the Romanians had loved the French, the French – to paraphrase La Rochefoucault – had just let themselves be loved!) Even today, Romania remains the principal bastion of French culture in Europe (except, of course, for Belgium and Switzerland). But this is only a relative position, as French has lost ground everywhere. In 1989, French and English were in more or less equal positions (with French perhaps slightly ahead). Nowadays, English has overtaken French by a long way; more and more young people can express themselves in English but do not know French at all. Some still study in France, however, just as plenty of 'nostalgic' intellectuals still look towards Paris. The economic presence of France in Romania is also relatively strong. But the sentimental connection is no longer what it was: France, for the Romanians, is now just a 'normal' country again. The old France, once loved with passion, belongs to the Romania of the past.

The Romanians can get along better with the British nowadays, thanks to the English language. In fact, English has a strong presence because of America, not because of Britain. Relations are closer than before, since the world is a smaller place, and the network of contacts is everywhere denser. But comparatively speaking, the two countries remain far apart. Britain is an island at one end of the continent, while Romania is, in its own way, an 'island' at the other.

In the nineteenth century, and also in the inter-war period, Romania had one of Europe's largest Jewish communities. Between the wars, its Jewish population was the third largest in Europe both in absolute terms (after Poland and the USSR) and as a proportion of the total population (after Poland and Hungary). In 1930, the number of Jews was calculated at 728,115 by nationality and 756,930 by religion, signifying 4.0 and 4.2 per cent of the population respectively. Today, only some 9,000 are left. While it could be said that the history of the Jews in Romania is almost over, it is still a history that arouses passion and resentment.

Extreme interpretations present two completely opposite faces of Romania. Some (but not all) Jewish authors consider that Romania has always been a fundamentally anti-Semitic society in which overt outbreaks can be traced back to the Middle Ages; evidence for this lies in the fact that nowhere in Europe was the right of Jews to citizenship recognized so late (only after the First World War).[5] This hostility reached the point of paroxysm in the violent anti-Semitism of the Legionaries and the Antonescu regime; after Hitler, Marshal Antonescu directed the most thorough campaign of extermination (albeit more hesitant than the Nazi 'final solution', and never brought to completion). Even today, in a Romania almost without Jews, anti-Semitism is said to persist to an alarming degree, in explicit or latent forms. In other words, the Romanians are not fully cured of it.

Most Romanians, on the other hand, will not hear of such accusations. Romanians, they say, have never been anti-Semitic! They are by nature very understanding with foreigners, including Jews. The latter can hardly complain that they did not get on well in Romania; if things were so bad, they would not have settled and remained for generations. Antonescu did not exterminate the Jews; he actually saved the greater number of them, refusing to implement Hitler's 'final solution'. Also, the Jews did not behave well towards the Romanians in welcoming the Soviet invaders and then occupying high positions during the most repressive phase of Communism.

Reality, as always, is more complex. It is impossible to deny that the Romanians have shown an inclination towards anti-Semitism. This must, of course, be seen in the context of a European Christian civilization in which the treatment of Jews as foreigners was imprinted on the collective imaginary. For centuries, Jews were the most pronounced figures of alterity, of the 'other', in European culture. In the case of Romania, certain relevant factors may be noted. In the nineteenth century, the number of resident Jews increased rapidly, most of them coming from Galicia and, later, from Russia; smaller numbers came from south of the Danube, from the Ottoman Empire. They settled especially in the towns, above all in the towns of Moldavia (in some of which they came to be in the majority). Around 1930, Jews represented 14.3 per cent of Romania's urban population but only 1.6 per cent of its rural population, with the majority concentrated in the north and north-east; more than two-thirds lived in Bessarabia, Moldavia, Bukovina and Maramureş. As with any massive population influx, it is only natural that this would have created tensions. Furthermore, Romanian nationalism, including anti-Semitism, was strongly motivated by economic factors. The Romanians, most of whom were peasants or boyars, closely bound to the land and to traditional activities, have never excelled in economic and commercial pursuits. Numerous foreigners – not just Jews but also Germans, Greeks and Armenians – occupied this sector, thus inspiring a sort of inferiority complex on the Romanians' part. The presence of Jews was particularly evident in commerce. In fact, Jewish society was itself highly polarized: while there were a number of rich Jews – bankers, merchants and industrialists – there were also plenty of Jews living in precarious circumstances in poor districts. In terms of educational attainment, they tended, on average, to do better than Romanians; there were many Jews in the liberal professions: doctors, lawyers, journalists etc.

It is beyond doubt that the Legionaries killed Jews, as did Antonescu's regime. However, only the Jews of Bessarabia and Bukovina, accused by the regime of siding with the Soviet occupiers in 1940, were actually subjected to exterminatory treatment. Almost all of them were deported beyond the Dniester, to 'Transnistria', the territory controlled by the Romanian army between 1941 and 1944. Although there were a number of summary executions, most died as a result of the hardships they suffered in camps. The number of dead can be estimated at between 110,000 and 120,000 (assuming that some 100,000 had managed to escape to the Soviet Union with the retreating Red Army). The Romanian authorities were also responsible for the disappearance of a large number of 'non-Romanian' Jews who had previously been living in Transnistria (these also were massacred or died in camps). In the rest of Romania, there was a single major bloody episode (after the Legionary murders of January 1941, in which 120 Jews died in Bucharest), namely the pogrom in Iaşi at the end of June 1941; based on documentary evidence, the number of Jews killed on that occasion was at least around 3,000. Otherwise, the Romanian authorities, perhaps after some hesitation, refused to apply the 'final solution' which the Germans were calling for.[6]

Jews were nonetheless subjected to all sorts of persecution in the context of a large-scale policy of 'Romanianization': their property was confiscated, they were excluded from schools and universities etc. They were not sent to the front (being thought unworthy to die for Romania), but they were forced to do compulsory labour, more humiliating than useful (such as clearing snow from the streets), and to pay duties in kind (for example, by giving up articles of clothing). Worst of all was the fact that they lived in fear for years: anything could happen to them. The recently published *Journal* of the Jewish Romanian writer Mihail Sebastian (1907–1945), an exceptional document for these years, highlights the trauma experienced by people who had previously considered themselves to be integrated and now found themselves abandoned or treated with condescension even by old friends.[7] But the fact remains that these Jews survived. Finally, the fate of the Jews of Northern Transylvania, which had been ceded to Hungary in 1940, must be mentioned. Deported to Auschwitz in 1944, most of them died there, some hundred thousand people in all. In their case, however, it was the Hungarian and German authorities who were responsible, not the Romanian government.

These are the facts and figures. The Antonescu regime exterminated rather more than 100,000; Romanian Jews and 'saved' some 300,000; in strictly arithmetical terms, the merit would thus be three times greater than the guilt! But killing is a crime, while there is no merit in not killing. On the other hand, Antonescu cannot be isolated from the troubled context of his time – an age dominated by discrimination, hatred and violence. Dresden and Hiroshima were hardly noble acts either, not to mention the millions of victims of Hitler and Stalin. There is no doubt that Romanians regard Antonescu differently from the way Jews regard him. The Marshal led the Romanians in the war to make the country whole again and fell victim to Communism. So not everything favourable said about him today necessarily implies an anti-Semitic or anti-democratic attitude, although such attitudes are characteristic of those (relatively few in number) who keep alive a veritable cult of the Marshal.

Another sensitive point concerns the role played by Jews in the early years of Communism. Around 1950, they were prominent in both the Party leadership and the *Securitate*. But this, too, has a historical explanation. First, in the small Communist Party of 1944, Romanians were in the minority and Jews were numerous. Even after the Party multiplied its ranks and became predominantly Romanian, the restricted circle of its leaders and of faithful Communists was slower to be Romanianized. Such a 'cosmo-politian' leadership also suited the Soviets initially, in as much as it was a way of striking at Romanian national tradition. Not only Jews but also Hungarians and other nationalities held sensitive posts in the apparatus of politics, propaganda and repression. After 1944, many Jews had embraced Communism since occupation by the Soviet army meant the long-awaited liberation. What reasons did they have to reject the Soviets and the system they brought, when 'traditional' Romania had come close to wiping them out? By supporting the Communist regime, they were, in a sense, getting their own back for what the Antonescu regime had done.

This argument should not be taken too far, however. There were also Jews who were persecuted by the Communists, driven to emigrate or thrown into prison, just as there were also – whatever anyone says! – a great many Romanians who supported Communism, starting with the head of the Party himself, Gheorghe Gheorghiu-Dej. To present Gheorghiu-Dej as a 'good man' who had no choice in the face of Russian pressure from outside and Jewish pressure from within, in contrast with his Jewish colleague and rival Ana Pauker, is not the most honest of approaches. Both leaders had their share of the responsibility for setting Romania on the road of Stalinist Communism (along with many others). And indeed, the Jews became disenchanted with Communism quickly enough. Already in the 1950s, they began to emigrate, leaving the Romanians to create a particular brand of national Communism for themselves.

As for contemporary anti-Semitism, I believe that it seems more of an issue when seen from the West than it actually is. Ultra-nation-alists (like those of the 'Greater Romania' faction) target Jews, especially to display their hostility to international 'high finance' and the West in general. But their 'favourite' enemies are still

Hungarians and Gypsies. There are Western commentators who believe that they can detect a 'potential' anti-Semitism in the remarks of certain intellectuals regarding recent Romanian history. What the West, which suffered the effects of Nazism and other forms of fascism, does not understand very well is that for the Romanians, the great drama was Communism, and in this respect their pains differ from those of the Jews.

Nowadays, relations between Romanians and Jews are as good as they could be, having largely been cleared of former prejudices. In Israel, and all over the world, there are numerous Jews who speak Romanian and feel attached to Romania; from time to time, they return to their country of origin. There is also an Israeli literature in Romanian. Romanians, too, travel to Israel, and many of them find work there (often in far from favourable conditions – but that is another problem, one that reflects the Romanians' status in the world in general).

In losing Romania's Jews, the Romanians lost, without realizing it, not only economic ferment (now, when the economy is scarcely moving, they have every reason to think nostalgically of the Jews and Germans who have left) but also part of the Romanian soul. It was not only ethnic Romanians that created Romania and Romanian culture: Jews also contributed a significant dose of nonconformism, together with intellectual curiosity and flexibility. Some of the most important researchers into Romanian language and folkore (the purest areas of 'Romanianism') were Jews, for example: Lazăr Şăineanu (1859–1934), author of a classic work on the oriental elements in Romanian language and culture, who worked first in Romania and then in France; H. Tiktin (1850–1936), author of the first systematic Romanian grammar and of a highly regarded Romanian-German dictionary; and Moses Gaster (1856–1939), who was particularly preoccupied by Romanian folk literature (he settled in London, where from 1887 he was Chief Rabbi of the Sephardic community). Jewish writers also made important contributions to inter-war Romanian literature, tackling a wide variety of subjects and literary forms, from the evocation of picturesque Jewish districts (now vanished) to science fiction, Dadaism and surrealism. (I shall return to these contributions in Chapter VII.)

Resentments between Romanians and Hungarians feed on a twofold frustration. Until 1918, the Romanians of Transylvania were generally looked down on by the Hungarians. They were largely peasants, with few townspeople and intellectuals among them, while Hungarians made up the ruling class. After 1918, the roles were reversed. Moreover, the Hungarians are concerned at their ongoing decline in the Transylvanian population. At the beginning of the century, Hungarian speakers constituted almost a third; now they are less than a quarter. Then, they were in the majority in the towns; now, they are in the minority even there.

The central square of Cluj in the inter-war period. The city was then still predominantly Hungarian. In front of the 14th-century Gothic Church of St Michael is the equestrian statue of King Matthias Corvinus, Hungary's greatest king. The 'she-wolf' monument set up by the Romanians – a symbol of Latinity – somewhat attenuated the scene's Hungarian character. Although the she-wolf is no longer there, the city has become predominantly Romanian. Excavations have been carried out in the square that have brought to light the remains of the Daco-Roman town of Napoca, which preceded the Hungarian city. In the time of Ceauşescu, the name of Cluj (in Hungarian, Kolzsvár) was expanded to Cluj-Napoca.

213

Greater Hungary had tried to include the Transylvanian Romanians in the Hungarian nation. However, the Romanians remained Romanian, preferring Bucharest to Budapest. Now, the situation is somewhat similar for the Hungarians. To which nation do they belong? They now look towards Budapest as the Romanians once looked towards Bucharest. Their project is to gain as many concessions as they can in linguistic, cultural and administrative matters within the context of a political system as decentralized as possible – exactly the opposite of the Romanian tradition of centralization and the 'unitary national-state'. At least in the present context, there can be no question of autonomy for Transylvania (where the Hungarians would have a greater weight than they have in Romania as a whole). Even autonomy for the two Hungarian-majority counties in eastern Transylvania would not be accepted by the Romanians – nor would it be completely favourable to the Hungarians, whom it would divide. So the Hungarians' demand is for an enhanced degree of administrative decentralization, coupled with the official use of the Hungarian language alongside Romanian in areas where they make up a significant proportion of the population.

The problem of a Hungarian university has proved to be a thorny one (and is unresolved). Hungarians enjoy a complete system of pre-university education, but feel that since they pay taxes like the rest of the population, they are entitled to their own state university. The Romanians do not look kindly on the idea. Such a university would put in question the very philosophy of the 'national state'; Romanian opinion is that it would end in the creation of a sort of cultural apartheid. The compromise solution currently being tried (but without much conviction!) is a multicultural university, with classes taught in Hungarian and German, as well as in Romanian.

The feeling of many Romanians is that the Hungarian leaders are preoccupied exclusively with their own problems rather than those of the country as a whole, and that if present demands are met, they will be followed by an endless succession of others. The Hungarians of Romania and their fellows in Hungary are seen as having worrying intentions where Transylvania is concerned. As in Romania, there are extremist nationalists in Hungary too; now and then, voices are heard talking of Greater Hungary, or bemoaning the plight of the Hungarians who live outside the country's borders. However, all of this has been much exaggerated by Romanian nationalists, as it was at certain moments by the pre-1996 governments (for whom the 'Hungarian peril' proved to be an efficient election slogan). Some find it suspicious that Hungarian businesses prefer to invest their money in Transylvania, instead of crossing the mountains into the other Romanian regions. What is certain is that Hungary is 'attractive', not only to Transylvanian Hungarians but also to plenty of Romanians along the western border. The explanation is simple: Hungary seems to be doing better than Romania in every respect.

All the same, political relations between Romania and Hungary are generally good. A Romanian-Hungarian reconciliation on the Franco-German model is in sight; there is still a long way to go, but a few steps have been taken. The tendency is towards resolution, not conflict. Europe can rest easy: Transylvania is not, and is in no danger of becoming, a Bosnia or a Kosovo. European integration will resolve many things. As borders become more abstract, the Hungarians of Transylvania and those of Hungary will find themselves much closer together, without Romanian unity being threatened. If the European project succeeds, the problem of minorities will also be resolved.

THE GYPSIES

Nowadays, the Romanians' principal obsession is the Gypsies,[8] who make the Romanians feel as if they are living in a castle under siege. Almost all crimes are attributed to Gypsies, whose population seems to be rising every day. Although the figure given by the 1992 census is not a spectacular one – 409,723, or 1.8 per cent of the population – the number is misleading, since many Gypsies were recorded as Romanians. Their real number is certainly higher. But they are even more numerous in the collective imaginary than they are in reality. There is talk of a million, two million or even three million (in other words, more than one in ten of the total population of Romania). While Romanians are having fewer and fewer children, the Gypsies are having many. They continue to show Third World demographic behaviour, compared with the European behaviour of the rest of the population. What will happen? Some say that Gypsies will be in the majority in 50 years' time.

Originally, the Gypsies came from the direction of India, and their presence in the Romanian lands was first recorded in the fourteenth century. They were divided from the Romanians not only by their 'race' but also by their social condition. For centuries, they were slaves, working on the estates of princes, boyars and monasteries. Their emancipation occurred in Wallachia and Moldavia towards the middle of the nineteenth century (shortly before the liberation of the Black slaves in America). Once they were free, many Gypsies remained in villages, but in districts of their own, where they did not mix with Romanians. Others went to the towns, where they are likewise generally concentrated in certain districts. Nomadic Gypsies have almost disappeared. The Romanians' impression is that Gypsies do not work, living instead by stealing or begging. In fact, some are skilled craftsmen with a tradition of fine work in iron, wood and gold. At least no-one denies that they are born musicians. Fiddlers are by definition Gypsies, and Gypsy music is an important element of the artistic sensibility of this part of Europe.

The Gypsies are the most widespread minority in Romania, being more or less evenly distributed throughout the country. Despite the generic name used to designate them, they are also the most heterogeneous minority. They think of themselves as a diverse ethnic group divided into subgroups. They also vary greatly in terms of integration: many remain exclusively within their own community, in an archipelago of Gypsy 'islands', while others are integrated to varying degrees, and some are even assimilated. 'Authentic' Gypsies speak their own language and have maintained their customs and laws. 'Gypsy justice' still operates, in parallel with the law of the land. In a republican Romania, Gypsies have remained monarchists after their own fashion: they have a 'king', and also an 'emperor'. The majority live in poverty. Many of their children do not go to school, or do not complete their schooling; abandoned children and 'street children' are more often than not Gypsies. But a Gypsy bourgeoisie or aristocracy has also emerged. Being by nature reluctant to accept constraints, the Gypsies have shown more 'economic imagination' than the Romanians since 1989. Some have become rich, often by less than orthodox means (this could be said, of course, of plenty of the wealth in Romania). The 'Gypsy mafia' regularly features in the mass media, in connection with kidnapping, fighting, prostitution and so on.

Gypsy 'palaces' have been built almost all over the country; they are not exactly palaces, but large, striking houses with countless turrets: a kitsch synthesis in which Disneyland meets the Far East. A traveller approaching the town of Strehaia from Craiova, the capital

Traditional Gypsy woman and child in the slums.

Another sort of Gypsy, outside her 'palace'.

of Oltenia, for example, will enter the town through an entire district of such palaces. The Romanian district on the other side, by contrast, has people crowded into sordid blocks of flats. Here, the Gypsies are rich and the Romanians are poor. The Gypsy men do not attract attention by any specific costume, but the women still dress in their traditional wide multicoloured skirts. The maids who work in the Gypsy 'palaces' are evidently Romanian. For Romanians, this is an upside-down world.

While it is certainly abusive to imply an equivalence between 'Gypsy' and 'criminal', it is no less true to say that Gypsies live in a world of their own, in which the constraints imposed by modern society have not yet made themselves felt. In recent years, Gypsy intellectuals and politicians have emerged – there is a Roma Party with representation in the Romanian parliament. Their mission is not an easy one: on the one hand, they have to convince their own community of the necessity of respecting certain rules, and on the other, they must convince the Romanians that they need to show more goodwill towards the Gypsies.

When Gypsies want to leave the country, they go without troubling much about visas, as Romanians have to do. Wherever you go in the West, you will meet Romanian Gypsies; the Romanians might be expected to be delighted that at least some Gypsies are leaving the country, but they tend not to be, as they consider that wherever

218

Gypsies go they make a laughing stock of Romania. A well-known anecdote tells how Romanian Gypsies ate the swans in the lake of Schönbrunn Palace near Vienna. Their recent presence in London did not go unobserved as they exercised their traditional practice of begging.

The Romanians are very offended by the assimilation, current in the West, of the terms *Romanian* and *Gypsy*. Although Gypsies who leave Romania are Romanians, at least according to their passports, Romanians are unable to understand how someone who is not ethnically and culturally Romanian can nevertheless be considered to be so. Another matter irritates Romanians intensely. As the word *Ţigan* ('Gypsy') has come to be pejorative, Gypsies insist on being called by the name they use themselves, *Romi* ('Roma'). 'Roma' is uncomfortably similar to 'Romanian', although the two words have quite different origins. How can foreigners be expected to make such fine distinctions? What is amusing is that in the time of Ceauşescu, the Romanians campaigned – thinking of their ancient Roman origins – for the English spellings 'Rumania' and 'Rumanian' to be changed to 'Romania' and 'Romanian'. And they almost completely succeeded in imposing this modification on the English language (although not on French and German). Now, they are having second thoughts, but what can they do?

There have also been bloody confrontations between Romanians and Gypsies. In a village, a Gypsy kills a Romanian. The indignant villagers fall on the whole Gypsy community. Houses are set on fire, and people burn to death. Even if such episodes are few and far between, they constitute danger signals. The only solution is acceptance and integration. There is a need for goodwill, imagination and perseverance on both sides.

THE ROMANIANS AMONG THEMSELVES

The Romanians like to think that they have certain features in common, a combination of qualities, and perhaps defects, that is specifically Romanian. They are ready to confess to a lack of discipline, perseverance and organizational spirit on condition that they are recognized as people with an intellectual coefficient probably superior to others. If they have not been able to produce something better out of such resources, the fault is partly their own (being less hardworking than they are intelligent), but mostly the fault of 'others'. Some interpretations see in Romanian spirituality, with its openness to the boundlessness of the cosmos and the great questions of existence, a synthesis superior to the positive and technological spirit of the West. (Such haughty interpretations were expressed by the philosophers Lucian Blaga, in his 1936 book *The Mioritic Space*, and Constantin Noica, in his 1978 work *The Romanian Sentiment of Being*.) If 'others' are more efficient, Romanians are more profound, subtle and sensitive.

Romanians are much inclined to meditate on their identity and that of others. The 'national specific' has preoccupied the theoreticians of Romanian culture for decades. The 'psychology of peoples', a rather suspect science, all the rage in the nineteenth century but generally abandoned nowadays, cast its spell on many Romanian authors and is not yet completely forgotten in Romanian intellectual exercises. The question 'What are we like?' is an obsessing one which in its very insistency reflects an insufficiency rather than a surfeit of national specificity. Having come together relatively recently in a single nation, and having borrowed so much from others, the Romanians have continually been in search of arguments to underline their personality. The Romanian village, as the repository of the national soul, in contrast to the cosmopolitan town, became the principal reference point in this quest. But what happens nowadays, when most Romanians are no longer peasants? In fact, folklore was made use of everywhere when the nations of Europe were taking shape, as a way of highlighting the specific genius of each one (generally an adapted folklore, if not actually an invented one, as in the classic case of the poems of Ossian). Folklore was obliged to demonstrate a sort of national unity, a task for which it had no vocation. It is beyond dispute that Romanian folklore is among the richest and best preserved in all of Europe. But 'Romanian folklore' is a generic term covering all sorts of local variations. Folk costume, the peasant house and homestead, customs and beliefs differ from one zone to another. There are, of course, similarities between zones, but there are also similarities with the folklore of neighbouring peoples, especially with the Balkan cultural area. The idea of an elementary Romanianism concentrated in folklore and symbolized by the peasant is mythological. It is not traditional folklore but the ideology of the modern nation that gave unity to the Romanian space (and to all other national spaces).

Romanians do not just differ from foreigners but also among

themselves. Here, too, we come across stereotypes which generally serve to delimit the country's three main regions. The Muntenians are considered to be lively, the Transylvanians slow moving, the Moldavians contemplative. Anecdotes about Transylvanians play on a certain difficulty in understanding and acting rapidly (this is, of course, Transylvania as seen from Bucharest). Those about Oltenians centre on an overturning of values, on out-of-the-ordinary solutions; Oltenia is the most rural part of Romania, and although it has long been attached to Muntenia, it preserves a distinct individuality. Along with the Banat and Bukovina, Transylvania is considered to be the most civilized part of the country – the result of German influence, in contrast to the Balkan and Turkish influences on the other side of the mountains!

The classic antithesis, however, as expressed not only in elementary stereotypes but also in various theoretical attempts to define the national spirit, is that between Muntenia and Moldavia. E. Lovinescu, one of the foremost Romanian critics and literary historians and a theoretician of culture, saw these distinctions in immutable 'racial' terms (in his work of 1924–5, *History of Modern Romanian Civilization*). According to Lovinescu, the Moldavians were 'by virtue of their contemplative character inclined to poetic creation', while 'through their mobile, comprehensive and practical nature, the Muntenians have directed their activity more towards the political and economic fields'.[9] It is a fact that the Moldavians produced the largest contingent of writers and artists, and even of scholars, especially in the nineteenth century. Iaşi was then a sort of Athens of Romania; however, the excessive centralization of the country subsequently led to the decline of Iaşi in favour of Bucharest, which absorbed most of the nation's energies and values. As for the political class, even if we cannot talk of actual discrimination, Muntenia clearly played the leading role (and continued to do so in the inter-war period, to the annoyance of the Transylvanians, who felt – and probably still feel – somewhat out of place in what they considered to be the excessively Balkan environment of Bucharest). Economically, too, Moldavia has fallen behind both Muntenia and Transylvania (with the result that an internal migratory flow has developed from there to the other regions).

For ideological reasons, there has been much insistence on unity in Romania. But what is striking is precisely the diversity of the country, of its places and people. There is no typical Romanian landscape, nor is there a typical Romanian. It is true that urbanization, and even more the uniformizing project of Communism, have progressively reduced this diversity. But anyone who passes from Muntenia to Transylvania, or vice versa, will be conscious of having also crossed a border between zones of civilization. If differences are considerable between regions, they are even greater, indeed disturbingly great, between social environments (in spite of the levelling attempted by Communism). The villages remain far behind the towns (even if the towns do not look so great either). The Western traveller will be surprised to see how people still draw their water from wells or drive horse-drawn carts on unmetalled roads of dust and mud. But there is also an appreciable hierarchy among the towns. Anyone who travels from Bucharest to a provincial town is likely to change their opinion of Bucharest for the better; for all its disadvantages, life in the capital is still rather more comfortable. Another problem is that of the peripheries, which present a demoralizing appearance, whether they are old, semi-urban districts or the famous new districts of blocks of flats, now looking the worse for wear after only two or three decades of existence.

Since 1989, social and above all financial inequalities have taken on disturbing proportions. The problem is not the emergence of very rich people, but the fact that the number of poor people has increased, and that they have become poorer. Romania remains the prisoner of an oriental model (or its own traditional model), in which social discrepancies are very great. In these circumstances, 'national unity' is more a matter of discourse than of real life. The Romanians are proud of their intellectuals and of the cultural values which they have produced. And this pride is substantially justified: Romanian intellectuals (excluding a type of 'pseudo-intellectual' created by Communism) are certainly closer to Western intellectuals than Romania as a whole is to the West. There is probably no other European country where the difference between the top and bottom levels is so great. This is why, in spite of its relative intellectual achievements, Romania is placed at the bottom of European statistical tables, below even some Balkan countries which do not have its intellectual tradition. Statistics do not measure intellectual life! From a social point of view, Romania is a dismembered country, in which Romanians seem foreign to other Romanians.

The Romanians who are most different are the Bessarabians. They themselves say that they are Moldovans; the Romanians cannot see how the Bessarabians could be anything other than Romanian. They belonged first to Moldavia and then to Romania, and they speak Romanian: thus they are Romanian by birth. However, such an interpretation implies the overvaluing of certain factors (language and history) at the expense of others. What counts in the first place in any national construction is the desire to be: to be (or not to be) Romanian or Moldovan. The term *Moldovan* (which in Romanian refers to Moldavians in general) can be a cause of confusion; Moldavians west of the Prut are a constituent part of the Romanian nation, just as Muntenians and Transylvanians are, while those east of the Prut still have to clarify what they are for themselves.

At the time of the break-up of the Soviet Union, the Republic of Moldova seemed ready to throw itself into the arms of Romania. The Romanian language (not 'Moldavian' as it had been called in the Soviet period) was declared the state language, and even the colours of the Romanian flag – red, yellow and blue – were adopted. Then, the atmosphere became cooler. Only a minority openly expressed the desire to unite with Romania, and a referendum approved Moldova's existence as an independent state. It does not seem to be a country based on very solid foundations, but it is not the only such case in this part of Europe (consider Bosnia, for example). The fact is that Moldova does not resemble Romania. The Russo-Ukrainian minority (a third of the population) give it a distinctive profile. (And the proportion of Russian speakers is even higher in the strip of land beyond the Dniester — Transnistria – which separated itself *de facto* from Moldova after a short military conflict and which is unlikely to accept re-integration except on the basis of autonomy; here, there can certainly be no question of union with Romania!) But the Romanians of Bessarabia are also different. The cultural level is lower than in Romania, and the Russian stamp is still strong; the old Romanian élite either took refuge in Romania after the cession of Bessarabia or was wiped out by the Soviets. Romania has concluded treaties with both Ukraine and Moldova, thus recognizing the new political configurations and the existing borders. Romanian nationalists have protested: how can territorial dismemberment be acknowledged, especially Moldova's existence as a state? In the meantime, of course, there are two Romanian states, or, more correctly, a Romania and a Moldova.

More remote relatives of the Romanians can be found in the Balkans, at an appreciable distance from the country's southern border – the last survivors of what was once Balkan Romanity. As well as the Romanian language itself, known also to linguists as 'Daco-Romanian', there are another three dialects of Romanian: Istro-Romanian, which continues to be spoken only in a handful of villages on the Istrian peninsula; Megl600-Romanian, spoken by some 15,000 people north of Salonika; and Aromanian or Macedo-Romanian, which is used by a rather larger community, perhaps some four hundred thousand people.[10] For linguists, there is no doubt about the similarity of these dialects to Romanian, but it is less evident in everyday speech; a Romanian and an Aromanian speaking their own dialects would not understand each other. About half of the Aromanians are scattered across Greece (especially in the Pindos mountains), and the remainder live in Albania, Macedonia and south-western Bulgaria. Their traditional occupations are cattle rearing and commerce. Around 1900, with active support from Romania, they had schools in their own language, but these no longer exist. At that time, they played an important role in Romania's Balkan policy, serving as something of a exchange token in 1913, when Romania obtained the Quadrilateral while the Aromanians, who lived far from Romania's borders anyway, were incorporated within the other Balkan states. Many Aromanians migrated to Romania, especially to Dobrogea. Perceived by the Romanians as very enterprising and persevering, they have displayed their qualities above all in commerce, but have also contributed some important names to the country's intellectual life. The Balkan states practically deny the existence of an Aromanian minority, which is now on its way to losing its identity. (Officially, the Aromanians have already lost it, as they are not counted in censuses, which also makes it difficult to estimate their number.) Indeed, the existence of the Romanians who live in the north of the Balkan peninsula, immediately south of the Danube, in Bulgaria and especially in Yugoslavia (in the Timoc valley) is not recognized either.

How many Romanians are there in the world today? Answers vary. In Romania, there are some 20 million ethnic Romanians (possibly slightly fewer: it depends how the Gypsies are counted). In addition, there are almost 3 million Bessarabians (Moldovans). Almost 500,000 Romanians are recorded in Ukraine (in the ceded parts of Bessarabia and Bukovina, but also beyond the Dniester and in the Ukrainian part of Maramureş). In Hungary, there are only some 10,000 left according to official figures (20,000 according to other estimates), and there are another 40,000 in Voivodina (Serbia). In the Balkans, as I have explained, it is hard to say. Then there are hundreds of thousands in Western Europe, and further hundreds of thousands in America (although those who have been settled there for several generations are not so much Romanians as Americans of Romanian origin). I do not believe that the total number can be much over 25 million – and in fact, on top of the statistics there is also a problem of identity: not all Bessarabians, Aromanians or American Romanians would include themselves in a Romanian identity. But even statistics can be approached in a nationalist spirit: in spite of their apparent rigour, they are very dependent on ideology. And thus the number of Romanians expands – in the imaginary – to 30 or even 35 million! What is certain is that they have begun to spread through the world. It is now a common thing to hear Romanian spoken in the streets of Western cities. In the past, foreigners came to Romania, while the Romanians stayed at home. Now, not so many foreigners come, but the Romanians have started to leave.

VII Who's Who in the Romanian Pantheon

DRACULA

The most famous Romanian of all is Count Dracula.[1] Only Ceauşescu can claim a place alongside him. There are foreigners who know nothing about Romania, but who at least know these two names. For them, the Dracula-Ceauşescu duo seems the most concentrated expression of the Romanian pantheon. Two dark legends mirror each other across the centuries, reinforcing one another. This selection is less than advantageous for the Romanians; while it may render the country attractive to enthusiasts of the weird and wonderful, it casts a disturbing cloud over it. The land of Dracula, the land of Ceauşescu: is it not all a bit much?

In the case of Ceauşescu, the Romanians cannot escape responsibility: they produced him, and, even worse, they put up with him. But they are not to blame for Dracula; the responsibility for Dracula is British. Written into existence in 1897 by Bram Stoker, Dracula went on to enjoy an extraordinary career, particularly in the cinema. His name is a byword all over the world; he has entered the cultural treasury of humanity. Having discovered him more recently, the Romanians have every reason to be surprised that something like this could happen in their own backyard without their being aware of it.

In fact, the protagonist of Stoker's novel is not even Romanian; he belongs to the Szekler community, a Hungarian-speaking population in eastern Transylvania (who nowadays consider themselves to be simply Hungarian). But this does not prevent him from claiming kinship with a medieval Romanian *voivode*. Vlad Ţepeş, whose principal reign in Wallachia extended from 1456 to 1462, was indeed known, not so much to his compatriots as to foreigners, as Dracula. The name was inherited from his father, Vlad Dracul, who had been honoured with the Order of the Dragon by Sigismund of Luxemburg, King of Hungary and German Emperor. The Romanian word *drac* is the result of an interesting semantic evolution; it comes

The most famous portrait of Vlad Țepeș, alias Dracula: an anonymous 16th-century oil in Schloss Ambras, Innsbruck.

from the Latin *draco*, which indeed means 'serpent' or 'dragon', but in Romanian it has come to signify 'devil'. *Dracul*, 'the devil', is Satan. Thus Vlad Dracul and his son Vlad Țepeș, also known as Dracula, make us think of the Evil One himself.

And indeed, Vlad Țepeș did everything in his power to justify such an association. His cruelty was quite out of the ordinary, and he liked nothing so much as impaling people on stakes, whence his nickname *Țepeș*, 'the Impaler'. (Contemporary woodcuts show him sitting down to dinner in the shade of a 'forest' of stakes.) These monstrosities are recounted in a number of German chronicles and, in a somewhat attenuated form, in a Slavonic chronicle. The Germans of southern Transylvania, the burghers of Sibiu and Brașov (German towns in the Middle Ages, and until recently still known as Hermannstadt and Kronstadt), had no grounds for being sympathetic towards Vlad Țepeș; he had repeatedly attacked them, laying waste their settlements and slaying their people by the score. Thus

Vlad Țepeș dining in the shade of a forest of stakes, in a German engraving of 1500.

the German accounts may not be completely objective, and it is possible that they somewhat amplify the Prince's perverse behaviour. However, historical figures do not live in our memory just as they really were but as they were perceived to be, and have been adapted, distorted or recreated. Regardless of the accuracy of the accounts, this is the Vlad Țepeș we are left with! Of all the medieval

Romanian princes, he was the most talked about on a European level, thanks to his morbid fantasies – just like Ceauşescu half a millennium later. Extraordinary deeds, whether good or bad, confer celebrity, and it may even be that evil-doers arouse more interest than saints, human nature being what it is – Dante's *Inferno* is more convincing than his *Paradise*! Vlad Ţepeş was also the most 'depicted' of Romanian princes. The portrait that presents him in all his splendour can be seen at Ambras Castle in Innsbruck: not by chance, it is displayed in a gallery reserved for monsters, along with a 'wolf-man' and other such images.

Bram Stoker borrowed from Ţepeş first of all the 'nickname' Dracula, then a few features from the Ambras Castle portrait (the long moustache, the thin, hooked nose) and finally, though in a quite different register, the thirst for blood. But what he wrote was a work of fiction which in fact has not the slightest connection to the real Vlad Ţepeş, or even to the legends about him. The vampire Dracula is not a transfiguration of Vlad Ţepeş; he is an independent and completely fictional character. The quest for Dracula in Romania – accomplished by tracing, of course, the footsteps of Vlad Ţepeş, themselves far from certain – is no more than a game, and a rather puerile game at that, even if a number of historians have allowed themselves to be caught up in it. Tourists should be warned, even at the risk of disappointing them: the history of Vlad Ţepeş and the legend of Dracula are two stories which have nothing to do with one another.

Towards the myth of Dracula, which has emerged rather unexpectedly from their point of view, the Romanians cannot decide what attitude to take. In the first place, the transformation of one of their princes – and not just any prince, as we shall see – into a vampire inevitably arouses dissatisfaction and even indignation. On the other hand, they have no wish to discourage tourism. If foreigners want Dracula, let them have him! They are offered picturesque trails, complete with castles where Vlad Ţepeş – certainly not Count Dracula – spent a night or two, and an entire industry of kitsch souvenirs bearing the *voivode*'s image. Who knows, perhaps one day the Romanians themselves will forget about Vlad Ţepeş and come to believe in the authenticity of Dracula!

The fact that Dracula (the vampire) did not exist does not mean that he does not exist. The history we carry with us is not the same as real history; what matters is what we have in our minds and souls.

There are fictions that become more significant than reality, because they succeed in giving life to certain dreams, fears or hopes. Fiction is more exemplary than history. Thus real history – which is less significant in itself than we might wish – is adapted in the imaginary, revised and supplemented. Like his contemporary Sherlock Holmes, Dracula has come to be more real than many a real historical figure.

For the time being, however, the Romanians do not seem inclined to give up their Vlad Țepeș. His cruelties are explained by reasons of state. In his time, he succeeded in ensuring order and justice, albeit by extreme methods. No-one in Wallachia dared to steal or to treat someone else unjustly in those days: they would soon have found themselves in the Prince's forest of stakes. What times! 'Why do you not come again, Lord Țepeș?' is a well-known invocation among Romanians, thanks to the poet Mihai Eminescu. When they feel inse-cure and abandoned by those responsible for their country (which happens quite often), Romanians dream of Vlad Țepeș, or of a new Vlad Țepeș. And the bloodthirsty Prince was also a valiant defender of the country against Turkish invasion. Here, then, is the 'true' portrait: a fighter for his country's independence and guarantor of social harmony within its boundaries. The ideal Prince! Quite different from the vampire Dracula. Nothing could be more inter-esting, as regards the logic of the imaginary, than the fact that the same historical figure has given rise to two such different myths: on the one hand, a national and political symbol for the Romanians, and on the other, the gothic legend of the vampire. We can only wonder what the real Vlad Țepeș was like.

THE PRINCES

Vlad Țepeș leads us towards the Romanian typology of the Prince. Having such an insecure history, and having been tossed one way or the other for the last 200 years in an endless period of transition, the Romanians are attracted to authoritarian solutions. They put more trust in individuals, in providential leaders, than in systems and abstract projects. Their 'ideal Prince' is quite similar to Țepeș – and this is an inclination of which they must learn to beware. Perhaps a latter-day Țepeș would help to wipe out corruption and establish a bit more order, but then what about democracy?

The Romanians' princely gallery – which remains very present in the national consciousness even today – implies a resorting to authority and illustrates an enduring inclination towards the great models of the past. But places in the Pantheon are not guaranteed. There are promotions, demotions and even exclusions – dictated not so much by the 'absolute' merits of the figures in question as by the ever-changing way in which they are regarded. This game of heroes is not, of course, a Romanian peculiarity; it fits a universal typology. However, the Romanians stand out due to their Pantheon's high degree of instability (reflecting their country's instability over the last century), by the heavy emphasis placed on the principle of authority, and by the insistence with which historical precedents are invoked in matters relating strictly to the present – as though the heroes of the past could teach us what to do now, in a world that has changed completely and that is continuing to change increasingly quickly!

A complete roll-call would be tiresome; let us recall only the greatest of them. We begin with the Trajan-Decebalus tandem, the parents of the Romanian people. In a first phase, when the Romanians considered themselves to be Roman, the Emperor Trajan took first place by a long way. Then, as the voice of autochthonism was heard more and more frequently, the Dacian King overtook him, and it is Decebalus who now enjoys a privi-leged position. Burebista, the first King of Dacia (a contemporary of Julius Caesar, who reigned a century and a half before Decebalus), vegetated for a long time somewhere in the obscure beginnings of history, only to re-emerge abruptly around 1980, propelled forward by the nationalist historical vision of the Ceauşescu era. Thus Romania began as a great state, a great power of Antiquity. Burebista and Decebalus help the Romanians to forget that Romania has been in existence only since 1859.

The medieval period had its great princes, to whom the Romanians still feel very close. There is no need to say more about Vlad Ţepeş. Mircea the Old, defender of Wallachia against the Turks, is also well placed. With Iancu of Hunedoara (Hunyadi János), things are more complicated: the Romanians share him with the Hungarians (for whom he is more of a cult figure). The two great symbolic histor-ical figures are Stephen the Great and Michael the Brave. Stephen the Great of Moldavia enjoyed the longest reign of any Romanian Prince, a period of authoritarian rule in a powerful state, punctuated in equal part by victorious campaigns and cultural achievements. Michael the Brave was the Prince who achieved the union of 1600, the precursor of Greater Romania and of the Romania of today. As a symbol, he quite simply merges with Romania (while Stephen the Great, likewise a symbol for all Romanians, has nevertheless remained, in a somewhat contradictory fashion, a symbol of Moldavian particularity: he is currently the great patron of the Republic of Moldova, and his statue is on prominent display in Chișinău).

The modern period opens with a pair of figures who are complementary but difficult to harmonize: Cuza and Carol I. The former was the Prince of the Union of 1859 and of the reforms that made the modern Romanian state; he has also remained in the consciousness of the Romanians as a Prince of the peasants, to whom he granted property rights in 1864. In 1866, however, he was dethroned, and Carol I took his place. Carol's long reign filled with achievements became the starting point for a dynastic myth in which there was no room for Cuza; though not forgotten, he was placed in the shadow of Carol I and the new dynasty. Carol could not stand beside Cuza; his place in the symbology of the time was next to Trajan: the founder of the Romanian kingdom beside the founder of the Romanian people. Thus Cuza's founding role was almost done away with. His revenge came with Communism, when Carol was excluded from the Pantheon (although he had to wait a few years, until Communism became more receptive to national values).

Carol has been foregrounded again since 1989; however, the dynastic myth has lost much of its force. In the Romanian consciousness, Cuza is firmly established in first place; he has won, posthumously, his battle both with those who dethroned him and with Carol I. These myths are not, of course, constructed and demolished at random; they are the result of education and propaganda. In comparison with Carol, Cuza has a number of plus points: he was in truth Romania's first sovereign (even if, at the time, the country was officially called the United Principalities); he was a native prince, not an imported one (this sort of nationalism still functions in Romania); he gave land to the peasants, while Carol repressed the uprising of 1907; and so on. Thus Cuza appears as a progressive, Carol as a conservative; Cuza signifies an option for the Left, Carol for the Right. It is unnecessary to repeat that all of these are mythological simplifications: this is how the carousel of historical personalities turns round.

In an interesting opinion poll dated June 1999, people were asked to name 'the most important historical personalities who have influenced the destiny of the Romanians for the better'. Of those questioned, 24.6 per cent opted for Cuza, placing the Prince of the Union and of the peasants first among the great figures of history by a long way. He was followed, naturally enough, by Michael the Brave with 17.7 per cent and Stephen the Great with 13.4 per cent. Vlad Ţepeş scored 4.1 per cent and Carol I only 3.1 per cent – not much compared with his former glory, which may have been fabricated but was also deserved. This survey also marked the demise of the dynastic myth. Ferdinand, Carol's successor, did not even appear among the top ten. Yet at the end of the First World War, he had been presented as the modern equivalent of Michael the Brave; like Michael, he had achieved Romanian unification 'by his sword', not a fragile unification for one year but a unification for all time. Communism passed over Carol I and Ferdinand and so, quite simply, has time. Society today has other reference points.

So much for sovereigns. Did Romania also have a Bismarck? It did, and not just one, but three: Mihail Kogălniceanu (1817–1891), Cuza's close associate; Ion C. Brătianu (1821–1891), who headed, under Carol I, the most durable government in Romania's history; and his son Ion I. C. (Ionel) Brătianu (1864–1927), the strong man of King Ferdinand's reign and of the years when Greater Romania was achieved. The Brătianus constituted, in a sense, the country's second dynasty – a Romanian dynasty in parallel with the foreign one – and were perceived prior to Communism as symbolic figures, alongside the kings. The Communists excluded both kings and Brătianus, leaving Kogălniceanu, together with Cuza, in an unrivalled position. Initially, Communism embarked on an even more radical modification of the Pantheon, placing the historian and revolutionary of 1848 Nicolae Bălcescu (1819–1852) in the foremost position; Bălcescu personified the destruction of the dynastic myth – and of national mythology in general – in favour of a new revolutionary mythology. Gheorghiu-Dej shook Bălcescu's hand (without asking if he felt honoured by the company; it is unlikely that he would have done). Later, Ceauşescu returned to kings – albeit Dacian kings! – and to the Romanian voivodes of the Middle Ages. His favourite 'interlocutors' were Burebista and Michael the Brave; thus, once again, there was a shift – from the mythology of class struggle and revolution to that of the Leader and of the unity of the entire people around him.

After 1989, there was a series of 'comebacks': the kings, the Brătianus (symbolic figures for both Liberalism and the nation as a whole), Iuliu Maniu (National-Peasant symbol and martyr of democracy) etc. The return of Marshal Antonescu, in particular, calls for comment. Having been condemned to death and excuted in 1946, in a Romania already dominated by the Soviet Union and Communists, he was presented in a negative light during the Communist period (albeit with a certain softening of tone in the years of Ceauşescu's nationalism). Since 1989, many Romanians have come to see him as an embodiment of patriotism and anti-Communism. However, the hard core of his admirers is made up of those attracted to authoritarian and xenophobic solutions, in partic-ular the Greater Romania movement – much the same people who are nostalgic for Ceauşescu. Ironically, they are, in a way, the succes-sors of those who sent the Marshal to the firing squad. Precisely because of this multiplicity of ideological and political reversals, the Romanian case is a very interesting one for anyone seeking to trace the mechanism by which the heroes of history are manipulated according to current interests.[2] Let us not forget Ceauşescu among the great shades of the past. In the opinion poll referred to above, he scored 10.3 per cent, which put him in fourth place, after Cuza, Michael the Brave and Stephen the Great, and which was double the score of King Michael – not bad (for Ceauşescu) in a Romania which has emerged from the Communist catastrophe through blood and fire! In another poll, Ceauşescu was declared to be the best of all Romanians by 22 per cent of respondents, and the worst by another 22 per cent! He is still a presence, and his spirit continues to divide.

QUEEN MARIE

A special place in the Romanians' heroic gallery is occupied by a woman. This is rather surprising; while women are not exactly invis-ible in Romanian society, Romanian men (and quite possibly a majority of Romanian women) do not have a lot of confidence in women who launch themselves into the public arena. The act of lead-ership seems to be reserved for men. It may be that British women brought a new spirit to Romania: a more relaxed way of behaving and more active conception of life. At a time when Britain and Romania hardly knew each other (even today, they do not know each other very well), a handful of British wives made themselves noticed in Bucharest. I have already mentioned Mary Rosetti; it is also worth mentioning Elizabeth, the wife of Take Ionescu (1858–1922), one of the most brilliant Romanian politicians of the beginning of the twentieth century and a passionate advocate of alliance with France and Britain in the First World War. However, the great feminine presence provided by Britain was Marie, Queen of Romania.[3]

Marie was right at the centre of the genealogical table of European dynasties around 1900. In as much as Queen Victoria was known as the 'grandmother of Europe', it might be said that Marie was the 'cousin of Europe'. She was a granddaughter of Queen Victoria by the latter's second son Alfred, Duke of Edinburgh and Saxe-Coburg-Gotha (1844–1900), the brother of King Edward VII. This made her a first cousin of King George V. She was likewise a first cousin of Tsar Nicholas II, through her mother, Grand Duchess Maria of Russia, the only daughter of Tsar Alexander II and sister of Alexander III. And finally, she was a first cousin of the German Emperor Wilhelm II, through his mother, Victoria, the eldest daughter of Queen Victoria. It may be noted that on the eve of the First World War, in a Europe profoundly divided, what remained of the idea of Europe was concentrated in the continent's monarchies, which were all inter-related, forming in fact one large family (with the inevitable family quarrels, but also a sense of solidarity).

For Romania, the marriage in 1893 of the seventeen-year-old Marie (born in 1875) to Ferdinand, the heir to the throne, was a remarkable dynastic coup. Of course, the country had a Hohenzollern at its head, but not one from the family's imperial branch. Marie was more closely related to the Hohenzollerns of Berlin than Carol or Ferdinand; she nonchalantly made her appearance as a close relative of all of the principal European sovereigns. Pushed into this marriage almost without realizing it, she might equally have become Queen of Great Britain or Tsarina of Russia. There was the beginning of a romance between her and her cousin George, and it is said that the future King later regretted losing her. The British throne was more prestigious than that of Romania, even more so around 1900, when Britain was almost the ruler of the world, the centre of the largest empire that had ever existed. But it is hard to imagine Marie in this role; what could she have done in a well-established country with strict rules, where she would have had almost no freedom of movement? Romania suited her much better; everything was still to be done, and anything might happen.

To list only Marie's positive qualities (for of course she also had her faults; even a positive quality can become a fault in some situations), she was a beautiful, elegant, intelligent, strong-willed and sentimental woman, with a sense of humour and, above all, a

235

The future Queen Marie, shown on a contemporary postcard as a princess in a Byzantine setting.

Marie shown as an officer in the Romanian army.

longing to be free. The great struggle of her life was for freedom. And for a Princess or a Queen, nothing is harder to obtain than freedom. She may, of course, win it by running away. This sort of revolt and flight has given rise to two significant myths: that of Sissi, the Empress Elizabeth of Austria, who left the court of Franz Josef to wander through Europe until her tragic death; and, more recently, that of Princess Diana, who also came to a shocking end. Both Sissi and Diana were defeated; they won a painful liberty, but at what a price! Marie's case was more complex; she loved freedom, but she also loved power. She banked on being able to win her freedom while remaining Queen, and she succeeded.

Her great confrontation was with King Carol I. Marie was warm, unimaginably warm, while Carol was cold, unimaginably cold. He was cold, of course, by nature, but he had become colder in a calculated manner; only thus could he keep control of a country as heated as Romania for half a century – something which no-one else was able to do, either before or after him. Between Marie and Carol there developed a prolonged contest which resulted in a draw; although very different, both were endowed with the same willpower. Marie learned something from the lessons in princely duty which she

237

Marie shown on a contemporary postcard wearing Romanian folk costume.

received from Carol, and the old King 'softened' with time, until he finally turned a blind eye to some of her outbursts of freedom.

In a country where social distances were so enormous, Marie was fond of commoners, or rather she did not make distinctions of rank. She had nothing against luxury, and would not have given it up, but she seemed in her element wherever she went. She dressed in folk costume, travelled up and down the country, chatted with peasants and did not even avoid Gypsy hovels. It is no secret that she felt attracted to handsome men, especially in uniform. A great deal has been said about her life, much of it hard to prove or to disprove. She never hid the attraction she felt towards certain individuals; such frankness is rare even today, and Victorian morality (symbolized by Marie's own grandmother!) completely ruled it out, especially for a member of a royal family. It is thought that at least one of Marie's children, Princess Ileana, was the fruit not of her marriage but of her liaison with Prince Barbu Ştirbei (who was certainly her close friend and adviser); her eldest daughter, Maria (known as Mignon), has also been 'attributed' to a young lieutenant – all this is, of course, impossible to prove, but quite plausible. Marie effectively acted as she saw fit, in a truly impressive manner, since she never lowered herself in any situation, always remaining a Princess or a Queen and displaying a relaxed but no less 'imperial' dignity. She therefore resembled neither the kings of that time (too distant) nor the kings of today (too much 'like everyone else'). Marie combined distance with closeness, according to a recipe that was hers alone.

One of her great passions was riding; she could ride better than any cavalry officer. She loved the army, and its officers ('Honi soit qui mal y pense!'), but above all its common soldiers. She was very proud when King Carol, who did something to please her now and then, placed her at the command of a regiment of *Roşiori* (the élite cavalry). Marie's ambition was to be a soldier-queen! The image of her in uniform mounted on a horse is seductive, and Marie knew that it suited her!

There are few people who can claim to have the privilege of giving all that they are able to give. Marie had such an opportunity in the First World War. The death of King Carol, who had been faithful to the alliance with Germany, eliminated the principal obstacle in the way of Romania's entry into the war on the side of the Entente. The fighting was heavy, with unexpected reversals, and there were moments when all seemed lost. Only Marie – according to the testimony of friends and adversaries alike – never had a moment of doubt. She *knew* that the war would be won. She believed in the luck of Romania, but she believed above all – since she never forgot where she came from – in the invincibility of Britain. Faced with so much hesitation and cowardice, there grew in her a pride she could not conceal. She spoke bluntly to General Averescu as, forced by circumstances, he was preparing to negotiate a separate peace with the Germans: 'Don't trouble yourself anymore, General, to understand my attitude. The explanation is simple: I am an Englishwoman, and the English are not accustomed to lose.' With such unswerving confidence, she could hardly fail to win. Romania at the time was in need of a 'saviour'. King Ferdinand was totally unlike Marie; an intelligent and cultivated man, he was indecisive to an unhealthy degree. It was she who was the great sovereign in those moments, even if officially the country was personified by Ferdinand. The Romanians felt this, and invested their hopes in her.

Marie had yet another quality which gave her a considerable advantage in wartime: physical courage. Quite simply, she was afraid neither of bullets nor of epidemics. And when you are not at all afraid of these things, it seems that they never touch you. Dressed in nurse's uniform (a complementary symbolic image to her military outfit), Marie spent days and nights at the bedsides of wounded soldiers or victims of typhus. Advised to wear rubber gloves, she turned them down with an argument that was hard to contest: 'The soldiers want to kiss my hand; how can I offer them a hand of rubber?' With the same disregard for danger, she even went into front-line trenches. Out of all this, and out of a mixture of despair and hope, Marie's myth took shape. She became the symbol of confidence in victory and in the achievement of the Romanians' dream of unity.

On the day of the victory celebrations, Marie made a fitting entry into Bucharest, mounted and in uniform, beside King Ferdinand – not as the wife of a King, but as a Queen in her own right. And in 1922, in Alba Iulia, the historical capital of Transylvania, which Michael the Brave had entered victoriously more than three centuries before, Ferdinand and Marie were crowned King and Queen of Greater Romania. Marie must have loved all the pomp and ceremony. Just as her grandmother Victoria had been proclaimed Empress of India, she now had her imperial moment. Compared with the little Romania of pre-war days, an empire had, in a sense, been created by the joining together of so many distinct territories, and her role in this construction had certainly been greater than that played by Queen Victoria. With her expertise in staging and in all sorts of 'disguises', Marie appeared in Alba Iulia as her own version of a Byzantine Empress. There was certainly a large element of theatre in all she did, in her dress and her attitudes – not that she was insincere, but her sincerity was always given an 'artistic' form. Marie 'played' her life; she believed utterly in what she did, without ever ceasing to play a role, or a multitude of roles.

The 'normal' times that followed the war suited her less well. She played her part in the Romanian initiatives at the Paris peace conference of 1919 (where Romania insisted on pushing its border as far west as possible), quite unofficially of course, as from a strictly constitutional point of view she had no say in such matters. It seems that she managed to appease Clemenceau, who was angry with the Romanians for making a separate peace, and in this way she may have contributed (it is hard to say to what extent) to Romania's obtaining the maximum possible – less than it had asked for, but quite a favourable border settlement all the same. Thereafter, her effective role declined year by year, especially after the death of King Ferdinand, when she was not included in the regency, and even more after 1930, with the installation on the throne of her (not so well brought up!) son Carol II, with whom she never got on well. She died of cancer in 1938, not yet 63 years old.

It is possible to speak of a 'Queen Marie' style: a style of life, a style of dress, even an artistic style in the true sense of the word. Marie promoted a specific form of Art Nouveau in Romania, combining in a very personal manner Celtic, Byzantine and Romanian decorative elements, all bathed in gold as in Russian churches. One may like or dislike the result, but it is certainly original.

Anyone who wants to know the Romanian royal family on its home territory would be well advised to pay a visit to Sinaia, 120 km north of Bucharest, where a narrow pass cuts through the Carpathian Mountains to Transylvania. Outside this small town, in an alpine landscape reminiscent of his native land, Carol I put much care and love into the construction of his favourite residence: Peleş Castle, a corner of Germany in the heart of Romania. The castle's elegant profile, in German Renaissance style, conceals an eclectic interior in which all sort of styles are juxtaposed; unique in its own way, it is heavy and oppressive, a museum that ignores, even cancels out, its natural surroundings. Can one live in a museum? Carol could, and could even take delight in it, but Marie could not. A short distance from Peleş, a smaller residence, on a more 'human' scale, was built for her and Ferdinand, but particularly to suit her preferences: it is known as Pelişor. Its interior, decorated in an Art Nouveau style adapted, of course, to the Queen's taste, is the exact opposite of Peleş. In Peleş and Pelişor, Carol and Marie continue their confrontation.

Marie's great love, though, was Balcic, a village on the rocky coast of the Black Sea, in the Quadrilateral which the Romanians had won from the Bulgarians in 1913 (and were to lose again in 1940). At a time when she did not even dream of becoming Queen of Romania, Marie had spent some unforgettable years on Malta. Balcic was for her a sort of replica of Malta, but adapted to the local atmosphere. The little palace there bears the mark of her characteristic eclecticism: Romanian and oriental elements (including a minaret!) are combined, and there is, of course, an English-style garden.

Towards the end of her life, Marie wrote her memoirs, in English, under the title *The Story of My Life*. It is surprising to discover in her a true writer, with a great capacity for description and portrayal and a lively sense of humour; she parades before the reader almost the entire gallery of emperors and empresses, kings and queens, princes and princesses of Europe, nearly all of whom were her cousins, uncles, aunts, nephews or nieces, evoking them with a mixture of tenderness and irony.

Compared with what Queen Marie meant three-quarters of a century ago, her memory is now considerably faded, along with that of the rest of the royal family. Yet it seems that we are witnessing a come-back. The Romanians are rediscovering their almost-forgotten Queen, while outside the country her stature is still considerable. From time to time, books about her appear in English or French, certainly more than about any other hero of Romanian history. The Romanians have their own hierarchy of personalities in which, as we have seen, Michael the Brave and Cuza are well ahead of Marie. But as well as national heroes there are also international ones, and it is possible that Marie occupies a place in this universal gallery. The explanation for this lies in the fact that her message is not just limited to what she did for Romania. She was in many respects a precursor, perhaps closer to the people of today than to her contemporaries. She was a rule-breaker, prefiguring a world in which women would be freer and rulers closer to those they ruled. Above all, she proved that a woman, while remaining feminine, could win a game normally reserved for men.

EMINESCU AND CARAGIALE

In the process of creating Romania, cultural action preceded the political act. Romania was made first of all in people's conscious-ness. It might be said that it is a country created by men of letters: writers, historians, teachers and so on. It was they who gave shape to a common history and a spiritual space, and through them the Romanians acquired an identity. Thus we pass from the Pantheon of political heroes to that of men of letters. Here, too, there is a hier-archy; here, too, some rise and others fall. If we limit ourselves to the most essential and symbolic expression of Romanian-ness, two names come to mind: Eminescu and Caragiale.[4]

Mihai Eminescu (1850–1889) is the Romanians' 'national poet'.

Romania has produced many poets, but not one has been able to compete with Eminescu for this unique position. This is unusual: neither the English, the French nor the Germans – none of the world's great literatures – possess a 'national poet', in other words, someone set above the rest as an unrivalled exponent of the national spirit. Eminescu is not just a great poet; he is a saint and a supreme symbol; if we were to mix the political and literary Pantheons together, his place would be at the very top. He is the first of all Romanians, the supreme fulfilment of the Romanian genius. At least so the myth would have it.

In a Romania which has identified for so long with its rural civilization, Eminescu appears as a transfigured image of the eternal Romanian peasant. Although he was educated in Vienna and Berlin, and was beyond question influenced by German philosophy and poetry, he remained a 'man of the soil' and of elementary essences (which indeed German Romanticism had not for a moment contradicted). He lives in a sort of atemporality, almost dissolving in the cosmos, in nature and in an immobile history, impermeable to modernity. He was nationalist and a 'reactionary' (in every sense, including the political). Some of his verses, and even more his political articles (he was editor of the conservative paper *Timpul* – 'The Time' – where he promoted not so much conservative ideology as his

Mihai Eminescu in a famous photograph from his youth.

own personal ideology), express a refusal of modernity and a fear of foreigners. Eminescu dreamed of an ancestral and eternal Romania.

He wrote all the time, but worked over each of his lines endlessly, so that a succession of variants of his poems exist in manuscript. His published poetic work is contained in a single volume, *Poems*, which appeared in 1883. (It was prepared for publication not by Eminescu himself but by the critic Titu Maiorescu after the poet had fallen ill; Maiorescu gathered and arranged as he saw fit poems scattered through the pages of *Convorbiri Literare* ['Literary Conversations'] together with some previously unpublished pieces.) In the early variants, especially those written in Eminescu's youth, the poetry is effervescent, characterized by an unrestrained grandeur and a torrential stream of images. At the other end of his creative career, we find almost abstract poetry, polished like a diamond – the waves stilled under an icy crust. What this poetry loses in materiality it gains in musicality. Ultimately, what sets Eminescu apart is not what he says, which is typically romantic in spirit (the misunderstood genius, unrequited love, extinction in the heart of nature, ancestral heroism, the creation and destruction of worlds etc.), and perhaps not even the way he says it, but the *sound* of what he says, a mysterious and haunting music that is his alone. This Eminescian musicality – which is difficult for a non-Romanian, even someone who knows Romanian, to sense fully – has a tyrannical effect. The Romanians have been under its spell for more than a century.

The myth of Eminescu is made up of several ingredients. First of all, there is, of course, the poetry, its stock of ideas and images, and its formal perfection, which raise it appreciably above the level of the Romanian literature of the time. Then, there is the tragic quality of a life of suffering, of the 'misunderstood genius' struck down by insanity at the age of only 33. Even his image contributes to the myth: a portrait from his early youth is imprinted on the retina of every Romanian, in which the poet appears as extraordinarily handsome, with an almost supernatural beauty (like Hyperion, his 'double' in the poem 'Luceafărul'). All of these factors – his handsomeness, the failure of others to understand him, his sufferings – are simplified and amplified according to the rules of myth; real life is always more prosaic and banal. Especially after his death, in the years around 1900, Eminescu's nationalism was added to these ingredients, and he came to be perceived not only as a great poet but as a prophet of Romanianism. What was then quite natural, given

Ion Luca Caragiale.

the period's nationalist atmosphere, now seems embarrassing, however. Today's nationalists have made Eminescu into a banner, not his poetry so much as his political ideas. Others appreciate his poetry, and keep the rest separate. But lately, some have started to distance themselves from Eminescu's poetry too. This is a completely new phenomenon, but in fact nothing could be more normal after more than a century; sensibilities and tastes evolve. Some carry their demythologizing to the point of highlighting the less seductive aspects of Eminescu's life and behaviour, outlining a portrait which no longer bears any resemblance to the fascinating photograph of his youth.

And so, among the Romanian conflicts of the present time, there is also a dispute over Eminescu. His challengers would probably not be so insistent if the promoters of the Eminescu cult (who are beyond doubt in the majority) did not deny the right of anyone to express the slightest reservation. The outcome remains to be seen. Meanwhile, Eminescu remains in the national consciousness as the most outstanding of all Romanians.

How, then, can Ion Luca Caragiale be placed beside him? A contemporary of the great poet, Caragiale (1852–1912) has no grounds for aspiring to sainthood, or even to be the eternal represen-

245

tative of Romanianism. Rather, he is a complementary symbol, who, alongside Eminescu, completes Romania's spiritual profile. With Eminescu alone, the Romanians would soon become tired. Fortunately, they also have Caragiale to relax them. While Eminescu represents rural and patriarchal Romania, Caragiale is a townsman, we might say a 'hardened' townsman, right at the opposite extreme. He is also a more Balkan figure, both in his origins (he had more Greek than Romanian blood) and in his attitudes. Balkanism implies a brand of disorderliness which Europe finds hard to bear, but in its more attractive aspect it also implies a way of looking at things with detachment, a high degree of sociability, and a substantial dose of relativism and humour. In contrast with Eminescu's Romanian 'purism', Caragiale personifies the cosmopolitan infusion typical of Romanian towns – in other words, precisely what Eminescu hated. Eminescu is humourless; Caragiale abounds in humour. Eminescu is the man of great truths; Caragiale observes and records the pulverizing of values. With Eminescu, everything is absolute; with Caragiale, everything is relative.

With the passage of time, the Romanians have got used to Caragiale and have come to take delight in his comedies (such as *A Stormy Night* and *A Lost Letter*) and prose sketches. But there were plenty of reservations and objections at first. The same Romanianism which glorified Eminescu delayed the recognition of Caragiale. Was he not making fun of the Romanians? In fact, his irony is quite without malice. Despite the fact that he settled in Berlin in the last years of his life – preferring the rather routine comfort of the German capital to the excessively picturesque and fantastical life of Bucharest – he cannot be separated from the environment he depicted, observing it lucidly from the outside, but also understanding it from within. In his own may, Caragiale illustrates Maiorescu's thesis of 'forms without substance'. The Romanians were playing at a modernity which they had no intention of applying in its rigid Western forms. To a severe observer, Romania could appear to be lacking in seriousness. The indignant words of Raymond Poincaré, the future President of France and a very serious gentleman, come to mind. 'Gentlemen,' he exclaimed in exasperation, 'here we are at the gates of the Orient, where everything is treated lightly!' Caragiale's heroes are the sort of people who drove Poincaré round the bend. He was a painstaking collector of the human weaknesses that are present everywhere, but that take on a heightened relief in a Romania caught in the unstable zone between tradition and modernity. Caragiale's work is complex, and it also has a less happy, even tragic, dimension, but the dominant note is one of irony and humour, and this is how he is generally received today. The humour results in the first place from the contrast between appearance and essence, a contrast which is beyond doubt universal, but which was apparent to a heightened degree in a Romania that was mimicking a borrowed civilization. It is also to a large extent a comedy of language, for Caragiale's characters talk incessantly, without necessarily saying anything in particular. This speech, which revolves in a void, challenging and almost cancelling out reality, looks ahead to the Theatre of the Absurd.

Caragiale captured, if not eternal Romanian characteristics, then at least characteristics which have proved to be long-lasting in a society perpetually in transition, a society with a voracious appetite for models but at the same time capable of taking these models less than seriously. For this reason, Romanians today still see themselves mirrored in Caragiale, and they will probably continue to do so for some time to come. Someone made the subtle comment that even Romanian Communism was destined to be a combination of Marx and Caragiale. To everything they do, the Romanians bring a note of improvisation and approximation, as well as an inclination to talk rather than act. This lack of rigour can be exasperating (and then you must take refuge, like Caragiale, in Berlin), but it also has its pleasant, relaxing side. Not taking things too seriously is a philosophy of life which has not made the Romanians rich (quite the contrary!), but it may have made them more able to endure their history.

Through Eminescu and Caragiale, the Romanians have said almost all there is to say about themselves. With the contribution, in a rather more limited register, of their contemporary Ion Creangă (1837–1889), the triad of the Romanian literary classics is complete. Creangă was an authentic Moldavian peasant (while Eminescu's peasanthood was more metaphysical). In his tales and childhood reminiscences, he transfigured the Moldavian village in an almost Rabelaisian style, with a hearty sense of humour and an extraordinary vitality. Even his supernatural characters, devils and all, seem to be Moldavian peasants too, albeit of a stranger sort.

All three men – and they open up so many directions – had a magical power with words. Their verbal inventiveness, the way they said things, defined them more than the substance of what was said. Another characterstic (except for Eminescu) was a massive dose of humour. The capacity to see the comic side of things, however serious they may have been, was a constant trait, and indeed it is one the Romanians amply put to the test in the less than happy times of Communism. Do the Romanians have too much humour? Perhaps. They often talk of 'making fun of misfortune'. The poet George Bacovia captured this Romanian contradiction perfectly in the line: 'A sad country, full of humour!'

THE ENCYCLOPAEDIC TRADITION

Mircea Eliade wrote:

> There is in Romanian culture a tradition which begins with Dimitrie Cantemir, and which we might name the 'encyclopaedic tradition'. A good proportion of the leading figures, great writers and cultural prophets of the Romanian people take their places within this tradition ... The same varied and contradictory preoccupations; the same thirst to cover as many as possible of the spiritual geographies of the world; the same multilateral activity, at times hasty, at other times improvized, but always springing from the desire to force Romanian culture to jump as many stages as possible, to raise it on a 'world scale', demonstrating the power of creation of the Romanian genius.[5]

This was the project which Eliade himself took up. Even at a time when specialization – stricter with each generation – had triumphed in the world, the Romanians continued to produce remarkable specimens of the universal savant.

The tone was set by Dimitrie Cantemir (1673–1723), who ruled Moldavia from 1710 to 1711, before taking refuge, following an unsuccessful war with the Turks, in Peter the Great's Russia. He was a man of action as well as a political thinker, writer, historian and philosopher. His *Description of Moldavia* (written in Latin and first published in German translation) is an encyclopaedic tableau of his country, bringing together geographical, historical, political and ethnographic information. A massive history of the Romanians remained unfinished, apart from the early section, in which he displays outstanding erudition in the treatment of their origins (up to the thirteenth century). Cantemir knew the Turks as well as he knew his own people. He had spent his youth in Constantinople, the most cosmopolitan capital of the time; as well as studying in Greek, he had learned Turkish, Arabic and Persian. He also wrote a treatise on Turkish music. No European came so close to the culture of the

Islamic East. In a book entitled *The System of the Muhammadan Religion* (published in Russian in 1722), he offered a synthetic sketch of Islamic civilization. However, it was as the historian of the Ottoman Empire that he won European fame. The Latin manuscript of his *Incrementa atque decrementa aulae othomanicae*, unpublished at his death, was brought to London by his son, Antiokh Cantemir (1708–1744). The son, like the father, was inclined towards multiple activities: he was Russian ambassador to London and Paris, and a writer and translator of various genres; he is considered one of the founders of modern Russian poetry. Antiokh Cantemir arranged for his father's manuscript to be translated into English by the Revd Nicholas Tindal; it was published in two volumes in 1734 and 1735, under the title *The History of the Growth and Decay of the Othman Empire*, and this version was translated into French (1743) and German (1745). This was the first book written by a Romanian to achieve European fame, and for almost a century it was the principal work of reference on Ottoman history and civilization.

The nineteenth century saw a multiplication of 'encyclopaedic' figures. Such 'universal spirits' were needed in a culture that was trying to make up as rapidly as possible for its delays in relation to the West. In Wallachia, Ion Heliade-Rădulescu (1802–1872) devoted himself to education, published a *Romanian Grammar* (1828), edited the first newspaper in the Romanian language (*Curierul Românesc* – 'The Romanian Courier' [1829]), wrote poetry – even an epic in honour of Michael the Brave – took a leading role in the revolution of 1848, embarked on the elaboration of a comprehensive philosophical system, and set himself up as prophet of the Romanians! In Moldavia, Gheorghe Asachi (1788–1869) fulfilled a similar mission; combining a background in the humanities (as poet and author of historical stories) with studies in science (engineering and astronomy) and visual art (he illustrated his own works), he was the founder of Romanian-language education in Moldavia, the leading promoter of the theatre, and the editor of the first Moldavian newspaper (*Albina Românească* – 'The Romanian Bee' [1829]). In his old age, Asachi was an opponent of the union of Moldavia with Wallachia which was to lead to the creation of Romania.

In the second half of the nineteenth century, the universal savant *par excellence* was Bogdan Petriceicu Hasdeu (1838–1907). A native of Bessarabia (then under Russian domination), Hasdeu was a polyglot with a particularly good knowledge of Slavic languages which provided him with the key to historical investigations previously unattempted by Romanians (it should be remembered that the Romanian lands developed in a Slavic environment, and that their official language in the Middle Ages was Slavonic). Hasdeu eventually became Professor of Comparative Philology at the University of Bucharest and Director of the State Archives. However, the strict borders and rigid methods of a profession did not suit him. Although he discovered and published countless documents, and brought important arguments to bear on controversial problems of Romanian linguistics and history, he could not resist the temptation to go further, far beyond the line which the professional dare not cross. He liked to compare himself to Cuvier, the famous palaeontologist, who had astounded his contemporaries by reconstructing the entire body of a prehistoric reptile on the basis of a single tooth. Hasdeu proceeded in the same way. Fascinating and confusing, with the impeccable, but no less fantastic, logic of an Edgar Allan Poe of linguistics and history, he continually wandered across the border between reality and fiction, constructing a 'possible' history, one in which real facts are embedded but which nevertheless carries us into a 'parallel world'. As much a poet, playwright and writer of literary prose as a linguist, philologist and historian, Hasdeu was apparently not conscious, or refused to be conscious, of the distinction between these fields. There have been many authors of fantastic literature; Hasdeu belongs to the rarer breed of creators who combine scholarship with fiction. Towards the end of his life, taking his 'quest for the absolute' to its logical conclusion (and under the influence of the death of his only daughter), he became a spiritualist. He had a tiny castle built in the town of Cîmpina (between Bucharest and Sinaia), intended as a privileged place of dialogue with those 'on the other side', and completed his oeuvre with texts on spiritualism (*Sic Cogito: What is Life? What is Death? What is Man?* [1892]).

No less spectacular, although rather more in accord with the demands of professionalism, was the career of Nicolae Iorga (1871–1940).[6] It is almost impossible to imagine how this man managed to do everything he did. It no longer matters how perfectly or imperfectly he did things; the question is how he ever found the time. After studies in Paris and a doctorate in Leipzig, Iorga became Professor of World History at the University of Bucharest at the age of only 23. He wrote some 1,400 books, some mere pamphlets but others massive multi-volume works, to which must be added no less than 20,000 articles. It is probable that no human being has written so much since the invention of writing; he ought to have a place in the *Guinness Book of Records*. It is not just the quantity but the variety that is amazing. History comes first, of course: almost every aspect of Romanian history (it is hard to approach any subject today without coming across contributions by Iorga), but also substantial ventures into world history: the Balkans; Byzantium (including *The Byzantine Empire*, a work of synthesis published in London in 1907); the Ottoman Empire (the five-volume *Geschichte des osmanischen Reiches* published in Gotha in 1908–13); and so on, culminating in a four-volume synthesis of world history, *Essai de synthèse de l'histoire de l'humanité* (Paris, 1926–8). Iorga also wrote poetry, literary prose, memoirs and – last but not least – plays. The bibliography of his dramatic works, many of which are historical five-act plays in verse featuring personalities from Romanian and world history (including Jesus Christ, Cleopatra, Dante and St Francis), comprises some 30 titles, almost as many as the plays of Shakespeare! He also wrote countless newspaper articles, particularly for *Neamul Românesc* ('The Romanian People'), which he ran for more than three decades. He succeeded in combining a nationalist-conservative ideology with a European spirit; however, he was not only an ideologist but an active politician as well. He made a considerable contribution to the mobilization of the nation in the First World War and was subsequently the first President of the Chamber of Deputies of Greater Romania, as well as Prime Minister from 1931 to 1932. His death, at the hands of Legionaries, was also politically motivated; he had given his support to the dictatorship of Carol II and to the King's suppression of the Legionary movement. So much activity! Was it not perhaps too much? Quantity was indeed achieved at the expense of quality. There are many original ideas in the writings of Iorga, but to find them one must search with a magnifying glass through a mass of printed paper. His work is effervescent, but not very systematic. Like it or not, however, he remains an almost cosmic phenomenon.

Some of the young men who grew up in his shadow were tempted to follow Iorga's example, although it was now the time for specialists rather than 'demiurges'. Perhaps the one who most closely approached the level of his achievement was Mircea Eliade (1907–1986). To place Eliade in the same 'family' as Hasdeu and Iorga is in no way to diminish his originality. Though he followed his own road, like his great predecessors he saw culture as a whole, its multiple pathways leading towards a single goal: the decipherment of the human spirit and the destiny of humanity. Seen from this perspective, there can be no uncrossable border between fiction and scholarship. Certain themes circulate between Eliade's literary and scholarly work. The great revelation for him as a young man was India, where he lived from 1928 to 1931. There, he immersed himself in an ancient and almost immobile civilization, which maintained mysterious relations with the cosmos and the world beyond: a more essential and profound civilization than the technological West. *Maitreyi* (1933) is the novel of Eliade's Indian experience; it can be read equally as a love story and as a philosophical novel, dealing as it does with the relationship between a man and a woman, but also with the impossibility of communication between civilizations.

Eliade continued to divide his energies between his literary work (partly 'realistic' and partly fantastic) and his research into mythology and the History of Religions. He saw mythical thought as a fundamental dimension of the human condition; myth was not untruth, but the attempt to penetrate beyond the surface appearance of things. *Noaptea de Sînziene*, his most elaborate novel, which appeared first in French as *Forêt interdite* (1955), is a combination of realism and fantasy (but who can tell if the fantastic is not more real than the real?). History is present, even overwhelmingly so, particularly in the impressive evocation of London during the Blitz (in 1940, Eliade was Cultural Attaché of the Romanian Legation in the UK). But equally present and obsessive is the quest for an escape from history, for liberation from the constraints of Time. According to Romanian folklore, on the night of Sînziene (24 June) the heavens open. It is a privileged moment, suggesting the way to another dimension of existence, beyond space and time.

Eliade's international career in the field of the exegesis of myths and religions took shape after his departure from Romania, first of all in France, between 1945 and 1956, and then in America, where he became Professor of the History of Religions at the University of Chicago. With works such as *Le Mythe de l'éternel retour* (1949), *Traité d'histoire des religions* (1949) and the three-volume *Histoire des croyances et des idées religieuses* (1976–83), he established his position as a leading authority in the field. However, he was not without his opponents, and more recently a campaign has emerged which draws attention to his youthful involvement with the Legionaries and argues that his orientation at that time also affected his scholarly work. This is certainly possible: an interest in mythology often goes hand in hand with a Right-wing orientation, while the more prosaic Left prefers to settle for rationalism. However debatable some of Eliade's interpretations may be – and what is beyond debate in this world? – he ranks among the handful of scholars who have extended the field of human sciences considerably during the past century. His work is truly universal; the mysterious beliefs of the Dacians (in a less than critical reconstruction), Indian mythology, the religions of Australian tribal groups, and a host of other sources all contributed to his profiling of 'essential humanity'.[7]

WRITERS, ARTISTS, SCIENTISTS, ATHLETES

Just one of the Romanians' many frustrations involves their belief that the world unfairly ignores their contributions, that they are discriminated against in the cultural sphere – that both the cultural and the political games are rigged by the great powers.

There is a certain amount of truth in this. If you want to be famous as a writer, it is better to be English or French than Romanian; at least you will then be able to express yourself in a world language. Assuming equality of value (but what does equality of value mean anyway?), the Romanian, as the exponent of a small culture and a little-known language, is evidently at a disadvantage. And if you are a scientist, it is easier to make your name in an American than in a Romanian laboratory. Many of the glories of Romania are in danger of remaining local glories: great creators within Romania, illustrious unknowns outside its borders. There is another factor at work: more and more cultures are demanding recognition, while, as history accelerates, celebrities are multiplying at an alarming rate. It is harder and harder to enter the gallery of world fame, and those who succeed in doing so have no guarantee that they will not be excluded the next day to make room for someone else.

The writers whom the Romanians consider to be the most representative are not well known in the world. (They may have been translated, but what does a translation mean? It is one thing to be translated and another to enter the world's consciousness, or even the consciousness of a significant category of intellectuals.) The case of Eminescu is eloquent. It seems that the national poet cannot be separated from the Romanian language. Translations yield nothing very convincing; the charm of Eminescian musicality is lost, and one is left with the rather banal profile of a Romantic poet – nothing much to get enthusiastic about, the more so as a century and a half has passed since the age of Romanticism. The Romanians do not give up, however; efforts to promote Eminescu continue, but what chances do they have? Similarly, Caragiale is too dependent for effect on language and on a specific Balkan atmosphere.

The Romanians have many excellent writers. Their literary landscape is all the more remarkable if we consider that modern Romanian literature, of Western type, began late; it can scarcely be traced back before the middle of the nineteenth century. Poetry and short prose emerged first; the Romanian novel did not come to maturity until after the First World War, when it suddenly blossomed. Indeed, the inter-war period is considered the golden age of Romanian letters. Outstanding novelists include Ion Rebreanu (1885–1944), with his vigorous epic frescoes of village life; Mihail Sadoveanu (1880–1961), in whose archaizing prose there is a meeting of novel, myth and epic; Camil Petrescu (1894–1957), with his subtle intellectual analysis of certain types of uneasy and ill-adapted heroes; and Hortensia Papadat-Bengescu (1876–1955), a novelist of morbid states and complicated psychological meanderings. However, the novel currently most highly regarded by Romanian critics – according to a recent survey – was written by Mateiu Caragiale (1885–1936), the son of I. L. Caragiale. His *Rakes of the Old Courtyard* (1929) is an evocation, 'decadent' in character and highly elaborate in style, of a nocturnal Bucharest, indolent and haunted by vice (a representative text for the Romanian inclination, in literature and real life alike, towards a flight from history). Among the most notable poets may be mentioned Tudor Arghezi (1880–1967), a poet with an extremely wide range who did not hesitate to turn the most vulgar material into poetry; Lucian Blaga (1895–1961), a philosopher-poet of pantheist and bucolic inclinations; and Ion Barbu (1895–1961), a mathematician who carried some of the secret rules of his profession into poetry written in a hermetic and abstract style. The *History of Romanian Literature* by George Călinescu (1899–1965), a monumental work published in 1941, combines critical intuition (resulting in conclusions which are generally accepted even today) with an almost novelistic reconstruction of the writers' lives and times. The years of Communism also produced many poets and novelists who are much appreciated by the

Romanians (although on the whole their 'standing' is lower than that of the great inter-war writers). Yet the Romanians have not won a single Nobel Prize for literature, and their great writers remain almost unknown outside the country.

Other writers, in fact a considerable number of them, have chosen to use a language with wider circulation – initially, respecting a strong tradition, French – thus improving their chances in the competition. It would be possible to compile an entire literary history on the basis of what Romanians living in France have written in French. Among them are number of women who had moments of celebrity, including Anna de Noailles (1867–1933), Elena Văcărescu (1866–1947) and Martha Bibescu (1889–1973); today, they are almost forgotten. But Panait Istrati (1884–1935) is still read, thanks to his Balkan and oriental exoticism and the defiant characters that populate his novels (for example *Kyra Kyralina* [1924]). There followed, after the Second World War, the famous Romanian-French trio of Eugen Ionescu, Emil Cioran and Eliade. Eliade continued to write his fiction and memoirs in Romanian (although they were promptly translated into French and other languages), but his works on mythology and religion were written first in French and later also in English. Eugen Ionescu (or Eugène Ionesco; 1909–1994) became, with *La Cantatrice chauve* (1950), the principal exponent of the Theatre of the Absurd, alongside Samuel Beckett. And Emil Cioran (1912–1995) turned his disgust with existence (*Précis de décomposition* [1949]) into essays and aphorisms written in a French so polished that he, a Romanian whose education was initially more German than French, has come to be considered one of the greatest contemporary French stylists. To have three writers at the peak of French literature 'with one stroke' is no small achievement (although, unfortunately for the Romanians too, French no longer counts for what it once did in the world either). Linguistic considerations aside, it was both their good fortune and their merit that they were expressing ideas and attitudes in line with the new horizon of expectations. These three Romanians brought their own answers to then current questions, offering an infusion of Eastern mythology, of the absurd or of philosophical nihilism to a West weary of rationalism.

In the visual arts, too, the Romanians rapidly adopted Western recipes and applied them with talent. A visit to the art galleries of Romania provides an opportunity to discover painting of very high quality. Nicolae Grigorescu (1838–1907), an artist associated with the

Some classic Romanian paintings

Nicolae Grigorescu, *Ox-cart at Orății*, oil on canvas.

Nicolae Grigorescu, *The Girl with a Dowry*, c. 1886–7, oil on canvas. Apart from its artistic value, Grigorescu's work is a good introduction to Romanian society of the second half of the 19th century, especially village life.

Ion Andreescu, *Forest of Beech Trees*, 1880, oil on canvas.

Ştefan Luchian, *Anemones*, 1908, oil on canvas: the best-known flowers in Romanian art.

Gheorghe Pătraşcu, *Women on the Sea Shore*, oil on canvas.

Theodor Pallady, *Still Life*, oil on canvas.

Nicolae Tonitza, *A Mosque at Balcic*, 1936, oil on cardboard.

Barbizon School and Impressionism, is the 'national painter'; he painted the Romanian landscape, rural scenes, peasant girls in traditional costume and other subjects in a luminous and optimistic key. Similar themes are found in the work of Ion Andreescu (1850–1882), but rendered in a more sober and interiorized manner. The period around 1900 is represented by Ştefan Luchian (1868–1916), a brilliant colourist and inexhaustible painter of flowers. The great names of the inter-war period are Gheorghe Pătraşcu (1872–1949), whose landscapes and still lifes are unmistakable for their dense yet luminous materiality; Theodor Pallady (1871–1956), the most Parisian of the Romanian artists, the opposite of Pătraşcu it might be said, whose works are marked by a clear, expressive and ironic line and a discreet and refined use of colour; and Nicolae Tonitza (1886–1940), whose portraits of children, nudes and Dobrogean landscapes are striking for their formal expressiveness and decorative sense. But these painters are in a similar situation to the great Romanian

259

Constantin Brâncuşi, *The Table of Silence*, 1937. Together with *Gate of the Kiss* and *Endless Column*, the *Table* forms part of a monumental ensemble created by Brâncuşi in the city of Tîrgu Jiu.

writers; their standing outside Romania is not particularly high. They offered good painting of European standard, but none of them revolutionized modern art.

The Romanians did produce one artistic revolutionary, and one of the most important at that: the sculptor Constantin Brâncuşi (1876–1957). A peasant's son from Gorj County (in northern Oltenia), Brâncuşi settled in Paris, where his studio is now a museum. He introduced into European art the simplified and abstract elements of Romanian folk art. Indeed, the assimilation of archaic forms was one of the principal ways of breaking away from figurative and 'realistic' art. With his figures carved and polished to the point of abstraction – yet always carrying a philosophical meaning – Brâncuşi was among the first, if not *the* first, to point the way towards what was to become the sculpture of the twentieth century. Through him, the art of the Romanian peasant was inscribed in universality.

Folklore was also the main source of inspiration for George Enescu (1881–1955), the greatest Romanian musician: violinist, pianist, conductor and composer. Enescu composed rhapsodies, symphonies and sonatas which are played all over the world but which always retain a specifically Romanian tonality. (His name is particularly

260

associated with that of Béla Bartók, who also created a 'universal' music on the basis of Hungarian folklore.) Enescu was the revered teacher of Yehudi Menuhin, who never ceased to speak of him, and considered him to have been one of the century's great composers.

The role played by Romanians in the literary and artistic avant-garde of the twentieth century was considerable. Many of them did pioneering work between the two world wars. Urmuz (1883–1923), the author of tales of an impeccable absurdity, numbers among the precursors of the Absurd; his legacy was picked up by Ionescu, who carried it further and propelled it onto the world stage. In these years, too, Romania saw the publication of a number of avant-garde periodicals intended to shock bourgeois moral and aesthetic sensibilities. Tristan Tzara (1886–1963), a Romanian Jew, initially wrote poetry in Romanian; after settling in Switzerland, he invented Dada literature and stimulated the Dadaist movement. He later moved to France. Among avant-garde painters, another Romanian Jew, Victor Brauner (1903–1966), earned a European reputation with his surrealistic compositions and fantastic themes.

This substantial Romanian contribution to avant-garde tendencies might seem curious, given that the country apparently lay at the opposite extreme, as a markedly traditional society (and with plenty of traditionalist manifestations in its literature and art). The phenomenon has a threefold explanation. First, the famous Romanian 'forms without substance' almost begged for absurd humour; its multiple dysfunctionalities made and continue to make Romania a privileged place for the absurd, as could already be seen in Caragiale's sketches. The progression from Caragiale to Urmuz to Ionescu is a logical one. Second, the archaism and folklore of traditional Romania provided an important source for modernism. Finally, the important role played by Jews in the literary and artistic avant-garde is notable; they brought to the arts their own traditions, including a folklore steeped in humour and absurdity, but at the same time an attitude of nonconformism and rebellion. The combination of these factors produced the paradoxical situation of a country that was itself weakly engaged with modernity, but that transcended its own condition in the spheres of literature and art.

The Romanians likewise boast of a host of contributions to science and technology, which have also, they say, been minimized or ignored by others.[8] The metal bridge that connects Muntenia to Dobrogea across the Danube at Cernavoda, erected between 1890 and 1895 by the Romanian engineer Anghel Saligny (1855–1924), can still be admired today; at the time, it was the largest structure of its kind in Europe. A number of Romanian names also feature in the history of aviation; indeed, the Romanians like to believe that they have a special aptitude in this field. Aurel Vlaicu (1882–1913), the builder of an aeroplane of his own conception (in which he crashed while trying to cross the Carpathians), is a national hero. According to Romanians, Traian Vuia (1872–1953) made the first flight in an entirely self-propelled machine (in 1906), and Henri Coandă (1886–1972) built the first jet aeroplane (in 1910). Unfortunately, their achievements are seldom acknowledged in the West. Another Romanian engineer, George Constantinescu (1881–1965), settled in England, where he developed the theory of sonics (*Theory of Sonics* [1918]), the science of the transmission of energy by vibrations though solid and liquid mediums. In Romania, he is considered a great inventor, but how well known is he in England?

In the field of medicine, Nicolae Paulescu (1869–1931) came within an inch of a Nobel Prize, which he probably deserved. He succeeded in isolating insulin a few months before Banting and McLeod, who received the award in 1923. The only Romanian who finally did win a Nobel Prize (in 1974, for his work on cell biology) was George Emil Palade (born 1912), and he won it as a Romanian-born American citizen.

Romania has been home to a pleiad of notable doctors: the bacteriologists Victor Babeş (1854–1926) and Ion Cantacuzino (1863–1934), and the neurologist Gheorghe Marinescu (1863–1938), to name but three. The Romanians consider themselves very gifted in medicine, although unfortunately they lack the technical resources to match these gifts. Certainly, no other Romanian doctor can rival the world-wide fame of Dr Ana Aslan (1897–1988), whose name is linked to the 'anti-aging' drug Gerovital and to the rejuvenating treatments offered by her clinic in Bucharest. It is outside my competence to assess the scientific value of her research; what is certain is that the illusion of rejuvenation drew many Westerners to Romania, and the Communist regime saw the operation as an important source of prestige and, above all, of hard currency (although even without Dr Aslan life expectancy in the West is appreciably higher than in Romania!).

One of the most interesting Romanian scientists was Emil Racoviţă (1868–1947), the naturalist on the Belgian Antarctic expedition of 1897–9 (it was a cosmopolitan team; the name of one officer in particular was later to go down in the annals of polar exploration: Roald Amundsen). The *Belgica* was the first ship to remain for a year in the Antarctic, spending the polar winter embedded in ice. Consequently, the research carried out was more systematic than anything achieved hitherto. Racoviță returned with a diary and with the results of many observations (notably his research on whales); he also wrote a lively and colourful account of the expedition. Although, unlike Amundsen, he did not return to the polar regions, he found another way of researching the manifestations of biology in extreme conditions. He was the initiator of biospeleology, the study of life in caves, and on his return from France (where he had spent the first part of his career), he founded the world's first biospeleology institute at the University of Cluj in 1920.

Romanian culture also resounds with the names of mathematicians. The list is a long one: Gheorghe Țițeica (1873–1939), Dimitrie Pompei (1873–1954), Traian Lalescu (1882–1929), Octav Onicescu (1892–1983), Dan Barbilian (otherwise known as the poet Ion Barbu [1895–1961]) and Grigore Moisil (1906–1973), to mention but a few. The Romanians see their school of mathematics as one of the most significant national scientific achievements, and nowadays there are many Romanian mathematicians and computer scientists working outside Romania.

While the Romanians treasure their scientific and technological 'firsts', and easily fall prey to a persecution complex when they feel that these are not sufficiently appreciated, some, at least, can find consolation in sporting records. The ex-Communist countries still enjoy an advantage in this area. The Communist regimes promoted sport for at least two reasons: it represented the biological dimension of the creation of the 'new man', a stronger and more able humanity; and, most importantly, it was the only field in which the Eastern countries could outdo the West. It is not easy to train good athletes, but it is still easier than achieving a successful economy. The Romanians in general are less sporty than the British. Most of them do not participate in any sport; they are content to sit and watch at the stadium or on television. However, Romania can claim as many champions as Britain, out of a population two and a half times smaller. (At the Sidney Olympics, Romania won eleven gold medals, putting it in eleventh place, and 26 medals altogether, putting it in twelfth place, while Britain won eleven gold medals and 28 in total.)

Womens's sport is far ahead of men's in terms of records. (At Sidney, nineteen of Romania's medals were won by women and seven by men; in general, the Communist countries placed more emphasis than the West on high performance in women's sport.) Romanian female gymnasts are among the best in the world, and Nadia Comăneci (born 1961), the sensation of the Montreal Olympics of 1976, has remained a symbol. Another world-famous sportsperson was Ilie Năstase (born 1946), one of the most talented and admired tennis players of the 1970s. At present, the Romanians are proud of the runner Gabriela Szabo (born 1975). However, the sport which captures more attention than any other is football; as in other countries, it is almost a national religion. Romanian footballers have scored notable successes in the European and world championships, and have given the country a range of greater or lesser heroes, with Gheorghe Hagi, 'King Hagi', the idol of millions of Romanians, outshining them all.

When Romanians, whether Brâncuşi, Eugen Ionescu or Nadia Comăneci, have contributed something out of the ordinary, they have not been refused world-wide fame. For a small country, such achievements are not to be under-rated. But what the Romanians really need to do is to count less on their great personalities, recognized or unrecognized, and take a more attentive and responsible look at the great deficiencies of their society. While there is no need to give up sporting or other records, the Romanians' greatest achievement will have to be the raising of the country's general level and its bringing into line with contemporary European civilization.

VIII A Walk through Bucharest

What immediately strikes anyone the first time they look at the map of Romania is the eccentric position of the capital. Bucharest is a stone's throw from the country's southern border; the Danube is only 60 km away. By its very setting, it is an almost Balkan city. The explanation for this lies in the fact that before becoming the capital of Romania, it was the capital of Wallachia. Seen in this light, its position is somewhat more central: 60 km from the Danube, 100 km from the Carpathians.

The first residences of the princes of Wallachia were closer to the mountains, at Cîmpulung and Curtea de Argeş, nowadays small, picturesque towns with historical monuments recalling their former importance. (Unfortunately, they have also been affected, especially Cîmpulung, by the stupidity of the Communist policy of industrialization, according to which factories were built where tourism should have been encouraged.) Later, the capital descended from the mountains to Tîrgovişte, in the hill country. In a final phase, it moved from the hills to the plains, the chosen site being Bucharest. Bucharest's advantage was that it lay at the crossing of a number of important trade routes, linking the Danube and the Balkans with Moldavia, Transylvania and Central Europe. From here, it was also possible for the princes to keep watch on the line of the Danube, the uneasy border between Wallachia and the Ottoman Empire. But it was also in the Turkish interest that the Wallachian rulers should stay in Bucharest; from the Danube port of Giurgiu, which they had annexed, they could quickly reach the capital to restore order whenever the situation required it.

The first document attesting to Bucharest's existence dates from 1459 (although it is assumed that the town had already been there in the previous century). And this is not just any document: it is signed by the Wallachian Prince of the day, the inevitable Vlad Ţepeş! Thus the Romanian capital entered history under the sign of Dracula! Țepeş had a 'citadel' here, in fact probably a relatively modest residence fortified with timber beams and clay. Subsequent rulers hesitated between Tîrgovişte and Bucharest, with the latter finally becoming established as the sole capital around the middle of the seventeenth century.[1]

The city's name (*Bucureşti* in Romanian) has a pleasant ring to it. It is related to the word *bucurie* ('joy'), and thus could be interpreted as 'the city of joy'. At one time, Bucharest was indeed an easy-going place, although it is less so today. However, this does not appear to be the real meaning of its name. It seems more likely to have come from the personal name Bucur, which is common among the Romanians. Someone called Bucur must have been the real or mythical ancestor of the rural community out of which the present big city evolved. According to legend, it was founded by 'Bucur the shepherd' (or fisherman, boyar or merchant). With or without Bucur, it is clear that initially Bucharest was nothing more than a village, and it retained its rural aspect for a long time.

ON THE BANKS OF THE DÎMBOVIȚA

It is a city of the plain, situated at an average height above sea level of 70–80 m. In the Middle Ages, this part of the plain was covered by an extensive forest. Nowadays, when concrete and asphalt have swallowed up almost everything, it is hard to imagine that Bucharest was born in the middle of a forest – a woodland city! All that is left are a few patches of the old 'Wood of Vlăsie' (such as the Băneasa Forest to the north, today a place of recreation); in the heart of the city, a few ancient trees may still be observed here and there, spared through who knows what miracle.

Through the forest and across the plain flowed the calm Dîmbovița, the river on whose banks Bucharest was to develop. The river rises in the mountains not far from Cîmpulung, the country's first capital, and flows for 266 km before finally joining the Argeş, a tributary of the Danube. The Dîmbovița of the mountains and that of the plain might be two different rivers. In the mountains, the water is cold and clear, and flows in a torrent through a narrow rocky valley. By the time it reached Bucharest, it was a lazy, murky river, winding its way through all sorts of meanders and separate channels, and scattered with tiny islands. On either side, there were lakes and pools, fed from both their own springs and the waters of the Dîmboviţa, whose normally modest volume was capable of rising spectacularly as a result of heavy rain or melting snow. In the past, the Dîmboviţa also had a number of small tributaries right in the centre of the capital. Bucharest was oozing water! To the north of the city, another rather smaller river, the Colentina, formed a series of lakes. In contrast to the 'fantasies' of the Dîmboviţa, of which nothing remains, the Colentina lakes have been landscaped and surrounded by parks, and today form the capital's largest 'natural' area, helping the city to breathe a little.

The Dîmboviţa's destiny was a sad one. Without it, Bucharest could not have existed, but as the city grew, the river became an inconvenience. Its meanders got in the way of systematic planning; its stagnant waters had an unpleasant smell, and were a breeding ground for mosquitoes (which even today do not show much mercy to the people of Bucharest) and thus a hotbed of malaria; its floods were often catastrophic. The modernization of Bucharest meant at the same time an offensive against the Dîmboviţa. Step by step, its lakes and meanders were drained, and its tributaries disappeared under the streets. There followed the work of channelling the river, between 1880 and 1883. The Dîmboviţa was lowered several metres below street level (to put an end to flooding), and grassy slopes were raised on either bank. All the meanders and tiny islands disappeared; the river's new course was plotted with a ruler, from where it entered the city to where it left. Thus disciplined, or rather imprisoned, with its water coffee-coloured and reduced in volume by the needs of the city, with all the sewers that emptied into it, and all the smells that still emanated from it from time to time, the Dîmboviţa became a source of embarrassment for the people of Bucharest. Hardly a little Seine for Little Paris! What could be done? People with imagination dreamed of a grandiose solution: to enrich its waters by means of a canal linking it to the Argeş and the Danube, so that it would become a great river and Bucharest a Danube and Black Sea port. This was a rather utopian project for a poor little river like the Dîmboviţa. But there was also a more straightforward and radical solution: simply to cover the river with a concrete floor. The Dîmboviţa would become invisible, and above it a wide boulevard would traverse the capital from one end to the other. The construction of the concrete cover began in the 1930s; a portion measuring around 1 km was completed in the city centre, but the work was not

267

taken any further.

The story does not end there. In the 1970s, the Dîmboviţa made a nuisance of itself once again, producing floods on a spectacular scale, considering that it had to increase its volume several times over in order to get out of the trench into which it had been channelled. As always, Ceauşescu found the solution. His new Bucharest was to have a new Dîmboviţa, a beautiful Dîmboviţa (at least according to his taste), whose water would be clean and inoffensive. Where the Dîmboviţa enters Bucharest, several villages were sacrificed to excavate a great accumulation lake, capable of absorbing any variation in the river's volume. The residual waters of the old, dirty Dîmboviţa continued to flow under a concrete cover. Above them appeared a new Dîmboviţa, whose waters were more or less clear but almost unmoving, a concrete channel filled with water. It was initially suggested that this channel would even be navigable, at least for small boats. But of course, it is not. It is no more than a mere canal, whose only distinction is that it has to be cleaned from time to time to remove the mud that accumulates in it and the endless range of objects that the people of Bucharest throw into the water. So periodically, the Dîmboviţa is emptied, offering the sorry sight of a ditch full of filth. And thus, unless some further episode occurs, the river's sad history comes to an end.

The plain of Bucharest is not quite flat. On either side of the Dîmboviţa valley, there is higher ground, rather more on the right bank, where a series of low hills rise 15 or 20 m above the level of the river. It is on these modest heights that some of the most symbolic religious buildings of Bucharest were erected: the Cotroceni Monastery, the Mihai Vodă Monastery (founded by Michael the Brave at the end of the sixteenth century), the Metropolitan Cathedral (mid-seventeenth century) and the Radu Vodă Monastery (following the direction of the river from west to east).

Curiously, the Prince's residence was not placed in a dominant position, but on low ground on the river's left bank; it may initially have been surrounded by water. Vlad Ţepeş's original palace was followed by a new construction in the time of Mircea the Shepherd, around the middle of the sixteenth century, which was enlarged and enriched by later rulers, especially Constantin Brîncoveanu. Then, in the course of the eighteenth century, the palace deteriorated and fell into ruin, becoming a shelter for vagabonds. In 1775–6, Alexandru Ipsilanti erected a new palace, this time looking down on the

The mid-16th-century Church of the 'Old Courtyard', the oldest building in Bucharest.

Dîmbovița, slightly upstream from the Mihai Vodă Monastery. But this new residence lasted even less time. Abandoned after it had burned down several times, it came to be known as the 'Burnt Courtyard'. Only its foundations remained; they, too, have now disappeared. However, it is possible to visit the ruins of the previous palace, the 'Old Courtyard', and beside them the princely church, which is still intact (although it has undergone restoration). The oldest church in Bucharest, this is a characteristic example of the style of Muntenian churches, which are Byzantine in character and quite similar to those of Serbia. (The Moldavian style is more expansive and shows traces of Gothic influence combined with the basic Byzantine structure.) The curious history of the vanished palaces – when those of other capitals have been preserved for centuries and are still used as royal residences or museums – says much about the instability and unpredictability of the evolution of Bucharest, and of the Romanian space in general.

FROM THE VILLAGE OF BUCUR TO LITTLE PARIS

No city has changed more from its origins to the present day than Bucharest. There have been many changes everywhere since the

269

Mihai Vodă Monastery at the end of the 18th century, shown in an aquatint by William
Watts after a drawing by Luigi Mayer. The Dîmbovița flows by the foot of the hill.
Apart from the monastery, the scene seems more rural than urban.

Middle Ages, of course, but there are reference points – links with the
past, monuments or sections of cityscape – that have lasted for
centuries. Bucharest developed against its own past. The destruction
of the princely palaces and the disappearance of the Dîmbovița
inscribe themselves within this tendency. Nowadays, three quarters
of the city consist of districts of blocks of flats, built in the Communist
period. The people of Bucharest have become a race of flat-dwellers.
This is not just an evolution, such as can be seen in all the cities of the
world, albeit in less brutal forms, but a complete reversal. Prior to
1800, there were hardly any buildings with more than one storey in
Bucharest. All of the city's people lived at ground level and emerged
from their houses straight into a courtyard or garden.

Bucharest was, and remained for centuries, a large village, or a
conglomerate of villages. Its countless churches, even the largest of
which were of modest dimensions, and the handful of princely or
boyar palaces (which were actually little more than larger and

270

Ceaușescu's 'House of the People' (now the Palace of the Parliament) seen from exactly the same place as the Mihai Vodă Monastery. Not only the monastery but also the hill has disappeared. In the foreground, the channelled Dîmbovița can be seen.

better-built houses, a far cry from the monumental palaces of the West) enhanced the relief of a rural agglomeration. Western cities began life as citadels, tightly enclosed within their walls, with multi-storey buildings and little free space (the same pattern can be seen in Transylvania, especially in the Saxon towns). Bucharest is scattered, like a Romanian village. From the boyars to the humblest of towns-folk, everyone had their own house, whether 'palace' or hovel, with a piece of land beside it, to cultivate or raise animals in. There were extensive orchards and, even more importantly, vineyards; vine-yards surrounded Bucharest and penetrated deep into the city, as far as the princely court. Each district was a village, a group of houses around a little church. This explains the multitude of churches that so amazed foreign visitors. It was not just Ceaușescu who destroyed the churches; many were demolished in the nineteenth century to make way for the civic buildings of the modern city.

Such a village/town had no need for a developed network of roads (except, of course, those required for access and trade). The first of the modern city's main arteries was laid out by Constantin Brîncoveanu, starting in 1692. This Prince had a passion for construction. He gave his name to the Brîncovenesc style, one of the most interesting syntheses of early Romanian art, remarkable for its

271

carved-stone elements (columns, window frames etc.) in which the Western Baroque meets the decorative traditions of the East. Brîncoveanu had a palace, separate from the princely residence but situated not far from it, close to the Dîmboviţa at the foot of the Metropolitan hill. He then built another, the most renowned of all and the purest model of Brîncovenesc art, at Mogoşoaia (today restored as a museum), outside Bucharest beside the first of the Colentina lakes. He wished, naturally enough, to be able to go from one palace to the other without too much difficulty. But how was he to cross Bucharest, with all those gardens and orchards in the way? Brîncoveanu had a road marked out, cutting across many properties, and it might be said that he combined utility with pleasure, as in this way he expropriated part of the estate of his great opponent Constantin Bălăceanu (who was favoured by the Austrians as a candidate for the throne). Thus Podul Mogoşoaiei, which was to become the most famous street of Bucharest and even, for a time, of the whole of South-eastern Europe, came into being [2]: 'Mogoşoaiei' because it led to the Prince's palace at Mogoşoaia, and 'Podul' because it was paved, or 'floored' (*podit*), with oak beams laid transversely. This was how the few paved streets of Bucharest looked well into the nineteenth century. The explanation lies in the fact that Bucharest had no stone, while it had timber in abundance.

The old Podul Mogoşoaiei, in 1878 renamed Calea Victoriei ('The Way of Victory', in memory of the 1877–8 War of Independence), is striking nowadays for its sinuous route, as well as its variable width and the no less variable height of the buildings that line it. No two sections of Calea Victoriei are alike. Sometimes, the street widens into a square; sometimes, it becomes so narrow that its pavements almost disappear. In its lack of orderliness, it perfectly illustrates the eclecticism and improvisation of Romania in recent centuries. Its winding course originates in the fact the road clung to the side of the hill that rose from the bank of the Dîmboviţa, leaving the lake (or rather swamp) that would later be landscaped to form Cişmigiu Park well to its left; nowadays, the slope can hardly be felt, but the difference in level was more pronounced then.

In the eighteenth century, Bucharest experienced a strong oriental infusion. The Phanariot rulers, who came from Constantinople, would have liked to make the city into a replica of the Ottoman capital, so as to feel more at home there. They hardly had time to do much, as their reigns were extremely short. However, the network of

A corner of the Orient in the very centre of Bucharest: the early 19th-century Manuc's Inn.

streets was extended, squares (*maidane* – a Turkish word – modelled on the *maydan*s of Constantinople) were laid out, and private houses and inns were provided with verandahs (*cerdacuri*: another Turkish word), following the same model. The most representative extant monument is Manuc's Inn, built in 1808 by a rich Armenian merchant, with a magnificent wooden gallery extending on two levels around all four sides of its inner courtyard.

But even those buildings which survive from the Phanariot period (which continued until 1821) rarely date from before 1800. Of pre-1800 Bucharest almost nothing survives; just some churches which have themselves been largely rebuilt. Although it is old by virtue of its history, Bucharest is new in its appearance. How could the past be wiped clean to such an extent? There are many answers to this question. In the first place, it was almost inevitable that when a true city was established on the site of the enlarged village of former days, little would remain of the village. In addition, Bucharest's buildings were rather improvised, rarely built under the direction of true architects, and made of less than durable materials (in the absence of stone, timber was used on a massive scale). If even the princely palaces have not lasted, how can lesser buildings be

273

expected to have survived? An uninterrupted series of calamities –
wars, floods, fires and earthquakes – also played their part; I shall
return to these shortly. A certain state of mind also played its part.
Ultimately, anything can be preserved or restored, however harsh
the conditions; all that is necessary is for people to consider it worthwhile and be willing to pay the price. The people of Bucharest seem
not to have considered it worthwhile. Romanian nationalism is not
much in evidence when it comes to palpable traces of the past; it
serves to mark their identity and to distinguish them from others,
but it has not helped to save their historical monuments. As history
progresses, the people of Bucharest wipe their past clean, or let it
disappear of its own accord; it is the sign of an unstable history, but
also of unstable behaviour.

The nineteenth century, especially from around 1830, and with
increasing intensity towards 1900, was the period of modernization.
In an impressive transfiguration, the 'big village' became 'Little
Paris'. Houses began to have more than one storey, and public buildings worthy of the name began to be erected. The most
representative of these were sited, naturally enough, along Calea
Victoriei. The National Theatre was built between 1846 and 1852 to
designs by the Viennese architect Joseph Heft. (After being hit by
German bombs in August 1944, instead of being restored, it was
demolished: thus yet another monument of Bucharest disappeared.)
Further along Calea Victoriei stood a boyar house more imposing
than the rest, that of Dinicu Golescu (1777–1830), well known to the
Romanians also for his cultural activities; after his death, this
became the princely residence. Grand as it may have been by
Bucharest standards, it gave Carol I a shock when he first saw it.
Initially, he could not believe that this could really be his palace;
'Where is the palace?' he asked. Following the proclamation of the
Kingdom, Golescu's 'house-palace' was extended (between 1882
and 1885) by the addition of a new wing (the work of the French
architect Paul Gottereau), which gave it a rather more regal appearance. But even this palace no longer exists; destroyed by a fire in
1927, it was replaced by the present royal palace, much larger in
scale and monumental in appearance, built between 1930 and 1937.

In the last two decades of the nineteenth century and in the years
immediately after 1900, increasing numbers of buildings were
designed by French architects or their Romanian disciples in a variety
of French styles (eclectic, neo-Classical etc.). Thus along Calea

An engraving of Prince Carol's entry into Bucharest in May 1866. At the time, the city still had a quasi-rural character.

Victoriei from the Dîmboviţa to the palace, the following may be seen: the imposing Savings Bank (P. Gottereau, 1900); across the road, the even more imposing Post Office Palace (Alexandru Săvulescu, 1900); the Military Club (Dimitrie Maimarolu, 1912); the Carol I Foundation, today the Central University Library, right opposite the palace (P. Gottereau, 1891–5); the Romanian Athenaeum (Albert Galleron, 1886–8), designed as a venue for lectures and concerts, a symbol of Bucharest, with its Greek temple façade and dome; and, next to the Athenaeum, the Athénée Palace Hotel (Théophile Bradeau, 1912), for a long time the top hotel of Bucharest with a place of honour in the history of the last century (it plays a central role in Olivia Manning's trilogy). Other representative buildings away from Calea Victoriei include the National Bank (A. Galleron, 1883–5); the Palace of Justice, in French Renaissance style (Albert Ballu, 1890–95); the Ministry of Agriculture (Louis Blanc, 1896); and the Faculty of Medicine (L. Blanc, 1903). (Of the architects named, Săvulescu, and Maimarolu were Romanians, Blanc a Swiss settled in Romania, and the others French.)

Even after the laying out of the great boulevards, Calea Victoriei remained the city's central axis and symbol. Everything lies along it: the representative buildings of the state, cultural institutions (including the Romanian Academy and the Academy Library, the most important library in the country), aristocratic residences (like

The Romanian Athenaeum (1886–8); in front, the statue of Mihai Eminescu by Gheorghe Anghel.

The Palace of Justice (1890–95).

The Savings Bank (1900).

The Faculty of Medicine (1903); in front, the statue of Carol Davila by Carol Storck.

The symbolic axis of 'Little Paris': Calea Victoriei in the inter-war years. On the right (with a small cupola) can be seen the famous Capşa restaurant.

the imposing 'House with Lions', the palace erected between 1898 and 1900 by Gheorghe Grigore Cantacuzino [known as 'the Nabob'], Conservative leader and the richest man in Romania), hotels, restaurants (including the famous 'Capşa') and shops. It is at one and the same time a political, intellectual, commercial and social axis charged with mythology, a veritable path of initiation. It was once walked by dense crowds who occupied the middle of the street as well as the pavement, rendering it difficult for carriages and, later, cars to make headway.

Perpendicular to Calea Victoriei on either side, the first axis of great boulevards was laid out in an east–west direction in the last decades of the nineteenth century, bearing the names of the royal couple, Carol and Elizabeth. Work on a second, north–south, axis, almost parallel to Calea Victoriei, commenced after 1900 and was completed in the 1930s. The resulting Brătianu Boulevard (renamed Magheru by the Communists and today divided into stretches carrying both names) is the widest and most monumental of the Bucharest boulevards. The city's centre is shaped by Calea Victoriei and these two lengths of boulevard. At their crossing, the centremost point in Bucharest, stands the University building

278

University Square, the symbolic centre of Bucharest, with the University building, the statue of Michael the Brave and, to the right, the new National Theatre.

(inaugurated in 1869 and extended after 1900). A number of representative statues stand in University Square, the first and most symbolic being an equestrian representation of Michael the Brave (unveiled in 1874): however patriotic it looks, this too is the work of a Frenchman, the sculptor Carrier-Belleuse; rumour has it that the statue was adapted from one of Joan of Arc!

It was not planned that modern Bucharest should gravitate around the University, but as a result of the crossing of the boulevards it has turned out that way. The symbolic centre was at first the Metropolitan Hill (where, alongside the Cathedral and Metropolitan, subsequently Patriarchal, residence, the parliament was later established); then it was the Royal Palace; now it is the University. In the early years of Ceauşescu, when architects still enjoyed a measure of freedom, two important buildings were added to the site (across the Brătianu Boulevard from the University), both completed in 1970: the Intercontinental Hotel, the tallest tower construction in Bucharest, and the new National Theatre. (The latter was initially a composition of geometrical forms, but this did not suit Ceauşescu's more 'classical' tastes; as a result, the geometrical structure was subsequently masked by a surrounding arcade in

A commercial street of old Bucharest.

unmitigated bad taste.) It was on the stretch of boulevard between these buildings and the University that the large-scale, dramatic 'University Square' demonstrations took place in 1990 (so called rather inaccurately, as the real University Square lies round the corner, in front of the University's main façade). Since then, the site has acquired an even more pronounced symbolic charge.

So what about 'Little Paris'? Like any myth, this was a combination of truth and illusion. To a large extent, the city's modern architecture, at least until the First World War, was French-inspired, and some corners of Bucharest do have a Parisian look to them.[3] But we should not let our imagination carry us away. The overall effect was not French. Everywhere, there was a quite un-French absence of regularity. New buildings stood alongside traditional constructions, some of them almost rural in character (single-storey houses with gardens), in the very centre of the city, not to mention the peripheral districts of *mahala* which extended the city until it blended imperceptibly with its rural surroundings. There were also some streets, like Strada Lipscani (a well-known commercial street which takes its name from Lipsca, the old Romanian name for Leipzig, whence merchants brought their goods), which retained a typically oriental aspect.

The people were not exactly Parisian either. What connection did the *mahala*-dwellers of Bucharest – an intermediate category between village and town – have with the French capital? Or that petty bourgeoisie whose very approximate relation to modern culture so delighted Caragiale? Moreover, even in the inter-war period, authentic peasants, in their characteristic costumes, could still be seen in Bucharest, coming to buy and sell, or on some other business, and wooden carts still circulated among the cars and trams! The upper layers of society had certainly adopted French culture, as had the intellectuals (though this did not mean, except in extreme cases, that they had completely broken with all Romanian tradition). The cultivated or snobbish citizen of Bucharest read French literature, keeping up to date with the most recent publications, and dressed according to the latest Paris fashions. Even foreigners, who found much wrong with the city, were impressed by the elegance of the women. The shops and restaurants strove to be as close as possible to French style. But not even the most Francophile of Romanians could ever actually become French! In their lifestyle, in their sociability, there was always something Balkan. It is sufficient to look at their gastronomy: nothing is more revealing of a person's soul than what they eat (if I may be permitted such a typically French remark in the present context). Refined Romanians did, of course, eat in the French manner, but they did not forget their own local specialities – related to Balkan, particularly Greek, cuisine, and often known by Turkish names. As a first course, they would drink *ţuică* (the Romanian national beverage, a strong alcoholic drink distilled from plums) and eat *mititei* (meat balls). To mark themselves off even more clearly from the French, the people of Bucharest were also great lovers of beer, and their brasseries followed the German or Austrian model, never the French – like the famous 'Carul cu Bere' ('The Beer Cart'), whose sophisticated wooden décor, frescoes and stained glass give it the appearance of a temple of beer. There were all sorts of places of refreshment in Bucharest, from the most refined restaurants (specializing in French or Romanian food) to the most popular pubs. The *cafenea* (coffee house), where Turkish coffee was drunk, but in an already Westernized atmosphere, was a veritable institution, but no less so was the *cofetărie* (cake-shop), which served an unimaginable variety of sweets, combining the flavours of East and West; in this domain, Bucharest had no equal.

With the passage of time, the coffee houses have disappeared, but the cake-shop is still a characteristic part of the Bucharest scene. Of all the eating and drinking places whose names were once symbolic, only 'Capşa' (a restaurant and cake-shop) survives; once, it was frequented by the élite of Bucharest, particularly, for a time, by writers and artists. The people of Bucharest liked going out, lingering over a glass of beer or wine or a cup of coffee, talking at length and 'setting the country to rights'. It was a lively and joyful city. And a very cosmopolitan one. The best-known places of refreshment went by a variety of European names: Hugues, Riegler, Giovanni, Fialkovski etc. Bucharest had attracted a large number of merchants and craftsmen but also all sorts of intellectuals, teachers, doctors and engineers, from many different countries. Nowadays, the city has become Romanianized, but then it was one of the most cosmopolitan capitals of Europe – and it should not be forgotten that the making of Romania was also due to a large infusion of foreigners who brought their competence and dynamism with them.

The parks also introduced a specific note. Bucharest started out as a green city, with more vegetation than built-up areas. The central park, known as Cişmigiu (which in Turkish means 'fountain-keeper', from *cişmea*, 'fountain'), was laid out around the middle of the nineteenth century by the German landscape architect Wilhelm Meyer, on the site of a marshy pond. Şoseaua Kisseleff (the Kisseleff Chaussée), a combination of boulevard and park which continues along the line of Calea Victoriei towards the city's northern edge, was begun in 1832, in the time of the Russian general whose name it bears; more than a decade later, the same Wilhelm Meyer continued the work. This was to become the city's most fashionable promenade; around 1900, Bucharest high society would ride out here in a veritable procession of carriages, providing an occasion for ladies to show off their fashions. Later, the lake zone, too, was landscaped. The Herăstrău Park (surrounding the lake of the same name) acquired its present form in the 1930s, in the time of Carol II. Even if something was borrowed from the structure of French parks, the Bucharest type of park is closer to the English model. The straight line, so beloved of the French, does not suit the Romanians; they prefer to let nature take its course.

Around 1900, the French architectural stamp began to be counterbalanced by the rise of the 'national' style inaugurated by Ion Mincu. Having imitated first the Orient and then Paris, Bucharest

The neo-Romanian architectural style

This monumental construction from 1912–39 was initially intended as the Museum of National Art. In the Communist period, it housed the Museum of the History of the Communist Party. Today, it is the Museum of the Romanian Peasant.

A Bucharest contrast: the 'classical' National Theatre, one of the first representative buildings in Western style (built in 1846–52 and destroyed by German bombing in August 1944), and the modern Telephone Palace, a little American 'skyscraper' of the 1930s.

now aspired to become itself. The 'neo-Romanian' style borrowed various traditional elements from local architecture: sculpted pillars, galleries, arcades etc. The 'Bufetul de la Șosea' restaurant on the Kisseleff Chaussée, designed by Ion Mincu in 1892, is a representative example. After 1900, this genre found expression in larger and larger constructions: the Ministry of Public Works (now the Town Hall), across the road from Cișmigiu; the Institute of Architecture, behind the University; and the monumental Museum of National Art (now the Museum of the Romanian Peasant) at the start of the Chausée (designed by Nicolae Ghica-Budești).

The 1930s saw the emergence of modern architecture, with its simple, rectilinear forms. Calea Victoriei augmented its stylistic range with a little American-style 'skyscraper': the Telephone Palace, sited right beside the National Theatre, which it dominated. The synthesis which emerged – it might be called the 'Carol II style' – combined modernism with the search for classical balance and a tendency towards monumentality (these are generally official commissions, buildings destined for state use). Brătianu Boulevard, as an axis of the

The Carol II style

The School of War (1939), now the Military Academy.

The Arch of Triumph (1936) beside Herăstrău park.

city, is representative of this period. The principal individual buildings of the time include the Law Faculty (Petre Antonescu, 1935); the School of War, nowadays the Military Academy (Duiliu Marcu, 1939); and, from the early 1940s, the Interior Ministry on Calea Victoriei, across from the Royal Palace (later to become the building of the Central Committee of the Communist Party – with the famous balcony from which Ceauşescu spoke and the terrace from which he fled by helicopter), and the Foreign Ministry, in Piaţa Victoriei at the end of Calea Victoriei (now the seat of the Presidency of the Council of Ministers).

Bucharest never stopped growing. In the mid-nineteenth century, it covered an area of 30 sq km; towards the end of the century, this had risen to 56 sq km, and by 1939 it was 78 square km. The city's population in 1865 was 140,000; in 1899, 280,000; and in 1930, 630,000. By the time of the Second World War, it was already approaching a million. The city, or at least its central zone, no longer resembled the old 'village'. It had boulevards, multi-storey blocks and monumental public buildings. However, its modernization was only partial, as was that of Romania as a whole. At every step, modern Bucharest met traditional Bucharest, in a contradictory synthesis that was not without a certain charm.

Stalinist architecture of the 1950s: Casa Scînteii. In front, the plinth where Lenin's statue formerly stood seems to be waiting for another statue.

Communism changed Bucharest radically, just as it changed the whole country. In the first phase, the fabric of the city was less affected, as the money and means were lacking. A few symbolic buildings were erected quickly, foremost among them Casa Scînteii (at the end of the Kisseleff Chaussée, beside Herăstrău Park), completed in 1956. This is a Stalinist fortress, with a central tower flanked by lateral turrets, a corner of Moscow (reminiscent of Lomonosov University) transplanted to Bucharest; in it, publishing houses, newspaper offices and printing facilities were gathered together, according to the new totalitarian spirit. From the same period is the Opera House, which was inaugurated in 1953 on the occasion of the International Festival of Youth and Students – a Soviet-controlled movement – held in that year in Bucharest and considered a major event.

In the 1950s, the population grew very rapidly as a result of forced industrialization. At first, people were crowded into existing houses, which had been taken from their owners by force. Then, slowly at first but more and more insistently after 1960, the programme of constructing new districts began. The old *mahala* areas – where, it is true, the houses were generally modest and often insalubrious – and the villages surrounding Bucharest gave way to an endless expanse of concrete blocks. To see what they are like, it is sufficient to visit one district: they all look the same, and none of them is particularly attractive! The appearance of the city and the lifestyle of its inhabitants were changed completely. Little thought was given to green spaces; the parks remained within the limits of old Bucharest. The area of the city increased to three times that of inter-war Bucharest, reaching a figure of 228 sq km – smaller than London, but twice the area of Paris. While both Paris and London encouraged the development of a system of small satellite towns around them, no limit was set to the expansion of Bucharest. It swallowed up its surroundings; there is no urban zone around it, nothing but fields and villages. This unrestricted growth has given rise to serious problems of infrastructure, maintenance and administration. The settled population now exceeds 2 million.

In its preoccupation with 'workers' districts', Communism spared the historic centre for a time. The most ambitious development, dating from 1960, was built behind the Royal Palace (partly on the site of the Palace gardens). This consisted of a great 'congress hall' and a series of blocks of rather modest appearance. But this was not enough for Ceauşescu; his new Romania had to have a new Bucharest to match. The earthquake of 1977 came to his aid: old Bucharest was starting to fall down of its own accord, and all he had to do was complete the job! He had also been struck by Pyongyang, the capital of North Korea. What an impressive sight: a monumental city with wide, straight boulevards and immense squares, and all brand new, without any embarrassing traces of the past – a true Communist city! Old Pyongyang had been flattened by American bombing; although Bucharest, too, had been bombed, the destruction had not been so severe. The only solution was for it to be destroyed by the Romanians themselves, under Ceauşescu's orders.

The dictator's intention was to raise a new Bucharest on top of the old one. And not only to demolish and rebuild, but to change the city's plan completely. Only the name and location would have remained! It would certainly have been more rational, cheaper and less painful to build a new capital somewhere else, on empty ground. But this was not Ceauşescu's intention; he wanted to transfigure Bucharest, to make it the exact opposite of the traditional city: a monumental and solemn place. His attempt invites a psychoanalytical interpretation. In all of his projects, Ceauşescu sought to wipe out the memory of the squalid house in Scorniceşti where he himself had been born. Everything that had been small had to become big. Bucharest had been a picturesque and lively city; Ceauşescu dreamed of a Bucharest that would be grand and frozen in stony perfection.

He began by clearing the oldest part of the capital.[4] Here, nothing was to be left standing. The period of maximum intensity of demolition was 1984–6. Among the buildings destroyed was (incredibly!) the Mihai Vodă Monastery, a symbol of the city, and a foundation of Michael the Brave, Ceauşescu's favourite ruler. But even Michael the Brave could no longer cast his shadow over Ceauşescu, and still less could a monastery spoil the view of the dictator's new palace. It is true that the monastery church was spared, but it was shifted 200 m and hidden among blocks of flats. The city's most picturesque district was destroyed, with its old houses and gardens, churches and monasteries spread over the hillside. Tens of thousands of people were evacuated. It was not just the buildings that disappeared, but the hill itself. Ceauşescu had it flattened. Only in this

The Ceauşescu style

The 'House of the People', the world's largest palace.

The National Theatre.

The new Museum of National History: it remains unfinished, just as it was left in December 1989.

way could he raise the palace of his dreams on an empty, level site. This was a building site on a Pharaonic scale, where tens of thousands of people were treated like slaves – craftsmen, workers and soldiers brought from all over Romania. One day, the dead, too, must be counted: there were many. Ceauşescu was not content to follow the operations on a plan or scale model; he would intervene 'on the spot'. Whenever he did not like some element of the construction, it would be demolished and work would start from the beginning again. And so the palace rose, though its interior was not completely finished at the time of Ceauşescu's fall. It is in the neo-Classical style favoured by dictators, with immense halls and corridors as wide as boulevards. Taken in isolation, some parts do not look bad, as the country's most skilled artists and craftsmen were put to work there. Overall, however, it is the most imposing piece of kitsch in the world. The lower level, a parallelepiped with almost identical sides of 270 and 240 m, does not match the upper level, which completely destroys the symmetry, transforming the palace into a sort of ziggurat and raising it to a height of 84 m (for, of course, it had to be not only very wide and very long but also very high). The bet was won: only the Pentagon is bigger, and Buckingham Palace or even Versailles would look insignificant placed alongside Ceauşescu's building. From the front, a no less impressive boulevard extends for 3.5 km; it is said to be half a metre wider than the Champs-Elysées. Ultimately, there is nothing all that original in the appearance of all this; we cannot talk of a 'Ceauşescu style'. The architects did what they could, and what they were allowed to do. The overall effect is somewhat similar to the neo-Classical postmodernism of the Catalan architect Ricardo Bofill, especially the 'Antigone' district of Montpellier, which he designed around the same time (mid-1980s). The palace and boulevard completely cut through the fabric of Bucharest: in contrast to what had always been a north–south orientation of the urban network, the new orientation they imposed was east–west. They were to have been the new symbolic centre and new symbolic axis. Unfortunately, the boulevard is not quite as monumental and significant as it ought to have been. Its public buildings are few: two ministries right in front of the palace, and the new National Library further along (still unfinished). Otherwise, we see the same obsession of the regime: blocks of flats (which were still empty at the death of the dictator, as they could only be occupied by people with special authorization, which he never had time to issue). These blocks are more carefully built than those in the residential districts, but that is all. Carol II and his architects had done better than this. And as for the new symbolic axis, what is there to say? Calea Victoriei is still full of people, while no-one would dream of going for a walk on the 'Boulevard of the Victory of Socialism'. It remains a foreign body in the heart of the city.

At the same time, demolition and construction were proceeding in other districts too. About 2 km from the new palace, the Museum of National History (likewise largely designed to glorify Ceauşescu) was going up; only its façade, in a style somewhat reminiscent of Mussolini, was ever finished. It remained to be seen how the road between the two symbolic buildings would be opened up. The strip which would have joined them passed over the Opera House, the Law Faculty and a good part of the city centre. In the meantime, churches were disappearing one after the other to be replaced by new constructions (or were shifted behind these). At one point, it was thought that even the Metropolitan Cathedral would be demolished; its dominant hill-top position, looking down on the new boulevard, made it an embarrassment. In the end, a kinder solution was found: a well-placed block positioned in front of the esplanade leading up to the Cathedral hid it from view (except for one narrow angle from which it can still be seen).

Another crazy idea led to the next operation: the demolition of the Văcăreşti Monastery on the edge of Bucharest, the largest eighteenth-century monastic complex in South-eastern Europe, built between 1716 and 1724, with a church in the Brîncovenesc style. In its place, a new Palace of Justice was to be built (though in the end it never was), presupposing the demolition of the old Palace of Justice, which was situated rather too close to the centre; in a Communist city, the place of justice was towards the periphery, as the conflicts and dramas which led towards it were quite foreign to the 'radiant future'.

Ceauşescu had also confiscated the Cotroceni Palace, although he never lived there or used it for any purpose. (He proceeded in the same way with Peleş and numerous other palaces all over the country.) At Cotroceni, on one of the hills on the right bank of the Dîmboviţa, there was a monastery and a beautiful late seventeenth-century church founded by Prince Şerban Cantacuzino. At the end of the nineteenth century, a palace, surrounded by a park, was built on the site of the monastic cells. It was intended at the time for the heir to the throne, Prince Ferdinand, and Princess Marie, and was continually occupied by the royal family until the Communists came to power. They gave it as a present to their children, transforming it into the 'Palace of the Pioneers'. Ceauşescu evicted the children, added new wings and – could it have been otherwise? – demolished Şerban Cantacuzino's church. Between the palace park and the Dîmboviţa, the early twentieth century had seen the development of an elegant and pleasant, if not opulent, district of villas and gardens. For about ten years, the inhabitants of this district lived in fear. Ceauşescu had almost completely isolated it, even demolishing the Cotroceni bridge over the Dîmboviţa. Outside the palace park, police and *Securitate* officers were always on patrol, keeping watch on who knows what! People expected the worst: evacuation and demolition. There was even talk of a plan to excavate a lake in place of the Cotroceni district! And why not? Ceauşescu had just entered his waterworks phase!

We may imagine the macabre story of a Romania with Ceauşescu still at the helm for another twenty years. What would have become of Bucharest? Certainly, little of what formerly was would have remained. Less open to criticism is what Ceauşescu did underground, where there was nothing to demolish. In parallel with the works on the surface, the Bucharest metro was also constructed, and it must be acknowledged that without it the city would suffocate.

THE POST-COMMUNIST CITY

The great works stopped suddenly on 22 December 1989. And they were quite simply 'frozen'! Even today, huge cranes still stand immobile beside concrete skeletons, just as they were caught by the moment of the Revolution. (We may wonder how long both cranes and skeletons will last!) Only the 'House of the People' (as Ceauşescu named his palace; it was his gift not to himself and his wife but to the people) was completed, on the inside too, by the new regime. The offer of an American multi-millionaire to buy it and turn it into a casino met with no success. Some even saw it as an offence against the Romanian people. If it was the people's, then it must remain the people's! Tastes differ: there are Romanians who consider the palace a monstrosity, but others like it. What is there to say? Even the Eiffel Tower looked horrible at first. Finally, the Chamber of Deputies was installed there, leaving its former home beside the Patriarchal residence. The building is now called the Palace of the Parliament. Guided tours – countless tourists want to see this wonder of the world – make almost no mention of Ceauşescu's name, as if the palace had grown up of its own accord. What ingratitude! Let us render unto Caesar what is due unto Caesar: the palace is his!

Bucharest emerged from Communism with a quite different appearance, and above all with a different spirit, a different atmosphere. This once so lively city had stiffened. People just went to work and came home from work. At night, with the streets sunk in darkness, it was a sinister place. The few restaurants closed early, leaving the city deserted. In the 1950s, at the height of the terror, something of the old Bucharest had still remained. In the early years of Communism, there were still tradesmen and restaurateurs who had learned their trade before. With time, however, they disappeared, and those who took their places had lost touch with the refinement of pre-Communist life. A short time after the revolution, a Frenchman pointed out to me – and he was right – that eating in a

Romanian restaurant, even one of the best, was like eating in a canteen, the only difference being the price. Tastes have been spoilt (since most people are not even aware of bad quality). This shows in fashion too, and in the general appearance of the streets. The impression is of poverty and a lack of good taste. Where are the elegant women who rivalled Paris around 1900?

At least the city is no longer dead. Year by year, since 1989, it has gained in animation. Perhaps it is even too animated! However, it is far from the relaxed and happy Bucharest of former times. People are in a hurry, irritable, not very friendly. Commerce has established itself everywhere. Small vendors have taken control of the pavements, with improvised stalls or metal constructions known, in Parisian style, as 'boutiques'. Restaurants, too, have multiplied, offering the most varied cuisine, so that anyone with money can at last eat and drink better than at a canteen! Night life has also picked up. I have heard the ambassador of a European country enthusiastically praising the discotheques of Bucharest. There are erotic bars too, and prostitution under various guises, not yet regulated (like so many other things in Romania), but fully operational nonetheless, whether in full view on the street or more discreetly by way of newspaper announcements. And there are any number of casinos! Some

Two of Bucharest's canine inhabitants.

four or five can be counted just in the neighbourhood of the University. It has been claimed that Bucharest occupies a very honourable third place in this respect, after Las Vegas and Monte Carlo. Inevitably, one thinks about other operations that may be going on, money laundering being the first.

What is most striking is how dirty the city is. It is hard to find a square metre without at least one discarded piece of paper or cigarette packet. Heaps of rubbish accumulate here and there: behind the blocks, in front of the blocks, on the pavement, anywhere. So far, no attempt to clean up the city has succeeded. The citizens contribute to this condition themselves: too few of them give a thought to the cleanness of the city.

Bucharest is also a city of dogs. It might be said that two communities co-exist here: a human population and a canine one. This is not a new situation: foreign visitors have been noting it with astonishment for the last two centuries. I am speaking, of course, not of dogs with owners, but of those who live in the street. Their number is estimated as close to 200,000. People's attitudes towards them are very divided. Some love them, others hate them. Some feed them and so help them to survive, while others chase them away and wait in hope for the day when they will be exterminated. Alongside each block of flats in Bucharest can be found a variable number of this parallel community. They are commonly referred to as 'vagabond dogs', but, more recently, in an attempt to integrate them, the expression 'community dogs' has caught on. Their great problem is finding food, and fortunately there are plenty of people who will give them a bit. Some have almost been adopted. Others have turned wild and can become aggressive, especially at night. The measure which has been recommended for some years now, but only implemented to a very partial extent and with little effect, is sterilization. There can be no question of mass adoption: the dogs are too numerous. On occasion, however (and not just in Bucharest), they have simply been killed, openly or covertly. Most of them continue to live as they have lived until now. But for how much longer?

The people of Bucharest want order and cleanliness. But since they themselves do not make much of a contribution, they are looking – true to the Romanian system – for a providential leader, in this case a mayor, who will sort out everything. After a few unsuccessful attempts, it seems that they have found him, following the elections of 2000, in the person of Traian Băsescu, a rising political figure (who in May 2000 replaced Petre Roman as leader of the Democratic Party). He is authoritarian and likes to parade his authoritarianism. He seems determined to uphold law and order, without bothering much about the details. As his first major action, with the law on his side, but not in the most democratic manner, he began to 'cleanse' the pavements of small-scale commerce. (This was a bit of an eyesore, and some of the wide variety of goods on sale were counterfeit, but for years it was an important part of Bucharest's trade and provided work for tens of thousands of people.) The town hall came out in force, with bulldozers and cranes; the traders tried to resist, and fights broke out in the street. Victory, predictably, went to the mayor, who had both the law and force on his side. The people of Bucharest have been assured that the next step will be the cleansing of the city of 'vagabond dogs'. Neither law nor force is on the dogs' side either.

How will the Bucharest of the future look? A project entitled 'Bucharest 2000' has been adopted, in theory at least. The problem, as always for the Romanians, remains its application, the more so as funds are not available. The scale model presents an ultra-modern city, with high towers (which also serve to diminish the solitary immensity of the 'House of the People'). A few isolated buildings with glass façades, recalling the Parisian district of La Défense, have started to appear, including some on Calea Victoriei, where they hardly fit the historical atmosphere of the street. This Bucharest may be beautiful; it may even be clean. But it will certainly be quite different from the old Bucharest of small houses lost among gardens. Perhaps the rupture is more appreciable in Bucharest than elsewhere. But ultimately, it is just a particular case of a general evolution: the world that once was is being left further and further behind.

BUCHAREST AND ITS ASSAILANTS

Many adversities have come together to strike at Bucharest. From almost daily nuisances to major catastrophes, it is all one long chain. Perhaps it is precisely the insecurity of life that has imprinted a dose of fatalism in the Bucharest psychology, combined with the desire to live in the present moment without investing too much in the future.

The first great enemy is the climate. Far from the mountains and far from the sea, in a plain open to the Russian steppes, Bucharest experiences a typically continental climate. There is little precipitation. It is very hot in summer, with temperatures frequently approaching 40 degrees Celsius (and in exceptional cases even higher – up to 42 degrees in July 2000). Winters are cold, the record being 30 degrees below zero (though in recent years they have been less severe: the greenhouse effect?). The spring is short; autumn, on the other hand, is long, bringing pleasant weather in September and October. The trouble is that the new city is much less able to deal with this sort of climate than the old one was. Even today, summer temperatures in the green areas are a few degrees lower than in the zones of concrete blocks and asphalt. When people lived in a sea of greenery and among rivers, springs and lakes, the summer would have been bearable. Nowadays, however, the heat in the city is appalling. A temperature of 40 degrees recorded in standard meteorological conditions becomes in fact 45 or even 50. And the little flats heat up like ovens. In winter, the problem is the opposite. Of course, it is no longer as bad as in Ceaușescu's time, but it is still difficult to heat the multitude of blocks of flats adequately. In the past, things were simpler: everyone had their own wood fire, and there was wood in abundance.

The climate is a permanent annoyance. The other troubles are periodic. No generation has been spared at least some of them. For centuries, wars and foreign occupations have been uncommonly frequent. The Turks, and sometimes also the Tatars, sacked the town repeatedly. In the eighteenth century, the long series of wars between the Russians, the Austrians and the Turks, wars that were largely fought on the territory of the Romanian lands, gave rise to a succession of occupations by the three conflicting armies. The record for the last two centuries begins as follows: Russian occupation from 1806 to 1812, Turkish in 1821, Russian from 1828 to 1834, Turkish and Russian from 1848 to 1851, Russian from 1853 to 1854, Austrian from 1854 to 1857. Not bad for just five decades! And yet in these conditions, Romania was made and Romanian society was modernized. After half a century of peace, there followed the German occupation during the First World War, between 1916 and 1918. The Germans returned in 1940, this time as allies; however, this did not stop them bombing the city in the days following 23 August 1944. In the previous months, it had been bombed by the Americans and the British. The Russians made their triumphant entry on 30 August 1944 and hung around until 1958.

Nor has Bucharest been bypassed by epidemics. The plague struck there later than in the West, but it also lasted longer, taking its heaviest toll in the eighteenth century and at the beginning of the nineteenth (aided by wars and troop movements). The outbreak which has stuck in people's memory is 'Caragea's plague' of 1813 (named after the Phanariot Prince who ruled Wallachia at the time). This was comparable in scale to the great plague of 1665 in London; carts rolled through Bucharest, collecting dead and dying alike. It seems that between 25,000 and 30,000 people perished out of the capital's total population of 80,000 (an even higher proportion than in London in 1665). The last time the plague struck was in 1829; hardly had it passed when it was followed in 1831 by the cholera epidemic which raged throughout most of the continent at that time.

The periodic overflowing of the Dîmboviţa was a further source of calamity, at least until the post-1880 channelling of the river; entire districts of Bucharest ended up under water. And when there was no flood, there was fire. For centuries, fires were almost a speciality of Bucharest. As it was built of light materials, with much use of wood, the city easily fell prey to the flames. It would take too long to count all the fires. Suffice it to mention the great fire of 1804, which consumed the old princely court and a large part of the city (only to be followed in 1805 by the Dîmboviţa bursting its banks twice, as if to restore the 'balance' of the elements), and the most destructive of all, the fire of 1847, in which 1,142 shops, twelve churches and monasteries, ten inns and 686 dwelling houses were burned.

Earthquakes are also a regular occurrence. Bucharest is situated in a zone of high seismic risk, with an epicentre in the mountains of Vrancea (at the bend of the Carpathians), about 150 km to the north-east. The Vrancean earthquakes propagate in such a way that their principal target seems to be Bucharest. Seismic activity is permanent, and there are countless quakes of small or medium intensity. Every three or four decades, however, there is a major one, which can exceed a magnitude of 7 on the Richter scale. Such an earthquake took place in 1802. According to contemporary records, 'The earth trembled very powerfully, so that all the towers of the churches in Bucharest, and the belfries and other tall buildings crumbled, and the famously tall belfry that was the ornament of the city fell in pieces, and there was great fear at that time.'[5] Other tremors of comparable intensity followed in 1838, 1894 and 1912. Closer to our own times, the earthquake of the night of 9–10 November 1940 is still

298

a living memory for the citizens of Bucharest. Hundreds of people perished, most of them as a result of the collapse of the newly built 'Carlton' block on the Brătianu Boulevard. Catastrophes have the bad habit of coming in close succession, as if one invites the next: the 1940 earthquake struck during the period of Legionary terror, and only a few months before Romania entered the war.

But the most terrible catastrophe of all was the earthquake of 4 March 1977, which had a magnitude of 7.2 on the Richter scale. For a whole minute, the city moved as if on waves. Some tens of buildings collapsed, mainly old blocks in the centre (especially on Calea Victoriei and the Brătianu Boulevard). This was the moment when Ceauşescu decided to take advantage of the occasion and build a new Bucharest. The number of deaths exceeded 1,500, and over 11,000 people were injured. In addition, the quake left behind it a state of unease, which was subsequently fed by fresh tremors (without serious destruction or victims, but nevertheless on two occasions, in 1986 and 1990, of above-average magnitude), and nowadays remains acute. Another major earthquake is expected any time: specialists say it is likely to come after 2005. What will happen then? To make matters worse, many buildings that suffered damage have not been consolidated. When a self-styled specialist created a false alarm at the beginning of 2000, announcing an imminent catastrophe, the mass media and the public became extremely agitated. Nothing happened, but the incident showed how nervous the people of Bucharest are. Visitors from happier parts of the world, free of seismic manifestations, would do well to avoid bringing up the subject!

As the city expanded, some dangers were attenuated while others grew. Floods are no longer a problem, and when fires break out they no longer threaten to envelope the city. However, earthquakes were less destructive in the past. Their effect has increased as the city has 'risen', the more so as blocks of flats were built (at least until 1977) without taking this risk factor into account. Anti-seismic resistance is now a *sine qua non* for any construction; otherwise, there is the risk of a disaster of unimaginable proportions.

These accumulated miseries largely account for the disappearance of the old townscape of Bucharest. Their responsibility is, of course, shared with that of the people, who built badly and have not looked after the past. Bucharest's instability is a concentrated illustration of the instability of Romanian society in general. Everything is uncertain, fluid, provisional.

Even the names of the streets are caught up in this whirlpool of instability. Nothing is more instructive than a study of Bucharest nomenclature. With each generation, the streets have changed both their appearance and their names. A good illustration is provided by one of the streets which branches out from Calea Victoriei. On it stand St Joseph's Roman Catholic Cathedral, St Sava College (the oldest secondary school in Bucharest), the Ministry of Education and the Radio Building. However, many Bucharest people would hesitate to put a name to it. In the beginning, it was called Strada Fîntînii ('Fountain Street'), because it had a drinking fountain at one end. Around 1900, it became Strada Lueger, in honour of Karl Lueger, the Mayor of Vienna, an opponent of the Jews and Hungarians and a supporter of the Romanians of Transylvania. At the end of the First World War, Lueger surrendered the street to General Berthelot, the head of the French military mission in Romania. When the Communists came to power, Berthelot was replaced by Popov, the presumed Russian inventor of radio. But Popov, too, had to disappear, as Romanian-Soviet relations entered a less cordial phase. The street was then given the neutral and rather silly name of Strada Nuferilor: 'Water-lily Street'! After 1989, it was restored, of course, to Berthelot. Almost every street in Bucharest has a similar story – and every generation calls it by its own name – though Strada Berthelot seems to me to hold the record.

The bronze of statues has proved no more durable than street names. There never were all that many in Bucharest anyway. The Communists destroyed a good many of the symbolic figures, first and foremost the imposing equestrian statue of Carol I in front of the Royal Palace (the work of the famous Croatian sculptor Ivan Meštrović), and the statue of I. C. Brătianu that stood in the round-about at the crossing of the two main boulevards. Not much was put in their place. Ceauşescu had everything, but not statues. On the other hand, there was a huge Stalin at the entrance of Herăstrău Park (until its removal at the time of the denunciation of the 'personality cult') and a no less impressive Lenin in front of Casa Scînteii. Lenin, too, had to come down from his pedestal in 1990, leaving an empty plinth waiting for another symbolic figure. Who might this be?

The Stavropoleos Church (1724).

It would be unfair to judge Bucharest according to the model of other capitals. It is different. It does not stand out particularly by its monumentality, and still less by any unity of conception. From this point of view, Little Paris is at the opposite extreme to Paris itself. It is a disorderly city, striking in its inequality, an eclectic city, made in pieces. And this is its charm.[6]

As we can see, there are few old monuments in Bucharest. All that remains from before 1800, with the exception of a few houses, are the churches. With their modest dimensions, they are lost among the modern constructions that surround them. But they are worth discovering. The genius of the church-builders is displayed not on a large scale but on a small one, not in grand compositions but in the capacity to miniaturize and create fine details. The smallest are the most remarkable, like the minuscule Stavropoleos Church (1724), a striking example of the elaborate detailing characteristic of Brîncovenesc art. The contemporary Creţulescu Church (1722), with its delicate profile and exposed red brickwork, produces an unexpected effect of contrast, positioned as it is beside the former Royal Palace and across the square from the former Central Committee of the Communist Party; it is almost a miracle that it emerged unscathed from Ceauşescu's hunting down of churches.

Anyone who sets out to discover Bucharest is guaranteed plenty of surprises. In the monotonous districts of concrete blocks, you know in advance that one block will be followed by another, but in the old part of the city a new perspective opens up with each step. No two neighbouring buildings are alike, either in style, in proportions or in height – there is nothing more variable than the height of Bucharest's buildings, from tower blocks to houses that hardly rise above the ground. Beside a ten-storey block you may come across a little rustic house or a tiny church, and behind the block there may be a whole street that seems to have been forgotten by time.

Bucharest lacks a major waterway. In this respect, its rival Budapest (with which it is often confused, although they are not at all alike, because of the similar sound of their names) is incomparably better off, situated as it is on the Danube, with the fine bridges that link Pest, the city of the plain, with the hilly city of Buda. Bucharest also lacks views: the hills on the right bank of the Dîmboviţa are too low to offer a true panorama of the city.

An old street in Bucharest, with traditional houses (watched over by the inevitable tower blocks).

The lack of an 'authentic' river is compensated for, however, by the chain of lakes to the north of the city, and the extensive area of parkland that surrounds them. The Kisseleff Chausée and Aviators' Boulevard, themselves lined with trees, gardens and sumptuous villas, lead towards Herăstrău Park and Lake, which are impressive for their scale and harmonious landscape. The whole composition is one of the largest and most beautiful of its kind in Europe. Another green district is Cotroceni, which happily survived Ceauşescu's bizarre projects. A walk along its streets takes us back to 1900, to a pre-tower-block Bucharest of villas and gardens. In 1990, the Cotroceni Palace became the seat of the Romanian Presidency. Here, too, are the Botanical Gardens, and the faculty of medicine, watched over by the statue of Carol Davila (1828–1884), general and doctor and one of the great 'founders' of nineteenth-century Romania. A naturalized Romanian of French origin, he founded medical teaching and organized the Romanian health services.

Bucharest is also a city of culture. Its citizens were theatre-lovers already in the nineteenth century, and the tradition continues

303

unbroken to the present day. Theatre actors are among the best-known personalities; the repertory is varied, and the stagings are often daringly experimental. The Opera, too, enjoys a good reputation, as do the concert halls (the Romanian Athenaeum, the Radio Hall). However, for a foreign visitor, the best introduction to the country's history and culture is probably offered by the city's many museums.

The Royal Palace is home to the National Museum of Art, which includes a rich collection of Romanian art (illustrating all of the stages in its development) and a number of outstanding pieces from other countries, most of which were in the royal collections; among the principal attractions are works by the Flemish primitives and three splendid El Grecos. Under Ceauşescu, a 'Museum of Art Collections' was also founded, in the old Finance Ministry building on Calea Victoriei. The advantage is that all of the collections can be seen in one place; the disadvantage is that they have been taken out of their settings and exhibited in a place that is not particularly suitable for a museum. (The best known of them all, the Zambaccian collection, essential for anyone interested in Romanian painting, has since been returned to its original home.) The 'Museum of Art Collections' gathers together a wide variety of art objects, reflecting the tastes and preoccupations of those whose collections it houses. Most of the works are Romanian, but some are Western or oriental, and alongside the great Romanian painters, works of folk and religious art can also be seen (including the famous Romanian glass icons).

History is presented in the Museum of National History, which was set up also in the time of Ceauşescu, in the former Post Office Palace: the change of purpose was curious, but typical of the dictator's logic. The very idea of a museum of national history is itself open to discussion, in as much as it means a single discourse, a single interpretation. Not much has changed in its arrangement since 1989; only the post-1918 section has been given up, as it was too contaminated by Communist ideology (but nothing has been put in its place). However much its conception can be criticized, the museum is nevertheless extraordinarily rich. It brings together a multitude of original pieces, including prehistoric, Dacian and Roman pottery, ancient statues, inscriptions etc.; above all, it houses

The Cantacuzino Palace (1900), today the George Enescu Museum.

Romania's treasures, ranging from Dacian, Scythian and Gothic objects (with the famous treasure of Pietroasa, attributed to the Goths, in pride of place) to the Crown Jewels. Another remarkable exhibit is a faithful copy of Trajan's Column, not raised high like the original in Rome, but with the scenes displayed separately, allowing the whole 'reportage' of the Daco-Roman wars to be followed with ease. There is also a Museum of the History of the City of Bucharest, situated across the road from the University in a nineteenth-century aristocratic house (the Suțu Palace, built in 1832–4). Since the early 1990s, a wing of the Cotroceni Palace has housed the Cotroceni Museum, which presents significant moments in modern and contemporary history, especially those concerning the royal family.

The visitor to Bucharest may also get a picture of the whole country concentrated in a small space, thanks to the Village Museum, which is situated in the open air between the Kiselyov Chaussée and Herăstrău Lake, and which displays a large number of peasant houses and homesteads, gathered from all over Romania. It provides a synthetic image of rural civilization, which was, until not so long ago, the very essence of Romanian society. And the life of the peasants, their beliefs, customs and creations, are presented at the Museum of the Romanian Peasant, which has taken the place of the Museum of the History of the Communist Party in an impressive building in neo-Romanian style where the Kisseleff Chausée leaves Piața Victoriei.

Romanian music, too, has its museum, which bears the name of the composer George Enescu. This is none other than the grand and lavishly ornamented palace of the 'Nabob' Cantacuzino, on Calea Victoriei. After the death of his son, who had inherited the house, the latter's widow, Maruca Cantacuzino (a close friend of Queen Marie), married Enescu. Thus, by an unpredictable twist of destiny, the Nabob's palace became a home to music.

A museum of a completely different sort, which is also famous among the people of Bucharest, is the Museum of Natural Sciences (in Piața Victoriei, just before the Museum of the Romanian Peasant). At one time, it was one of the most important museums of its kind in the world: I do not know if it still is today. It bears the name of Grigore Antipa (1867–1944), the notable biologist who ran it for decades and built up its collections.

But I must stop here. My intention was to explain Bucharest, not to compete with the guidebooks.

Epilogue

Everything in this world must be explained in the first instance by history. From one historical stage to the next, peoples and individuals change, while still retaining something of the inheritance of the past. For Romanians, history is to a large extent a handicap. It pulls them back, with its accumulation of delays and dysfunctionalities and its excessive instability. Few European nations have such an unstable past. History, of course, is to blame, but people's character and behaviour have also ended up adapting to this prolonged state of insecurity. Romania has created its own undesired reputation as an unpredictable country.

On the other hand, history has also meant the crystallizing of a certain type of civilization and Romanian identity. It is a distinctive synthesis, combining a strong and tenacious rural base with no less strong and insistent influences from outside. Resistance goes hand in hand with receptivity. The Romanian synthesis is full of contrasts.

But not very much of the old Romania is left for the Romanians of today. Communism destroyed much of what went before, and then it too collapsed. Only disparate elements have survived: fragments of folklore and tradition, nostalgias, cultural and historical reference points. Romania today is a disarticulated country, a collage of ill-matched segments of traditional life, inter-war reminiscences, Communist attitudes and structures, and post-Communist evolutions. It is a system that functions with difficulty, in the expectation – somewhat prolonged – of a new beginning, capable of pointing the way towards a new synthesis. The present moment is a crucial one for the Romanians; while recovering what can still be recovered of the past, or what deserves to be recovered, they must construct something new, in keeping with the world of today and, hopefully at least, more durable and more stable. Will they succeed?

The points in their favour are not to be discounted. The upheavals of the last few years in South-eastern Europe have left Romania untouched. Its cohesion has passed the test. It has demonstrated that it has managed to weld what were formerly quite disparate

307

provinces into a nation. In the region in which it has evolved, Romania is the exact opposite of Yugoslavia. In the eastern half of tomorrow's Europe, it is the second-largest country after Poland in terms of area and human potential. On top of this, Romanians have always demonstrated an extraordinary capacity for receiving models. It is true that they have also shown a tendency to treat them superficially, and not to persevere in their application. Rigour, discipline and perseverance have never been their foremost qualities: this is what separates them most profoundly from the Western type of civilization. Without losing their soul, the Romanians have to take at least a step towards the West in their mentality and behaviour.

Romania needs Europe, since it is only in the European framework that it can find stability and develop. But Europe needs Romania too. A European construction without Romania would leave an unwarranted and dangerous gap at the continent's eastern gates. Romania is the best point from which to supervise the Balkans, and the last bastion before the immense, vague and unsettling space left behind in the wake of the disintegration of the Soviet Union.

December 1999 – December 2000

References

The present work is above all a personal account, in which the characterizations and interpretations are largely my own. For the last half-century – the period of Communism and the years after Communism – my principal source has been my own memories and observations. For this reason, I have not considered it useful to provide an extensive bibliographic apparatus. I cite here those works which seem to me to be indispensable, and in particular those published in languages of international circulation, especially English, as well as contributions which I have used directly or which support some of my statements. Finally, I mention some of my own works, in as much as something of their substance has passed into this book too.

INTRODUCTION

1 For a more detailed presentation of my ideas regarding the construction of the 'other', see Lucian Boia, *Pour une histoire de l'imaginaire* (Paris, 1998), pp. 113–35 ('Le Jeu des altérités').
2 Some of the characterizations and a few phrases here are taken from Lucian Boia, *History and Myth in Romanian Consciousness* (Budapest and New York, 2001).

I A LOOK AT THE MAP

1 Sabin Manuilă, ed., *Recensămîntul general al populaţiei României din 29 decembrie 1930*, 9 vols (Bucharest, 1938–41).
2 For physical and especially human data on the Romanian provinces, see *Enciclopedia României*, vol. I (Bucharest, 1938), pp. 47–8 ('Geografia României'), 133–60 ('Populaţia României').

II AN ISLAND OF LATINITY

1 For the problem of the Romanians' origins, and the various interpretations that have been advanced about them, see the chapter on 'Origins' in Lucian Boia, *History and Myth in Romanian Consciousness* (Budapest and New York, 2001).
2 Petru Maior, *Istoria pentru începutul românilor în Dachia* (Buda, 1812), pp. 8–22.
3 Herodotus' references to the Getae can be found in his *Histories*, IV, 93–6. For a critical interpretation, see Zoe Petre, 'Les Gètes chez Hérodote', *Analele Universităţii Bucureşti* (1984), History ser., pp. 17–23; and 'Le Mythe de Zalmoxis', *ibid.* (1993–4), pp. 23–36.
4 Mircea Eliade, *The Romanians: A Concise History* (Bucharest, 1992), p. 13.

5   Alexandru D. Xenopol, *Istoria românilor din Dacia Traiană*, vol. I (Iaşi, 1888), p. 307.

6   Ioan Bogdan, *Istoriografia română şi problemele ei actuale* (Bucharest, 1905), p. 21; *Însemnătatea studiilor slave pentru români* (Bucharest, 1894), pp. 17-19, 25; *Românii şi bulgarii* (Bucharest, 1895).

7   Marc Bloch, *Apologie pour l'histoire ou Métier d'historien* (Paris, 1964), p. 15.

8   See the chapter on 'Continuity' in Boia, *History and Myth*, from which I have borrowed, with some modifications, in what follows.

9   For the various interpretations of continuity, I have referred principally to the following: Bogdan Petriceicu Hasdeu, *Istoria critică a românilor* (Bucharest, 1873); A. D. Xenopol, *Une Enigme historique: Les Roumains au Moyen Age* (Paris, 1885); Dimitrie Onciul, 'Teoria lui Roesler...', in *Scrieri istorice*, vol. I (Bucharest, 1968); Nicolae Iorga, *Istoria românilor pentru poporul românesc* (Vălenii de Munte, 1908; latest edn Bucharest, 1993); and G. I. Brătianu, *Une Enigme et un miracle historique: Le Peuple roumain* (Bucharest, 1937; in English as *An Enigma and a Miracle of History: The Romanian People* [Bucharest, 1996]).

10 For the history and character of the Romanian language, a few classic works should be mentioned: Ovid Densuşianu, *Histoire de la langue roumaine*, vols I–II (Paris and Bucharest, 1901–38); Sextil Puşcariu, *Limba română: I–Privire generală* (Bucharest, 1940; in German as *Die Rumänische Sprache* [Leipzig, 1943]); and Alexandru Rosetti, *Istoria limbii române de la origini pînă în secolul al XVI-lea* (Bucharest, 1968; summarized in French as *Brève histoire de la langue roumaine dès origines à nos jours* [The Hague, 1973]). For the integration of Romanian into the family of Romance languages, Carlo Tagliavini, *Le Origini delle lingue neolatine*, sixth edn (Bologna, 1972) is invaluable.

11 B. P. Hasdeu, Introduction to *Etymologicum magnum Romaniae*, vol. I (Bucharest, 1886).

12 The standard work on the oriental element in Romanian remains Lazăr Şăineanu, *Influenţa orientală asupra limbii şi culturii române*, 3 vols (Bucharest, 1900); a French summary appeared under the title 'L'Influence orientale sur la langue et la civilisation roumaine', in *Romania* (Paris, 1901), pp. 536–66, and *ibid.* (1902), pp. 82–99.

13 I. I. Russu, *Limba traco-dacilor* (Bucharest, 1967).

III HOW ROMANIA WAS CREATED

1   The classic works of synthesis on the history of the Romanians as a whole are: Alexandru D. Xenopol, *Istoria românilor din Dacia Traiană*, 6 vols (Iaşi, 1888–93), with a more succinct version in French, *Histoire des Roumains de la Dacie Trajane*, 2 vols (Paris, 1896); Nicolae Iorga, *Geschichte des Rumänischen Volkes*, 2 vols (Gotha, 1905), and *Istoria românilor*, 10 vols (Bucharest, 1936–9; in French as *Histoire des Roumains et de la romanité orientale*, 10 vols [Bucharest, 1937–45]); and Constantin C. Giurescu, *Istoria românilor*, 5 vols (Bucharest, 1935–46). Of the works of synthesis published in the Communist period, the following may be consulted in English: Andrei Oţetea, ed., *The History of the Rumanian People* (New York, 1974), and its later version, *A Concise History of Romania* (London, 1985); and

Dinu C. Giurescu, *Illustrated History of the Romanian People* (Bucharest, 1981). Both are affected by the inevitable Communist distortions but are interesting even from this very point of view. For a synthesis free of Communism, written by a Romanian historian in exile, see Vlad Georgescu, *The Romanians: A History* (Columbus, OH, 1991). A recent synthesis, which nevertheless includes many 'traditional' interpretations, is Kurt W. Treptow, ed., *A History of Romania* (Iaşi, 1997). An older work which is also worth consulting is *A History of the Roumanians* (Cambridge, 1934), by Hugh Seton-Watson, a distinguished British specialist in the problems of Central Europe.

2   P. P. Panaitescu, 'Problema originii clasei boiereşti', in *Interpretări româneşti* (Bucharest, 1947; second edn 1994).

3   On the question of the relationship of vassalage to Hungary, which Romanian historians in general have sought to minimize, see Marius Diaconescu, 'The Political Relations between Wallachia and the Hungarian Kingdom during the Reign of the Anjou Kings', in *Mediaevalia Transilvanica*, II/1 (Satu Mare, 1998), pp. 5–42; and 'The Relations of Vassalage between Sigismund of Luxemburg, King of Hungary, and Mircea the Old, Voivode of Wallachia', in *ibid.*, II/2 (1998), pp. 245–82.

4   Panaitescu, 'De ce n-au cucerit turcii ţările române', in *Interpretări româneşti*.

5   Viorel Panaite, *The Ottoman Law of War and Peace: The Ottoman Empire and Tribute Payers* (Boulder and New York, 2000). The author concludes that Wallachia, Moldavia and Transylvania were integrated into the Ottoman system, with the status of 'tributary-protected principalities'.

6   Ovidiu Cristea, 'Frontul românesc antiotoman în secolele XIV–XV: realitate istorică sau mit istoriografic?', in Lucian Boia, ed., *Miturile comunismului românesc* (Bucharest, 1998), pp. 148–53.

7   The road towards the constitution of the Romanian nation and of Romania is traced by the American historian Keith Hitchins in *The Romanians 1774–1866* (Oxford, 1996).

8   The Union of the Principalities and the creation of Romania (the period 1856–66), seen in the context of the game of European diplomacy, form the subject of an excellent book by the American historian T. W. Riker, *The Making of Roumania* (London, 1931).

9   The founding role of French culture in Romania is treated, perhaps with a degree of exaggeration, by Pompiliu Eliade in *De l'influence française sur l'esprit public en Roumanie* (Paris, 1898); *Histoire de l'esprit public en Roumanie au XIXe siècle* (Paris, 1905); and *La Roumanie au XIXe siècle* (Paris, 1914).

10   According to Constant Maneca, *Lexicologie statistică romanică* (Bucharest, 1978).

11   Titu Maiorescu, 'În contra direcţiei de astăzi în cultura română', in *Critice*, vol. I (Bucharest, 1908), pp. 145–56.

12   The proposal of Amedeo of Savoy appears in a document which I discovered among the manuscripts of the Academy Library in Budapest, a projected Romanian-Hungarian accord dated 19 September 1865 which, among other matters, provides for a common action against Austria. See Lucian Boia, 'O convenţie româno-maghiară din anul 1865', in Lucian

Nastasă, ed., *Studii istorice româno-ungare* (Iaşi, 1999).

13 Carol I's maternal grandmother was Stéphanie de Beauharnais, the adopted daughter of Napoleon I, who married the Grand Duke of Baden; his paternal grandmother was also French, the niece of Joachim Murat, Marshal of France and King of Naples, who was married to a sister of Napoleon I.

14 Curiously, there is no complete monograph on Carol I. His very detailed memoires may be consulted, although they end in 1881: *Aus dem Leben König Karls von Rumänien*, 4 vols (Stuttgart, 1894–1900). For the early years of his reign and the preceding Cuza period, see Paul E. Michelson, *Romanian Politics 1859–1871: From Prince Cuza to Prince Carol* (Iaşi, Oxford and Portland, 1998).

15 The history of Romania in its 'royal' period is treated by Keith Hitchins in a balanced and very well-informed synthesis, *Rumania 1866-1947* (Oxford, 1994).

16 The same Keith Hitchins is the author of the most complete synthesis dealing with the situation of the Transylvanian Romanians and their national movement in the half-century preceding the First World War, *A Nation Affirmed: The Romanian National Movement in Transylvania, 1860–1914* (Bucharest, 1999). This work follows the author's previous contributions, which together make up a vast fresco of the history of the Transylvanian Romanians in the eighteenth and nineteenth centuries: *The Rumanian National Movement in Transylvania, 1780–1849* (Cambridge, MA, 1969), and *A Nation Discovered: Romanian Intellectuals in Transylvania and the Idea of Nation, 1700–1848* (Bucharest, 1999).

17 See Philip Eidelberg, *The Great Rumanian Peasant Revolt of 1907: Origins of a Modern Jacquerie* (Leiden, 1974).

18 For its great wealth of information, and in spite of its pathetic style, a useful work on the participation of Romania in the First World War remains Constantin Kiriţescu, *Istoria războiului pentru întregirea României, 1916-1919*, second edn, 3 vols (Bucharest, 1925). See also Glenn Torrey, *Romania and World War I: A Collection of Studies* (Iaşi, Oxford and Portland, 1998).

19 For a very well-informed treatment with precise details (including numerous statistics) on both the internal problems of the country and the military operations, see Dinu C. Giurescu, *România în al doilea război mondial, 1939–1945* (Bucharest, 1999).

20 The figures that follow are taken from *Enciclopedia României*, vol. I (Bucharest, 1938), pp. 133–60 ('Populaţia României').

21 An excellent analysis of the various ideological and cultural tendencies in inter-war Romania can be found in Hitchins, 'The Great Debate', in *Rumania 1866–1947*. See also Irina Livezeanu, *Cultural Politics in Greater Romania* (Ithaca, NY and London, 1995).

22 The most reliable work on the Legionary movement is by the German historian Armin Heinen: *Die Legion 'Erzengel Michael' in Rumänien: Soziale Bewegung und Politische Organisation: Ein Beitrag zum Problem des internationalen Faschismus* (Munich, 1986).

23 For the interdependence between the agrarian structures of Romania and its political evolution, see Henry L. Roberts, *Rumania: Political Problems of*

an Agrarian State (New Haven and London, 1951).

IV ROMANIAN COMMUNISM

1 For the logic of Communism in general – the construction of a new world through science and technology, and in accord with the 'laws of history' – I refer the reader to my own *La Mythologie scientifique du communisme* (Paris, 2000).
2 The first reliable study of Romanian Communism was that of Ghiță Ionescu, *Communism in Romania 1944–1962* (London, 1964). A succinct but comprehensive synthetic overview of the whole period with a good bibliography is provided by Dennis Deletant, *Romania under Communist Rule* (Bucharest, 1998; second edn Iași, Oxford and Portland, 2000). Essays dealing with Communist repression and Romanian Communism in general, recollections by victims of Communism, and a rich body of illustrations can be found in Ștefan Constantinescu *et al.*, *Archive of Pain* (Stockholm, 2000). An interpretation within the larger framework of East European Communism can be found in Vladimir Tismăneanu, *Reinventing Politics: Eastern Europe from Stalin to Havel* (New York and Toronto, 1993). The collective volume *Miturile comunismului românesc* (Bucharest, 1998), produced under my direction, touches on a wide range of social, ideological and cultural problems, with an emphasis on representations and propaganda.
3 Ion Ioanid, *Închisoarea noastră cea de toate zilele*, 5 vols (Bucharest, 1991–7).
4 For the Ceaușescu period in general, see Dennis Deletant, *Ceaușescu and the Securitate: Coercion and Dissent in Romania 1965–1989* (London, 1995). The best known of the dictator's official biographies is that by Michel Hamelet, *Nicolae Ceaușescu* (Paris, 1971), which perfectly illustrates how some Westerners allowed themselves to be caught in the web of Romanian propaganda (the author was a journalist with *Le Figaro*, a respected paper, and moreover of the Right!). Also worth consulting are: Mary Ellen Fischer, *Nicolae Ceaușescu: A Study in Political Leadership* (Boulder, 1989); Edward Behr, *Kiss the Hand You Cannot Bite: The Rise and Fall of the Ceaușescus* (London, 1991); and Mark Almond, *The Rise and Fall of Nicolae and Elena Ceaușescu* (London, 1992).
5 Ceaușescu's natalist policy is the subject of Gail Kligman's book *Controlling Reproduction in Ceaușescu's Romania* (Berkeley and Los Angeles, 1998), which shows that almost 10,000 women died between 1966 and 1989 following improvized abortions.
6 For an inventory of the demolition campaign, see Dinu C. Giurescu, *The Razing of Romania's Past* (Washington, DC, 1989).
7 On the cultural profile of Romania under Ceaușescu, see Katherine Verdery, *National Ideology under Socialism: Identity and Cultural Politics in Ceaușescu's Romania* (Berkeley, 1991).
8 The figures that follow are taken from *Recensămîntul populației și locuințelor din 7 ianuarie 1992: Rezultate preliminare* (Bucharest, 1992); and *Recensămîntul populației și locuințelor din 7 ianuarie 1992: Structura etnică și confesională a populației* (Bucharest, 1995).

V BETWEEN THE PAST AND THE FUTURE

1 In the absence of any overall treatment of Romanian evolutions from 1989 to the present, and given the purely personal character of my own evocations and interpretations, I limit myself to citing a few titles. On the Romanian revolution: Nestor Ratesh, *Romania: The Entangled Revolution* (New York, 1991). On the violent events of June 1990: Mihnea Berindei, Ariadna Combes and Anne Planche, *Roumanie, le livre blanc: La Réalité d'un pouvoir néo-communiste* (Paris, 1990). An interpretation of the political system, propaganda, representations and mentalities in the first years after the revolution can be found in Alina Mungiu, *Românii după '89: Istoria unei neînțelegeri* (Bucharest, 1995). The unpublished doctoral thesis of the French political scientist Jean-Jacques Sonny Perseil, *Le Factionnalisme partisan: Etude de cas: Les Organisations politiques libérales roumaines* (Université Paris I, 1999), offers an analysis not just of the liberal currents after 1989 but also of the new political élite and the disputes between parties in general. For statistical data, and the comparison of Romania with other European countries, my principal source has been *L'Etat du monde 2001* (Paris, 2000).

VI ROMANIANS AND FOREIGNERS

1 Some of the figures and interpretations that follow are taken from my articles 'Sur la diffusion de la culture européenne en Roumanie (XIXe siècle et début du XXe siècle)', *Analele Universității București* (1985), History ser., pp. 51–69, and 'Les Roumains et les Autres: La Quête des modèles dans la société roumaine des XIXème et XXème siècles', in Alexandru Duțu and Norbert Dodille, eds, *L'Etat des lieux en sciences sociales* (Paris, 1993), pp. 39–48.

2 Ion Codru-Drăgușanu, *Peregrinul transilvan, 1835–1844*, ed. Șerban Cioculescu (Bucharest, 1942), pp. 95–105, 205–15.

3 On the Romanians in America, I summarize here the findings of a study which I carried out long ago: 'On the History of Rumanian Immigration to America, 1900–1918', *Rumanian Studies*, III (Leiden, 1976), pp. 61–76.

4 The enquiry was published in the Bucharest magazine *Oameni în Top*, 4 (1999), pp. 93–7.

5 See, for example, Carol Iancu, *L'Emancipation des Juifs de Roumanie, 1913–1919* (Montpellier, 1992); the author considers Romania to be among the countries that practised 'a systematic state anti-Semitism'.

6 On the fate of the Jews in Romania in the years 1940–44, the very well-informed study of Radu Ioanid, *Evreii sub regimul Antonescu* (Bucharest, 1997), particularly deserves mention. A critical discussion of the various interpretations and an assessment of the extent of anti-Jewish repression can be found in Dinu C. Giurescu, 'Evreii din România (1940–1944)', in *România în al doilea război mondial, 1939–1945* (Bucharest, 1999).

7 Mihail Sebastian, *Jurnal, 1935–1944* (Bucharest, 1996; in English as *Journal, 1935–1944* [Chicago, 2000]).

314

8 The most up-to-date and complete monograph on the Romanian Gypsies is Viorel Achim, *Ţiganii în istoria României* (Bucharest, 1998), which includes a quite detailed English summary, 'The Gypsies in the History of Romania', pp. 179–92. See also Emmanuelle Pons, *Les Tsiganes en Roumanie: Des citoyens à part entière?* (Paris, 1995).
9 E. Lovinescu, *Istoria civilizaţiei române moderne*, vol. I (Bucharest, 1924), p. 118.
10 A well-informed treatment of the Aromanians can be found in Max Demeter Peyfuss, *Die Aromunische Frage* (Graz, 1994).

VII WHO'S WHO IN THE ROMANIAN PANTHEON

1 The 'Vlad Ţepeş / Dracula' file is presented in detail in Raymond T. McNally and Radu Florescu, *In Search of Dracula: A True History of Dracula and Vampire Legends* (Greenwich, CT, 1972).
2 For more extensive coverage of the mythologized figures, see 'The Ideal Prince' in Lucian Boia, *History and Myth in Romanian Consciousness* (Budapest and New York, 2001). The survey referred to appeared in *Oameni în Top*, 1 (1999), p. 13.
3 Queen Marie presents herself in her memoirs, *The Story of My Life*, 3 vols (London, 1934–5). The principle biographies are: Terence Elsberry, *Marie of Romania: The Intimate Life of a Twentieth Century Queen* (London, 1973); Hannah Pakula, *The Last Romantic: A Biography of Queen Marie of Romania* (London, 1985); and Guy Gauthier, *Missy, reine de Roumanie* (Paris, 1994).
4 Regarding the Romanian literary phenomenon, the principal work of reference remains G. Călinescu's great synthesis (itself a quite special work which has entered Romanian cultural mythology in its own right), *Istoria literaturii române de la origini până în prezent* (Bucharest, 1941; in English as *History of Romanian Literature* [Milan, 1988]).
5 Mircea Eliade, 'Introducere', in Bogdan Petriceicu Hasdeu, *Scrieri literare, morale şi politice*, vol. I (Bucharest, 1937), p. xxxviii.
6 On Iorga, see the monograph in English by Nicholas M. Nagy-Talavera, *Nicolae Iorga: A Biography* (Iaşi, Oxford and Portland, 1998).
7 The works mentioned have been translated into English under the following titles: *The Myth of the Eternal Return* (New York, 1955); *Patterns in Comparative Religion* (London and New York, 1958); and *A History of Religious Ideas* (Chicago, 1978–85). Of Eliade's novels, *Maitreyi* has appeared in English as *Bengal Nights* (Chicago, 1993), and *Noaptea de Sînziene* as *The Forbidden Forest* (Notre Dame, IN, 1977). See also Mircea Handoca, *Mircea Eliade: Biobibliografie* (Bucharest, 1997). Eliade's memoirs, published in English as *Autobiography I 1907–1937* (New York and San Francisco, 1981) and *Autobiography II 1937–1960* (Chicago and London, 1989), are important sources regarding his career (including his political self-justifications) and for the intellectual atmosphere of inter-war Romania. They invite a parallel reading with the journal of Mihail Sebastian (the two men were close friends, in spite of the fact that one was a Jew while the other allowed himself to be attracted by the Legionary movement).
8 Ideological distortions aside, the dictionary published under the title *Personalităţi româneşti ale ştiinţelor naturii şi tehnicii* (Bucharest, 1982)

remains a useful tool. The fact that Elena Ceauşescu is the beneficiary of an article twice as long as those accorded to the most distinguished Romanian scientists only adds colour to the work!

VIII A WALK THROUGH BUCHAREST

1 The most complete monograph on the evolution of the city, an impressive source of information despite the inevitable concessions to Communist ideology, is Constantin C. Giurescu, *Istoria Bucureştilor din cele mai vechi timpuri pînă în zilele noastre* (Bucharest, 1966). A shorter version is available in English, as *History of Bucharest* (Bucharest, 1976). A succinct recent work, suggestively illustrated and with a bilingual text in Romanian and French, is Dana Harhoiu, *Bucarest, une ville entre Orient et Occident* (Bucharest, 1997).

2 This famous axis of Bucharest – Calea Victoriei – is the subject of a beautifully written, meticulously documented book by Gheorghe Crutzescu, *Podul Mogoşoaiei. Povestea unei străzi* (Bucharest, 1943).

3 'Little Paris' is described in detail (with numerous photographs) by Frédéric Damé, a Frenchman who settled in Romania, in *Bucarest en 1906* (Bucharest, 1907), and, a few decades later, by his compatriot Paul Morand, in *Bucarest* (Paris, 1935, 1990).

4 I refer the reader to Dinu C. Giurescu, *The Razing of Romania's Past* (Washington, DC, 1989).

5 Dionisie Eclesiarhul, *Hronograf 1764–1815* (Bucharest, 1987), p. 83. Dionisie also gives a description of the fire of 1804. Overall, his work is a picturesque and naïve evocation of the period as it was seen and understood by an ordinary citizen of Bucharest.

6 A good guide to Bucharest, richly illustrated and containing much historical information, is Rolf Peter Reimer, *Bukarest: Kultur-Historisches Stadt-Führer* (Bucharest, 2000)

A Note on Romanian Pronunciation and Spelling

As the Romanian spelling system is basically phonetic, it should not be difficult for the reader to pronounce the Romanian names and other words that occur in this book, if the following basic rules are borne in mind.

1 CONSONANTS

S should always be pronounced as in the English *seat* (never as in *prison*). *C* and *g* are pronounced like the English *ch* in *church* and *g* in *gem* when they are immediately followed by *i* or *e*. In all other cases (including *ch* and *gh* before *e* and *i*), they are pronounced as in the English *coat* and *goat*. *R* is sounded in all positions, somewhat as in Scottish speech. The specifically Romanian letters *ş* and *ţ* are pronounced like English *sh* and *tz* respectively.

2 VOWELS

Romanian has seven vowels. *A, e, i, o* and *u* should generally be pronounced as in Italian. However, final *i* is usually silent (for example, *Bucureşti* is pronounced 'bookoo<u>resht</u>'), though it is pronounced in some personal names like *Rosetti*). The Romanian letter *ă* represents a sound something like the *a* in *about* or the *er* in *mother* (though not so weakly stressed). Finally, the sound represented by *â* or *î* (a notorious stumbling block for foreigners!) is something like the English *i* in *fill*, but pronounced further back in the mouth. In diphthongs, the second of the two vowels is emphasized (unlike in English). As a result, *i* or *e* before another vowel sounds like English *y* (for example, *Ion* sounds like the English 'yon'), and *o* before another vowel sounds like *w* (for example, *Timişoara* is pronounced 'teemee<u>shwa</u>ra').

3 STRESS

In general, the contrast between stressed and unstressed syllables is not as pronounced in Romanian as in English. However, there is a tendency, especially in longer words, for the stress to fall on the last syllable if the word ends in a consonant, and on the penultimate one if it ends in a vowel.

Since the adoption of the Roman alphabet in the nineteenth century, Romanian spelling has undergone a number of reforms and modifications. The most recent point of controversy concerns the use of *â* and *î*. The single sound represented by these letters had its own specific sign in Cyrillic script, but its representation proved more problematic after the Roman alphabet was adopted in 1860. The current official spelling was established by the Romanian Academy in 1993, and represents a return to pre-Communist practice, whereby the sound is represented by *â* unless it occurs at the beginning or end of a word, in which case *î* is used. However, many Romanian intellectuals (including the author of this book), and some of the most distinguished Romanian publishers, remain unconvinced by the somewhat dubious etymological arguments advanced in favour of this usage, and continue to follow the convention (established by a spelling reform at the start of the 1950s) whereby the sound is represented by *î* regardless of its position, though *â* is retained for *România, Român* etc. (a concession introduced in the mid-1960s in order to re-emphasize the Roman connection) and in certain proper names like *Brâncuşi, Pârvan* etc. In the present translation, it is this latter convention, favouring *î*, that has been followed in the rendering of Romanian names and other words (not least because for English speakers *î* is more suggestive of the correct pronunciation than is *â*).

Photographic Acknowledgements

The author and publishers wish to express their thanks to the following locations or sources of illustrative material and/or permission to reproduce it:

Courtesy of the Artexpo collection, Bucharest: pp. 19, 22, 94, 128, 131, 136, 141, 153 (top), 157, 213, 217, 218, 237, 238, 278; from *Ateneul român din Bucuresti. Marea fresca* (Bucharest, 1938): pp. 40, 80, 101; from George Calinescu, *Istoria literaturii române de la origini pîna în prezent* (Bucharest, 1941): pp. 243, 245; Eugen Ciocan: p. 136; courtesy of Editura Meridiane Publishing House: pp. 199, 256–260; courtesy of Editura Meronia, Bucharest: pp. 13, 14, 32; from *Enciclopedia României* (Bucharest, 1938), vol. 1: p. 70; National Museum of Romanian Art, Bucharest: pp. 199, 256 (bottom), 257 (bottom); from Raymond Netzhammer, *Aus Rumänien* (Einsiedeln, 1913), vol. 1: p. 93; vol. 2: pp. 88, 89, 96; after F. W. Putzgers' 1918 *Historischer Schul-Atlas*: p. 30; photos by the author: pp. 17, 26, 113, 153 (bottom), 179, 269, 271; photos M. Leaman/Reaktion: pp. 18, 118, 132, 276, 277, 279, 280, 285, 286, 289, 290, 294, 301, 303, 305.

Index of Personal Names

Index of Place Names